Compassion

Compassion

The Core Value
that Animates Psychotherapy

ROGER A. LEWIN, M.D.

JASON ARONSON INC.
Northvale, New Jersey
London

Production Editor: Elaine Lindenblatt

This book was set in 11 pt. New Baskerville by Alpha Graphics of Pittsfield, New Hampshire, and printed by Book-mart Press of North Bergen, New Jersey.

Library of Congress Cataloging-in-Publication Data
Lewin, Roger A.
    Compassion. : the core value that animates psychotherapy / Roger A. Lewin.
        p.   cm.
    ISBN 1-56821-678-5 (alk. paper)
    1. Psychotherapist and patient.   2. Psychotherapy—Moral and ethical aspects.   3. Psychotherapists—Professional ethics.
    4. Caring.   5. Listening—Psychological aspects.   6. Intimacy (Psychology)   I. Title.
    [DNLM: 1. Psychotherapy—methods.   2. Empathy.   3. Professional –Patient Relations.   WM 420 L673c 1996]
    RC480.8.L49   1996
    616.89'14—dc20
    DNLM/DLC
    for Library of Congress   95–23012

Manufactured in the United States of America. Jason Aronson Inc. offers books and cassettes. For information and catalog write to Jason Aronson Inc., 230 Livingston Street, Northvale, New Jersey 07647.

For Joan Lilienthal Lewin

and Rachel Julia Lewin

Contents

Acknowledgments

I owe a debt of gratitude to all those who, at the different stages of my life, have thought and felt with me and helped me learn to think and feel. Thinking and feeling are ongoing processes, journeys without ends as long as we live. My patients and students have had a special catalytic role in challenging me in this phase of my life to try to articulate in accessible form what I hold to be fundamental.

I also owe thanks to Sheppard Pratt, one of America's most distinguished institutions in the field of treatment of the seriously mentally ill, for making a place for me as a supportive and also critical presence in its deliberations during a trying time for all who care for the emotionally disturbed. I hope very much that this book is a help to psychotherapists of all trainings and backgrounds in maintaining their courage to care.

Under the auspices of Sheppard Pratt, Steve Sharfstein has continued to provide support for my writing. A portion of this book was presented at Grand Rounds at Sheppard-Pratt on April 26, 1995 to an audience that was very generous in its reception. Rudy Lamy and the other staff of the Kubie Library at Sheppard Pratt have generously provided me with the reading and reference materials I requested, however odd, even whimsical, they have sometimes found my requests.

1

The Perils and Promise of Listening

The Unwilling Explorer

"So what are you going to do? Are you just going to sit there in that chair for the next thirty years and listen to people's troubles? That's pathetic."

With this salvo, a young man in his late twenties began his therapy session. This broadside came after a little more than a year and a half of meeting with me three times a week. The therapy had been a help to him. Where before he had been depressed and anxious and stymied despite his very real talents and energies, now he was beginning to find his way. He was beginning to take steps to try things out both in work and in personal relationships that were very hard for him. He was beginning to be able to feel enough self-confidence to risk small reverses and yet repair his self-esteem when he experienced these. He was starting to call into question his scheme of expectations and requirements of himself.

Throughout our work together he had made it very clear to me that he had come to see me only because he felt that he had had absolutely no alternative, that coming to see me at all was a source of considerable shame whenever he thought about it and that he found the whole process of psychotherapy to be very strange indeed. Also, he found very strange much of what he himself had to say and much of what he was becoming more and more aware that he himself felt.

Not only strange, but also repugnant. Whereas we most often picture explorers as making their discoveries in a spirit of exultation, triumphantly expanding the realm of the known world, he was much more like an explorer who had never wanted to set out from home on his expedition, had done everything in his power not to go, had found every step of the way quite tedious and depressing, and yet now, for all his valiant resistance, found himself the discoverer of a new continent he fervently wished did not exist in the first place. Such an explorer feels not the least urge to lend his name to this continent. Not only are its flora and fauna repulsive, but also their behaviors are strangely unpredictable, so that he never knows quite what is going to happen next in this new continent he has discovered.

Worse yet, this continent he has so unwillingly discovered after the winds of life have blown him far off his intended course has the perverse quality that it does not seem always only strange. From time to time, in the midst of the strain of the exotic, in the midst of the horror of the new and as yet unintegrated, there are tinges of something familiar but long forgotten or long neglected, as if what he has stumbled on is an internal Atlantis, full at once of the dangers of memory and of prophecy.

These tinges give the experience of exploring this new continent an edge of special horror and fear, because when they come he feels as if he is in danger of losing his bearings not only in the world of this new continent but also within himself as he has known himself. He fears in these moments that he may lose his inner bearings so thoroughly that he might not ever be able to find his way home to a more familiar and sheltering place where things are simpler and clearer, with sharper edges and outlines.

He is confused as the result of his discovery and the confusion is frightening in itself. It does not strike him primarily as promising a new way to put himself together, but rather as threatening all the ways that he has been accustomed to view the world around him and to be in it. He feels that he is beginning to feel and act and understand in a new set of ways, as if something in the flora and fauna of this new continent (or is it a very old continent, older than currently accessible declarative memory, perhaps even older than declarative memory itself?) is contagious and beginning to influence him, even perhaps in ways that might be interesting and intriguing, if they were not so disorienting and did not put him so much at odds with his habitual ways of seeing himself and his environment. He finds himself worrying inside himself that he may go native on this new continent. He cannot even begin to fathom the implications of this for how he may come to live and how his life may take shape.

This young man, the unwilling explorer in our extended figure, looked at me as an object of fascination, of mixed horror and allure. I listened to him. I talked to him. He told me that he had said things to me that he had never considered saying to anyone else and never would consider saying to anyone else. He told me that he had said things to me that he did not even like to think that he knew about himself, although one of his troubles, as he saw it, was that he had so much trouble forgetting. In fact, his memory was uncannily good but unfortunately enlisted largely in the service of a conscience whose rigors were unrelenting and cruel. He wished often that his memory did not work so well, that he could put things out of his mind, that it would be possible for him not to notice and not to hold on to what he noticed.

As he presented himself to me, he was a man who had long half-known much too much and long half-known much too little, someone who had been hung up at a very painful and conflicted midway point in his development. He knew too much to go along with much that was conventional in the world in which he had grown up. So he had the loneliness of knowing too much. If he let himself feel and think with any clarity, then he did not fit. On the other hand, because of this worry about fitting, about becoming definitively estranged from those he knew and loved, he was in the habit of inhibiting what he started to feel and to think. He operated in a range that was at once too large for comfortable fitting with others and too restricted to make it possible for him to find a good fit with himself within himself. This was a very painful conflict for him, one that he had not had a way to put into words before therapy.

He told me that his approach to life involved never telling anyone anything about yourself, because whomever you told might at some future time, in some now unpredictable, even unimaginable way, use whatever you said against you. If no one knew anything about you, you could go on appearing to be perfect. Whatever you knew about yourself already had a lacerating quality because, to the extent that you were revealed as real, to that extent you fell short of perfection. If perfection was your ideal, then whatever you knew about yourself rendered you unacceptable in your own eyes. In a strange way that he could not articulate clearly, this young man explained all this to me precisely so that I could disagree with it, call it further into question, ask difficult questions as the external trustee and ally of the part of him that longed to break with it. Even to listen to it was already to call it entirely into question, because as I listened he listened, too, so that together we found ourselves struggling with the hurt of hearing and knowing.

The more he told me, the more he cherished and needed me and also feared and even hated me. I was struck and moved by his capacity to risk the disorienting power of a new attachment, a new kind of relationship with a person so unfamiliar in background and in life experience. Also, a new kind of relationship with himself. I often wondered why he kept coming back when he said that what was happening to him in therapy was so unsatisfying, even revolting to him. But come back he did, over and over, with a hunger for what we were doing together that showed in what he brought of what he had thought and felt during the time between our sessions, in his intense concentration during sessions, in the way that he lingered at the end of the sessions.

I took up with him his use of denial to defend himself against what he felt. I never used the term *denial*. I spoke with him instead about his being too scared to be scared, too angry to be angry, too hurt to be hurt, too worried to be worried, too embarrassed to be embarrassed, and so forth. He took on this idea by stages, getting to the point where he would say, accusingly, "I know what you're thinking. You're thinking that this bothers me too much for me to be bothered by it." Then his face would relax into a grin, as if to make it clear to me that he was on to all my tricks and that I should abandon all hope of trying to outwit him. There was a special closeness in these moments of accusation. After another few months, he graduated to asking himself on his own initiative whether the feeling he currently claimed not to feel was actually overwhelming him by its intensity so that he could not afford to let himself know that he was feeling it.

A Peculiar Exchange

When he began the session by asking me whether I intended to spend the next thirty years just sitting in my chair listening to people's troubles, I felt at once accused of sloth and immobility, of a paralytic approach to life that involved some horrible dimension of slacking off. I also felt cherished and endorsed. I heard the injunction to reliability. I appreciated his wish for my longevity. I was aware that both he and I had been in our lives near enough to death to be burdened with deep feelings of vulnerability on an ongoing basis. Both of us had had occasion to consider what it would be like to be unable to do anything at all but sit in a chair.

When he pronounced his verdict on the project that he had made up for me by declaring it "pathetic," I was struck by the etymological connection with the Greek word *pathos* or feeling. The project of sitting in the chair listening was, indeed, a feelingful one, just as the troubles that people told me were feelingful, pathetic both in that original etymological sense and in the sense that they were deserving so often of a pity and solace that they had not received either from the individual who brought them or from his or her near human environment.

Probably because of the warmth and because of the connection to mortality in his question about what I proposed to do with the next thirty years of my life, I found myself giving my patient what struck me as an odd and extensive answer, one that carried me forward in thinking about myself onto terrain with which I was not wholly familiar. He had given me a taste of my own medicine, rendering me self-conscious. He had made me aware of my inner diversity and so of myself as an unfinished and not wholly planned project. The ability of a patient to turn the tables may be at once quite disconcerting and a sign of how much the patient has in fact learned in therapy.

"I'm not sure what I'm going to do for the next thirty years of my life, if there are that many," I said. "Actually, the pattern of my life has been that I've done a lot of different things. I can imagine myself doing something else."

"Aha," said my patient, pouncing as if I had finally owned up to withholding essential knowledge from him, "then you have a plan."

"No," I replied, "I don't have a plan. I've made many plans in my life, but most of them haven't worked out. The best and the worst things that have happened to me in my life have taken me by surprise. I never could have imagined the life that I've actually led or that I'm now living. This probably means that I can't imagine the life I will lead, either."

"But you must have a plan," he protested. "You must know what you're going to do."

"I'm not sure that I do," I insisted. "I suppose that I have planned some things at some times in my life, but even then I've had to change my plans to accommodate circumstances. I've never known enough to make a plan and just stick with it. Plans always change as you go along with them."

"So you end up just sitting in a chair all day long listening to people's troubles. That's really pathetic," he shot back, as if I had disappointed and confused him.

After this conversation, I wondered whether I had said too much. Had a pincer movement of anxiety attacking from one side and vanity attacking from the other driven me to expose too many of my own worries and uncertainties? I found the thought of sitting in that chair listening to people's troubles for the next thirty years at once appealing and appalling. His question had made the end of my life suddenly feel very near and palpable. When we start to think of the end of our lives, the limit to all we are and do and propose, we are naturally impelled to think of the ends, the purposes, for which we are living. We are impelled to reflect on what really matters to us and how it matters to us.

Subliminally, as my patient asked the question, I had the thought, "So, is this all there is to me, this person sitting in this chair and nothing more? Is there not anything more creative than that to me? Am I just a man sitting in a chair, listening passively? Is this all I can expect of myself? What am I really doing here? How did I get here? What keeps me here?"

I felt disappointed in myself, without quite knowing why. I was very much aware that the question on my patient's mind was not so much what I was going to be doing for the next thirty years but what he was going to be doing for the next thirty years. He was trying to imagine his way forward into a life he could not picture, one that did not fit with what he had expected of himself and felt had been expected of him. When I told him that most of my life had not gone according to plan, I administered at once a jolt of reality and a jolt of reassurance.

My patient was often bothered by his inability to foresee and control things and often toyed with the notion of his own prescience in matters that actually were ruled by the laws of chance. This had to do, in part, with a very close and painful brush with death he had had as an adolescent. But it also had to do with earlier fears about the dangers of initiative. It had to do with his view of social position, of the role of money, of what made one valuable to oneself and others. My patient often felt hemmed in by the expectations of others so that the idea that life had an open horizon and that I did not have my own course precharted had its real allure for him. He was hungry to know about me. He wanted to know what made me tick as an aid to trying to figure out what made him tick. I often had the impression that he needed to know about me equally in order to choose for himself how to be and how not to be. That is, he needed to be able to learn from me by both positive and negative example.

My patient worried that he would never amount to anything, that his vast ambitions could never be realized, that, in fact, his life would turn out to be, to use his term, "pathetic." He longed to find a frontier where there was a margin of freedom but despaired of being able to do so. In fact, he was an extremely attached young man who longed to revolt precisely because of how attached to and implicated in others he felt, how much he felt he had to conform to what others wanted him to be or else be abandoned. If he tried to adopt the pose of being aloof and unconcerned, cool and ruthless, this was because underneath this pose (which did not fool him at all), he was so much the opposite, so warm, so concerned, so attuned to the hurts of others, so desperately feelingful. Inside himself, he felt so small.

Sitting in the Chair

This patient's questioning of me and of how I was now spending my life and how I meant to spend the rest of my life stimulated a familiar meditation in me, one that I had carried on before. I found myself asking myself what I was doing, why I was doing it, how I had come to do it, why I went on doing it, and so forth. I assume most, if not all, psychotherapists carry on meditations on these topics in the private recesses of their minds and hearts, in those internal workshops where we are perpetually revisiting and revising ourselves in order to try to be true to ourselves as people we both already know and are in the process of encountering for the first time.

Therapies change. In the course of a single treatment, focus and flavor and fervor can all change, so that a therapy that started out as one kind of experience becomes transmuted into something quite different. This can happen more than once in the course of the treatment of a single patient, especially if the treatment spans years and stages in the maturation and life experience of the patient. Often when a patient expresses a desire to leave therapy, this has something to do with wanting to change the focus or aim of therapy, to introduce a new element that produces a sense of unfamiliarity. Not only do theories of psychotherapy and emphases in ideas about and approaches to psychotherapy change, but, prob-

ably more importantly, psychotherapists themselves change
as they learn and grow and experience not only the triumphs
but the tedium and defeats that life brings them, not only in
psychotherapy but outside of it, too.

What we imagined we could do in psychotherapy, what
we set out to do in our early years as therapists, is not what
we necessarily find ourselves doing later on. It is not necessarily what we now consider worth doing. Psychotherapeutic
practice teaches us many things that we did not know were
to be known. Psychotherapy is one of those occupations in
which we have perpetual opportunity for remorse and regret
over what we did not understand earlier on when we had less
experience and less insight, not just into our patients but into
ourselves and our practices. By a simple act of extrapolation,
we realize that what we understand ten years from now will
necessarily be quite different than what we understand now.

Of course, it is possible that our different understand-
ings at different points in our careers and in different psychotherapeutic relationships cannot easily be located on anything
so simple as a curve of increasing knowledge and understanding. Perhaps what we know and do at each phase has its own
validity. Certainly, it is the case that persons early on in their
career often do very well with very difficult patients because
they bring so much in the way of goodwill and enthusiasm
to the work, because so much is at stake about themselves
and the project of the formation of their own professional
identities. Their patients can benefit from an attention that
is not only intense but also in some ways undivided, because
nascent. But it is also true that these same factors that can
be enormously helpful in some treatments can represent
major interferences in others.

What we psychotherapists do, in fact, is to sit in chairs
and listen to people's troubles, not that there is anything
essential about the chair. We could do what we do while we

walked with a patient along a path or road outside. We could do what we do sitting in the shade of a tree. Nor is there any uniform necessarily required. Nor is uniformity of the essence of psychotherapeutic practice. I have often enjoyed the thought that psychotherapy depends on what we have in our hearts and minds, not on anything external. I have also had the thought that psychotherapy is an example of such a high-technology activity that it lies well beyond the reach of any machine or algorithm.

There is no mechanical way to counterfeit the ingenuity and wisdom and attunement and staying power of the psychotherapist. Psychotherapy is, we should also note, therefore, one of those rare activities that is at once high-tech and high-touch. A psychoanalyst who had previously been a pianist and a composer remarked that one of the things he liked best about doing psychotherapy was that there was nothing he knew that he did not have the opportunity to use in the course of his work, often in ways that surprised him with their freshness. Needless to say, he did not tire of psychotherapy, finding in it threads of interest and sustenance that kept it new for him even as he had more and more experience.

Listening as an Internal Industry

We often hear it said that psychotherapists do "nothing," that all we do is sit and listen. This formulation sets listening equal to nothing and represents a very common and concrete form of thinking. In motor terms, the listener shows little. My patient, for example, had a very hard time understanding what either one of us did in psychotherapy. As he saw it, he "just" talked and I "just" listened—not that he did not listen and I did not talk. But, behaviorally, as he saw it, very little was going on that seemed familiar to him. I did not give him either advice or orders. I was clear with him that I often had no idea what he should do and that often what he said was confusing to me just as it was to him. Psychotherapy challenged him with a new notion of "doing," this particular kind of intimate dialogue between two individuals in which an integral part of the proceedings was a questioning of the "rules" of proceeding.

I did listen and I did think and feel about what he said, which meant that I lived with it not just during the time of the sessions but also through the rest of the day, consciously and unconsciously. From time to time, too, I dreamt about it. Also, I have been moved to write about him and his quandaries, which shows that they are still working on me even as I am working on them. When we work seriously in psychotherapy with a patient, the experience is much like acquiring, if not a chronic disease, then a new form of chronic unease. We find a new presence within ourselves.

When we really listen to someone else, when we really attend and try to understand, this is an activity of enormous complexity and requires the commitment of extensive resources. This is especially so when we consider that we are listening also for what a patient cannot yet say, cannot yet know, cannot yet make available to him- or herself in the form of experience that can be described and held in connection with the full range of his or her known experiences. Sometimes we hear hints of what will not be there to be known more explicitly and emphatically for years to come. I often remind myself that what is most interesting about what a patient says is what the patient will say next.

Listening is, however, an internal industry, not one in which we can see rows of factories clustered along the banks of a river, their smokestacks thrusting up into the sky, emitting vast clouds of steam or smoke. It is not one in which we can see lines of railroad cars and barges bringing raw materials and carrying away the finished product. It is sometimes very hard to figure it into something like a Gross Rational Product, let alone a Gross National Product.

The material of listening is different, intangible, more abstract, more internal, weighty in quite another sense than that of the industry we see in our great factories. When someone is listening, we see very little. We may, however, recognize the aura of concentration, the quality of receptivity that is at once reposed and active. To listen well, we have to be in a middle state where we are neither quite in control inside ourselves nor quite out of control but rather attuned to an ongoing flow of feeling and information. We have to have made a special potential space within ourselves.

We know when someone is listening to us and when we ourselves are listening by the interpersonal atmosphere that simultaneously shelters and engages us. Those of us who listen are well aware of how much we have *not* to do in order to listen and of how much effort we have to expend in order to get into the groove of listening and to stay there. We are also aware that we wobble in and out and that this wobbling can be extremely confusing, even painful, representing in itself a kind of experience that is hard to learn to use.

The Pygmalion Paradox

One of the most taxing aspects of the job of listening to another person in a psychotherapeutic way is contending with what I have come to call the Pygmalion paradox. In order to get to know someone else, we have to make up an image of that person, of their concerns and possibilities. We have to make of that person an actor on the inner screen of our minds. We do this largely unconsciously, in response to cues we get from the other. If we stop to think about it, these cues, abundant as they are, are also quite meager.

It is as if we used the cues we got from the other as dots and then proceeded to connect the dots in order to establish the outline of an integrated, meaningful, and active figure. However, inevitably we not only add a few dots here and there but also go on excursions with our line between dots, so that the figure we ultimately discern owes an enormous amount to our own acts of interpretation. In a certain number of persons, what we miss is that between one dot and what we took for the neighboring dot, there are abysses, virtual Grand Canyons that the person cannot span, not now, and perhaps not ever.

We operate in knowing others so much by extrapolation and interpolation. We operate in knowing an other so much by inference, so much of which we do so automatically that we can be unaware that we do it at all. So much of our knowing of another person involves the assimilation of the unfamiliar to the familiar. In short, we make the other person up, with some help from that other person, out of the inner mental-emotional material that is available to us, much as a sculptor works a figure out of the available stone or clay or wood. We have to make the other person up in our minds in order to animate him or her internally so that we can relate, so that we can be receptive, so that we can be of use to the person. This is a part of the essential work of relationship. However, it has its grave dangers.

Whether in sympathy or antipathy, we make others up to figure in our own dramas. The device we invent in our minds to relate to an other may act as a filter that screens out parts of the person that are essential but that disturb or upset us or simply do not fit with our own style of accustomed perception. Just when we think we are listening and attuned, we may be turning a deaf ear on the patient. Also, patients are often only too eager for us to make them up, to tell them how to be, to become caught up as a player in our lives and lies, because they despair of the work of making something out of their own lives and lies, their own particular situations. They want us to help them perpetuate inner states of being dumb and numb.

Whenever we become truly psychologically intimate with another person, the fundamental issues of boundaries, of what belongs to whom, of what passes back and forth across them and how it passes, are opened up again. In this area, there is so much that is so difficult to describe because it is fleeting, rapidly shifting, only partially formed. In this area, we often know by immersion and intuition, which do not permit that extra degree of abstraction that makes it possible for us to know what we know and so describe what we know. This knowing by immersion and intuition and participation is an essential dynamic and determinative aspect of every psychotherapy in any depth. Certainly, with many patients we make major contributions to the formation and the reformation of their personalities more by how we are with them than by what we think, know, say, or do.

In psychotherapy, we must, like Pygmalion, do our sculptural work. We must make of the other an integrated and meaningful figure in our lives. However, unlike Pygmalion, who was motivated by his disgust with the shameful acts of women and his urge to revise by compensatory idealization, we must strive to maintain an element of skepticism and openness in regard to our creation and its relationship to our own desires. Also, again unlike Pygmalion, we must strive to work in a medium that is much more readily reworked— over and over again, if necessary—than stone. After what we imagine we know of the other, we must leave a gap, a place where a spark of what does not fit, what we had not expected or suspected, may suddenly flash and call our design of the other profoundly into question. This spark may be the spark of the other's genuine existence and presence.

We must recognize and remember that we are working with illusions whose reality is nonetheless telling. The protection of this gap, of this margin of uncertainty, costs a great deal of effort, because it is a fundamental feature of human psychological nature that we like to believe in our own creations, our sketches of other people, our own illusions. We like closure. We like the feeling of assurance, that smug feeling that our synthesis suffices. The lesson of psychotherapy, however, is *at once* that we must synthesize and that our syntheses rarely suffice, unless we rework them over and over again. Even then, their sufficiency is only partial, momentary, relative to particular life situations and demands.

In psychotherapy we need always to operate in the mode of provisional knowing or, to put it less reassuringly, to operate simultaneously in the mode of knowing and in the mode of the willing suspension of belief. We must retain the capacity for an ambivalence about our illusions that itself changes and develops, allowing us to trust them and mistrust them as context and cues shift.

The discomfort with this process of illusionary making and remaking, this project that depends so much on remaking through illusions, may explain in large part the longing for the objective and the conventional in psychotherapy. It may explain the urge to remove the margins of uncertainty and doubt by making the product of psychotherapy seem more concrete, as in measurable changes in discretely, if arbitrarily defined, symptoms. It may explain in large part the urge to make psychotherapy focus on changes of behavior rather than on changes in internal states.

Certainly, the shorter the course of treatment, the more the treatment is likely to be biased in the direction of the external, the concrete, and the apparently measurable. We should keep in mind what Goethe (1782) said so presciently: "Nature delights in illusion. Who destroys illusion in himself and in others, nature punishes tyrannically" (p. 16). As is so clearly evident in borderline personality organizations, excessive concreteness is at once a defense against the fear of internal chaos and a serious limitation on human possibility (Lewin and Schulz 1992).

After a year of treatment, a woman described me as "not just one person, but a whole busload of people." A few years later, she used the occasion of recalling this statement to revise it in a most significant manner.

"It's not just you," she said, "who has been a whole busload of different people. I've been a whole busload of people here, too."

We go through many shifts in our view of a single patient in the course of a treatment of any degree of intimacy and depth. One patient can turn out to be a busload of people in many different senses. A common enough transformation is to see that the patient who seemed so compliant and pleasing is actually seething with rage and petrified of letting anyone near. We can also often see that the patient who seemed to be so angry is actually terrified of his or her own compliance. We come to understand the exhibitionist elements in the patient who seems the most inhibited to start with, to see the awesome clarity of mind of someone who seemed so confused, and so forth.

Sometimes, as a therapist, it is easy to feel very slow. Once we catch on to something that is very important and fundamental, we can see how many times in how many different ways the patient has tried to call this to our attention and how hard a time we have had making ourselves available for understanding it. This experience serves to sensitize us to the fact that we must be missing so much on an ongoing basis. If we know we are slow, then we can learn to be patient. The work of remaining open so that we can hear what patients have to tell us and themselves in our presence about the kinds of experiences they actually have is a subtle and difficult one. Like my patient, we are all at times extremely unwilling explorers, full of diverse doubts about the value of our expeditions.

The Listening Urge

In response to my patient's challenge as to whether I was going to spend the next thirty years just sitting pathetically in my chair while I listened to other people's troubles, I said that I had done a number of different things in my life and implied that I might yet do something else besides sit in this particular chair. It was certainly the case that I had done many other things and had not been, as one unsympathetic interviewer put it when I applied to medical school, "exactly a straight arrow shooting into medicine." However, I realized that, whatever I had done, the primary fascination for me had been in trying to make sense out of the people with whom I came in contact.

I had always wondered why they said and did what they said and did, why they acted so differently at different times, why they were sometimes so happy, sometimes so sad, sometimes so angry, and sometimes so utterly unavailable. I always listened for what was suggested by what they did not say, what was concealed in the incompleteness or peculiar structure of their verbal and bodily gestures. I had always wondered whether it was possible for me to feel what they felt. I was always confused about my own states and struggling to learn to describe and accommodate them better within myself.

I remembered vividly a series of recesses I spent in elementary school listening to a classmate explain to me the intricacies of how electrical motors worked, a topic about which I knew nothing and felt no particular urge to know anything. But we had been told that this classmate was about to leave school to have an operation on his eyes that I did not understand and that terrified me. As I listened to him explain about electrical motors, I was captivated by the monotony and urgency of his tone, by the implicit claim that there had to be a way not only to understand but to control extremely complex devices on which we depended. I heard his terror and, because my terror recognized his terror, wanted to provide him some measure of comfort.

So, as the others played baseball, I stood and listened to him talk about electrical motors, not understanding a thing, although to this day I can remember not only where we stood but how we stood. Perhaps what moved me was not so different than what moves a dog to come closer when it senses that its owner is upset. I met a frame of mind and body by matching my own frame of mind and body to it. I may even have known my classmate's terror more clearly than he did because I had a distance from it that let me give it more shape. I have often wondered what his experience of me was during those explanations of such extraordinary urgency. Certainly, the account I give now of the experience is not one I could have given then. Then, I was simply wordlessly there, held as by a magnetic field.

When I got seriously to thinking about this business of listening to others' troubles, listening both for what could be said and what could not be said, I realized that I had been doing it already for almost my entire life. I believe it to be the case that most psychotherapists begin listening to the troubles of others long before they realize that there is a name for what they are doing and a social structure, training, role that formalizes and sanctions it. When exactly does the listening begin? I think in many cases it begins with the dawn of personality.

I know I came from a family in which so many sorrows, so many losses, so many tragedies, so many terrors, so many resentments, so many hopes and ambitions were shrouded in silence, barely hinted at around the edges of what could be said. Yet, under the shroud of silence, their massive outlines could be discerned. But I wonder if this is the kind of thing that is decisive for the development of the listening faculty, this listening urge, the impulse to pursue a listening vocation.

I am not sure that it is not a much more fundamental quirk of temperament, an elaboration of a mammalian capacity for attunement as a style of both attention and social intervention. Listening in this sense, which goes far beyond the merely auditory, is a matter of an existential apprehension of how complex and variable and vulnerable the human situation is. There is no childhood so privileged as to make the promptings that lead to this existential intuition unavailable.

Probably, we listen because there is something in us that fits us for the job of active listening, of a complex investment in another human being across wide reaches of our personalities. There is something in us that fits us to this listening as a vehicle for the realization of the design of our own personalities. No doubt, this faculty requires development to reach maturity and be fully useful. No doubt, this development calls for hard and sometimes horrifying work. However, what is to be developed often already makes its presence known at the earliest stages and often in a decisive way.

Virtual Experiences

Part of listening to others involves living vicariously. I, for example, have not been to the movies for the past seven years, and yet, through the eyes of different patients, I have seen every movie that comes to town. During one especially interesting period, I had three young patients who were regular moviegoers and to whom movies were very important as vehicles for imaginative exploration of their own feelings. They could explore without acting in the real world. Naturally each one had his or her own take on the movies about which they talked to me. These takes were sometimes so different that it was hard to believe that they had seen the same movie. Clearly, they had not. Or perhaps they had seen the same movie but then subjected what they had seen to an internal remake that had transformed the original fabulously, almost beyond recognition.

It is a commonplace that, in order to do psychotherapy, we need to have lives of our own outside psychotherapy to counterbalance the pull of what our patients bring to us. What is not so well appreciated is that the vicarious life, the life of virtual experience brought to us through our patients, is a real life, too. We learn by simulating if we have the kind of imagination that lets us go deeply and freely enough into the simulation to find ourselves rather than to lose ourselves. Our faculty for experiencing goes well beyond the literal. What we experience as we sit with our patients and try to follow them leads us onward into territories of ourselves that we may not previously have known well, if at all. We find that the way we see people in our lives outside therapy is influenced by our lives in therapy.

I have a very troubled patient, one of whose deepest and most enduring loves is for dance. She herself as a young woman was an accomplished dancer of promise. Dance helped her survive a harrowing childhood. One of her enduring griefs is that she was not able, for a variety of complex familial, personal, and emotional reasons, to pursue her dream of a career as a dancer. I myself am a person who has never danced and have only a limited appreciation of dance. This exceedingly difficult treatment has been filled with long, desperate, and painful silences. Imagine my surprise during one of these interminable silences when I discovered myself simultaneously choreographing and watching the performance of a dance about despair in my mind.

It was set at the edge of a cliff. The performers were stylized, almost pipe cleaner figures, perhaps so thin because my patient suffered from an eating disorder that kept her always at the edge of fainting when she stood up. (Or perhaps she suffered from the eating disorder because the world was so filled with terror for her.) I watched these figures dancing, enjoying the counterpoint of the figures and their shadows, which were even longer and thinner than they were. These dancing figures were Giacometti sculptures that had come to life, preserving that tantalizing combination of grace and deformation that is so intimately evocative of loneliness and longing.

What impressed and thrilled me was that instead of suffering in silence, I found myself enjoying myself in a new realm, as if somehow the patient had found a way to lead me somewhere that was crucially important to her and, in so doing, made a major gift to me of a new avenue for understanding and enjoyment and creativity. No doubt my experience was defensive in a variety of ways. However, there is also no doubt that it was progressive and helpful. Certainly, it paralleled almost uncannily the patient's life experience, in which the world of ballet offered her the hope of another realm in which she could be active instead of passive, be noticed instead of ignored, be always accompanied, and, as she felt it, cared for by the music and the sequence of the steps instead of left to her own devices in trying to ward off chaos and cruelty as best she could.

Our patients instruct us in so much that is painful, but our patients lead us to love, appreciate, and enjoy so much that we would not otherwise have known to cherish. We come to care about what they care about because they care about it and we care for them. Our patients tell us the stories of their lives in the diverse worlds in which they live them. As we sit in our chairs, we are carried into so many different realms of experience. We come to appreciate how important what goes on outside therapy is for what goes on in therapy just as what goes on inside therapy is important for what will go on outside therapy. We come to know our patients as the children they once were and, in many ways, still are, as parents, workers, spouses, lovers, citizens of a vastly complicated society. They bring us news of so many trends in the world around us.

What impact does all this virtual experience have on us? What does it ask of us? How do we contain it? How does it affect the commitments that we make? In a basic sense the work of psychotherapy is much too important to be left to psychotherapy alone. We can no more expect to make fundamental repairs in the world around us simply by doing psychotherapy than we can hope to exert an effect on world history by reading the newspaper. The work of psychotherapy stimulates our concerns for a much wider world, but in so doing it can also make us feel very small and frustrated.

We can easily be moved to attitudes that are both defeatist and embittered. In fact, many psychotherapists fall prey to this danger and withdraw from their patients, often to a much greater extent than is consciously recognized either by patients or therapists. The therapist may call it neutrality or professional distance, while the patients take it in, often unconsciously, as yet another proof of their own lack of appeal, their own exile from human company. Some therapists withdraw not only from their patients but, in a crucial interior way that is fateful for their own vitality, from themselves.

A Wider Orientation

Sitting in a chair and listening to people's troubles in such a way as to be of use to them in making some headway in learning to live with these troubles is no easy task. The more we know of people, the more we know about the pain and suffering there is in the world, about the caprices of fate and fortune. We are continually faced with the job of changing to accommodate what we know and what it means not only to us but in us.

Therapists need support. They need holding environments. Much has been written about the importance of psychological theories as devices to hold and support psychotherapists, to help them, as it were, keep themselves and their chair afloat and on an even keel. The idea here is that therapists gain a security from their theoretical notions, as from a fetish or a teddy bear, that helps them stay organized and so be effective (Michels 1983).

Much less has been written about the importance of certain attitudes in therapists in providing holding for themselves. The complex of attitudes that I regard as decisive for therapists' capacity to hold and sustain themselves as they sustain their work is best described as compassion. Compassion is an orientation toward whatever comes our way in life.

It is nothing simple. It involves a broad caring that does not stop at the boundaries of a particular discipline.

If a therapist's work is to be vital, it must be founded in a personal ethics, a personal politics, a personal aesthetics, a personal account of what is near in life and what is dear and ultimate. It must be founded in a personal way of being. It must take its spirit from a broad orientation toward life and its problems and prospects as they present themselves both inside and outside the consulting room, which, after all, is a highly permeable membrane.

The broad set of attitudes I call compassion. It is the knowing pursuit of kindness; it constructs the bridges between the therapist's own life and the patient's life, between the therapist's positions in the consulting room and outside it, between the therapist's ethics and aesthetics and politics and spirit and his or her work specifically as a therapist. To be a therapist, to take on the burden and the promise of the care of other persons as persons in their full complexity and integration, to be the steward often of their emerging functions, sensibilities, and commitments, calls for an integration and commitment on the part of the therapist that goes well beyond convention, beyond the assumption and enactment of a social role. It requires an inner conviction and resiliency worthy of the name of a vocation.

The therapeutic instrument that the therapist composes for and plays is him- or herself, as the therapist actually is, grounded in the world of his or her own deepest concerns, in the world of his or her own ongoing peril and unfolding as a person. Certainly, psychological knowledge is important, but psychological knowledge is not like the knowledge of astronomy or geology. It brings with it questions about what we are, what we wish to be, what our commitments are, what values we will hold, explore, express, and defend, and how we will go about all this. Cleverness and perceptiveness may be of great help in doing psychotherapy, but a deeper devotion, which is not in any way simple-minded, is more decisive. In psychotherapy, what we are matters at least as much as what we know. What we do may be no more important than how we do it.

I do not believe that it is possible to do therapy without discussing politics, ethics, aesthetics, and religion. The discussions may not be explicitly so labeled. They may not involve the use of cumbersome or fashionable terms. When we treat a man who has no job or prospect of getting a job, a divorced person in the midst of a bitter custody fight, a person who has been homeless, an executive who is consumed with ambition and also suicidal and addicted to alcohol, we cannot help but engage on the terrain of ethics, politics, aesthetics, and religion, however strictly psychological we try to be in our approach. The fact is that all these different matters that matter are linked up together, that each one names a piece of the seamless fabric of living.

We cannot make a defense of life and its possibilities, a case for doing the hard work of change and compromise, without also being prepared to be critical of not just personal psychological arrangements but also social arrangements. We cannot help people with necessary disillusionments unless we have a faith, however rough and ready, however apparently untraditional or uncanonical to help temper the process of disillusionment. When we work with patients, we take on the whole package of the patient's living, with its ethical, aesthetic, political, and religious dimensions. Not only do we take it on, but also we take it in and we take it home with us.

Compassion is the core value that animates psychotherapy and gives it soul and staying power. As such, it is not something that can exist for the therapist exclusively or even primarily in the consulting room. Psychotherapy gives a privileged position from which to study and get to know the attitudes of people toward themselves and toward each other. This study is not simply detached and descriptive but inevitably linked to positions of advocacy. We are not neutral in our consulting rooms, if by neutral is meant something like without values or uninvolved or unengaged. When we care, we are no longer neutral, no matter how we try to retain our equanimity.

We are there as ourselves, and, no matter how hard we try to disguise or dissemble, our patients will read through to an experience of us as living people with living vulnerabilities, values, pretensions, and possibilities. Psychotherapy is a discipline of human involvement with the suffering and promise of particular people in the actual circumstances they find themselves. As such, it remains, at its source, a cure through love.

A middle-aged businessman who had been quite successful monetarily but not so successful either in his personal relationships or in his struggles for self-esteem and self-respect was sitting in my office when he heard the hospital operator announcing that someone had parked a luxury car in a parking space reserved for the handicapped. The operator asked whoever had parked there to be so kind as move the car.

My patient grinned from ear to ear and said, "They'll never track me down."

From the handicapped space to the regular parking lot was a distance of no more than 50 feet. I was shocked as much by my patient's sadistic glee as by his act of inconsideration. I found myself seething and having great difficulty listening to him. I thought this act was, in some real and important way, typical of him. I find it hard to explain in retrospect why I did not immediately take it up with him. I feel a certain shame about my failure. Perhaps I was frightened as well as

shocked. Or perhaps I was chilled and awed by what I felt as
the futility of taking it up. Possibly, I had gotten a felt sense
of just how isolated and removed not only from others but
from himself this man was. He seethed on a regular basis and
also complained of enormous difficulties in concentrating.
One of the things that bothered him the most about himself
was that he did not seem to be able to choose a direction
and stick with it.

After the session, I was still very upset. Only at the end
of a few days did it strike me that my patient was really handicapped. In an important way, his glee that he had taken up
a handicapped spot was a communication and a confession.
He did feel that he belonged in a handicapped space. Where
he parked was an act of self-recognition. Nor was this feeling without a certain justification, even if his handicap was
the result of a different kind of heart disease. What he was
missing was a sense of the reality not only of others but of
himself, a sense of what he had to give and what others
needed that would have made possible a compassionate attitude and some pleasure in it. I struggled hard to help this
man become aware of his inner desolation, all the while
wondering about the complex series of factors—personal,
natural, historic, and social—that had helped produce it and
now helped maintain it.

As he told it, his mother had been deeply humiliated
and fanatically interested in money and social position. His
father had not had the courage to stand up to her. His mother
had had scant respect for him. They were often gone and
paid little attention to the impact of this on him. Even when
his parents were there, their investment in him was not reliable. He had always felt inadequate and inferior and had been
surprised to discover how easy it was to make money, not
that he had always been terribly scrupulous about how he
went about making it.

In many ways, what he perceived as the rift between his mother and father still existed within him. What was sad and startling was the extent to which he had reproduced the familiar pattern in his own marriage and functioning as a parent. He failed to understand that what was motivating his teenage children in much of the behavior that made him so angry was exactly what he felt himself and had felt since he was a small child. They had a sense of not mattering. They could not acquire a secure sense of making a difference even to themselves. So they were driven to a search for the reassurance of sensation and discord, much as he was.

Patients bring the whole world with them into therapy, if in a highly personalized manner. Just so and in just as personalized a manner, we therapists bring a whole world in as well. What follows is a reflection on the role of compassion in helping us care for patients and the world in which we and they live. It is an effort to provide a holding environment for reflections on the kind of commitment involved in taking care both in therapy and outside therapy. It is an effort to provide a holding environment for reflections on how what goes on outside therapy links with what goes on in therapy. We have to be able to think and feel globally in order to be able to think, feel, act, and be locally.

What follows is an effort to make a contribution in the linked domains of the culture of psychotherapy and the psychotherapy of culture. When we know single persons in depth, this can make possible a breadth of understanding and point of view not available without this degree of immersion. It is a tragedy of our times that so much in the way of political rhetoric and social policy is based on simplifications of the existential status of individual persons that amount to tyrannical distortions.

So much of what concerns us in psychotherapy is too big to be managed as only a set of psychotherapeutic issues.

We must be concerned with prevention as well as with care and cure, with provision as well as with repair. The social, cultural, and historic conscience we bring to and take from psychotherapy provides the basis for starting to imagine public and community health measures of great importance. Meaning is an important dimension of communal life and exerts a major impact on community health. Initiatives in our community life, after all, depend for their success on widely shared cultural attitudes and values. Changes in these must begin with intimate investigations of ourselves and our close associates.

What follows is an effort to stimulate and support therapists' efforts to take care of themselves, to understand and maintain their own commitment and sense of a personal orientation in the wider troubled world of which the consulting room is a small part. To reflect on compassion is to seek a tuning fork for the heart so that we can both keep our hearts in that part of our living and loving we call work and also take heart from our work. This kind of reflection can help us to be both active and receptive. While such reflection may make us uncomfortable, the comfort that comes from remaining numb is much more dangerous.

2

The Vital Link

A First Look

A psychiatric resident was struggling in weekly appointments to make a relationship with an HIV-positive woman who was episodically very suicidal. She had cut her throat during one such time. She had previously been diagnosed, probably wrongly, as schizophrenic. She had spent ten years as an IV drug-using prostitute, then given that life up after she had a child who, fortunately, did not acquire the HIV virus in utero. Her T cell count had recently dropped. She was searching for a way to find meaning in staying alive in the face of the prospect of a very difficult death, one that had a special vividity for her because she had watched her sister die of AIDS. As she put it to her therapist, her child and her mother were her main reasons for wanting to live.

When she told her therapist that she had recently held a loaded gun to her own head, he was moved to ask her whether she had ever had to survive someone's suicide. She said she had not. Then she asked him whether he had ever had to live through losing someone to suicide. The resident was moved to talk with her about the history of suicide in his family, a topic that was not easy for him. He spoke of how much impact a suicide had on the survivors, in this way conveying to the patient his sense of her importance.

He used his knowledge of his own suffering to help her feel that she mattered. He encountered her in a genuine and human way and came away full of sorrow, with what amounted to awe for the difficulty of her predicament. He encouraged her to call him if she got to feeling that way. When she said that she had thought about that but felt she did not want to disturb him at eleven o'clock at night, he replied that he would find it much more disturbing to hear that she had killed herself.

Compassion is the virtue that comes from a considered appreciation of the links that bind us each to the other. Compassion depends on the understanding that we are, to use Harry Stack Sullivan's memorable phrase, "more simply human than otherwise" (1953, p. 16). Why should we be compassionate? The answer is simple, deep, old, and honorable: We should be compassionate because we are each one implicated in the other. As the knowing pursuit of kindness, compassion is a central feature of the search for realization of the creative potentials of our kind.

If we appear to be islands, it is only because we have not looked beneath the surface to see the enduring connections. When we close our hearts and turn our backs on the other, we are actually hardening our hearts against ourselves and turning our backs on ourselves. The eventual consequence of this is a sense of inner impoverishment and terror, often coupled with a bitter sense of having been cheated. This sense of bitterness and of having been cheated all too easily issues in violent and destructive behavior.

"I don't know why everyone didn't give up on me. I gave up on myself over and over again. I did my best to push everyone away, too. I was good at pushing people away, too. I didn't care about them any more than I cared about myself. I was mean without even knowing that I was mean. I just couldn't find any other way to be. I was totally lost," said a young woman who had been living self-destructively and longing to die for years. In the process she had almost alienated everyone she knew, including her family. Yet, they had persisted, ultimately compelling her against her expressed will into a treatment situation that proved to be useful to her.

Some would object that being compassionate brings no personal advantage. This objection only demonstrates a failure to understand either what is truly personal or what genuine advantage is. If virtue is its own reward, the reward is a deeply satisfying one that renews itself whenever the virtue is practiced or contemplated. Virtue nourishes growth from inside. We can please ourselves by living well in a way that gives us strength and sustenance. If we fall into the habit of believing that rewards can only be external and material, we have abandoned any real respect for the human spirit. We have closed off our prospects and imprisoned ourselves, subjecting ourselves to a regimen that is as bleak as it is implacable. We have sent ourselves into an exile from which there may be no return.

Even when compassion involves sacrifice, sacrifice is not without its rewards. Nor are these rewards necessarily masochistic in nature. For example, we may discover that our needs are much less or different than what we thought they were. We may come to understand what is truly essential in us and to us. We may enjoy the pleasures of traveling lighter and so having more inner room for maneuver. We may find that what we gave up, even though we had to struggle hard to give it up and missed it, was a deadening force in our lives. In human design, as in other forms of design, less can be more. What we give up outside we may find ourselves able to take up inside. Sacrifice can help us become less literal and material minded. It can help us become more aware of the extent of the inner domain and its creative possibilities. It is in the inner domain that the fate of humans will be decided.

A young man had been very successful in many different endeavors, none of which meant very much to him. He was a star student and seemed to have an intriguing future ahead of him. However, nothing rang true for him inside, so that the more successful he was, the more desperate and empty he felt, as if he were trying to live someone else's life, not his own. Almost by accident, he became involved in teaching. After he had taught a very disturbed teenage girl how to read, he had the spontaneous thought, "I've done something that makes my existence worthwhile. I can go on living." He had found that he enjoyed taking care of other people, and this piece of self-knowledge helped him chart a way forward in life.

Beyond Human Darkness

The dark enlighteners of the last century and a half, themselves the heirs of a critical tradition dating back at least to Spinoza, have instructed us in humans' limitless capacity for deceit, folly, cruelty, and destructiveness, including self-destructiveness (Yovel 1989). All this has become commonplace. It has passed into reflexes of thought nearly as automatized as the spinal ones that mediate the withdrawal of a hand from the fire. The dark enlighteners made it their business to puncture the self-congratulatory sentimentalism that allowed people to turn away from the dark side of their acts, intentions, and inactivity. Freud was certainly one of the most distinguished of these dark enlighteners, teaching that even the most apparently selfless acts had a selfish underside, that the best and the worst in people were the nearest of neighbors. Indeed, Freud taught that they cohabit in profound and disquieting intimacy.

These dark enlighteners performed a useful service. Certainly, no person of feeling or decency can fail to have been moved to a measure of despair by the record of this last century, the orgies of cruelty, the extravagances of destruction, the gross and growing disproportions between the material chances of the haves and have nots, the wanton disregard for the environment. All this continues even now. If material poverty kills by pressure, material wealth often destroys by moral vacuum as the things get the upper hand and exercise a tyranny of numbness all their own. This tyranny of the thing is one of the forces that we spend so much of our time and energy trying to combat in therapy.

Gross injustices in distribution of resources are bad for those who have too much as for those who have too little. No orgy of consumption can make up for an empty heart. The fable of King Midas, whose greed turned everything to gold and led him to a horrible death by starvation, still resonates. We might say that he invested himself in a way that had disastrous results. Investment in a world of things alone is certainly a very bad investment policy. "I find myself buying things I don't even want," said one patient. "I wonder if it's just too frightening for me to want anything." As I listened to her, I thought her words had a special importance. I longed to hear them spoken more publicly, as I felt they had wide applicability. The topic of how a person can become so frightened of her own genuine needs as to find knowing about them unbearable is important both for therapy and for politics.

The dark enlighteners had only a part of the story. A pessimistic and self-deprecatory sentimentalism can serve to excuse us from responsibility on the grounds that to hope or to strive is to be naive. How luxurious this kind of pessimism can be! Trying is hard, especially when the odds seem against us, as they almost always do when we are seeking to find a way that is genuinely our own and feels genuinely human to us.

How superior we can sometimes feel if we give up before we have even begun! We close our eyes and start to flatter ourselves that we have been so adept at accepting just what a hard world it is, when actually we should be shamed at our own complicity in injustice, at our failure to be moved by what is happening around us. There are so many ways that we can drug and delude ourselves. Pessimism without limit about human nature is certainly one of them. When we do not try our hardest in the name of ideals that we believe in, we have some real reason to feel pessimistic about ourselves. It is much better to try to come to grips with our own inner sense of our own failings than to celebrate it in a generalized pessimism.

A failure to contend with what is difficult, rationalized on the basis of superior insight, can make a plush lining for a coccoon in which an awful metamorphosis takes place. The creature that emerges is no butterfly but more a parasitic worm quite unaware of its brutality and lack of any self of real human scope. We cannot afford a pessimism that makes us forget that to do even a little in dire circumstances can be very satisfying. An essential resource in a dark hour is the capacity to imagine and work for even a slightly brighter one. Our concerns are what animate us. They give us both spunk and soul, neither of which we can live without.

Compassion, a local virtue with global implications, starts its work where it finds itself. There is always plenty to do. The question as to whether these myriad local tasks were always there waiting to be discovered or whether compassion created them is best left moot. After all, human history is not simply the history of advances in cruelty and destructiveness. There has also been an enormous series of advances in the capacity to conceive kindness and practice it, to conceive the broadest human kinship and give it practical meaning.

We should not allow these advances to go unremarked but should retain our capacity to be both astonished and inspired by them. The expanding record over the centuries of the capacity to be kind, to appreciate and respond to the predicaments and possibilities of others, should serve us as a series of prophecies in deeds that summon us to a fuller awareness of ourselves and a worthy standard for our own efforts and aspirations.

Think, for example, of new ways of viewing women, children, old persons, and persons who are disabled. Think of the creation and at least partial implementation of ideals related to nonviolent resolutions of disputes. Think of the development of systems of law and justice. Think of the capacity to listen to and respond to appeals to conscience from those who know themselves to be oppressed.

Acts of compassion are small, like blades of grass. Like blades of grass, they take root and hold the human soil that holds and nourishes them. They protect it from being blown away and stripped bare. They protect it from being reduced to the status of a desert whose human carrying capacity is virtually nil. Acts of compassion are acts of emotional fertility. Physical fertility without emotional fertility is ultimately barren. We need meaning every bit as much as we need milk. We need the milk of human kindness to make us grow, to help us develop immunity against the blandishments of cruelty.

Acts of compassion counter acts of aggression and neglect. Acts of compassion have the capacity to demonstrate the ultimate futility of neglect and aggression. Acts of compassion enrich the local human environment in ways that are real and practical. Their reality is of the mind and the heart, not merely "thingish." Acts of compassion matter in ways that go beyond what is literally material. Acts of compassion build on one another. There is an architecture of compassion that can make human cities graceful and pleasing places to live, each person possessing an alcove that has a different point of view, not so much in opposition as in complementarity.

A borderline patient came for a consultation in part because her insurance company was not willing to trust her therapist's judgment concerning the need for two sessions a week, in part because the patient herself felt "stuck" both in her therapy and in her life. In addition to a very difficult childhood, she had suffered a staggering series of losses in the previous three years. While she felt stuck in therapy, she was careful to tell me that this therapist had done more for her than any other. I was tempted to translate "stuck" as attached and vulnerable both to the dangers of losing and to the dangers of fusing.

In particular, she pointed out the therapist's willingness to go to court to speak for her needs in a complex piece of litigation involving her divorce. She described with relish how badly the opposing lawyer had treated her therapist and spoke with surprise and pride of her therapist's resilience and commitment.

"She didn't need to put herself on the line for me," said the patient.

Her sense of this as a novel act was as saddening as her gratitude for it was touching. Actually, the therapist did need to put herself on the line for the patient. What made the attachment possible was the therapist's willingness to be as uncomfortable as the patient was and the patient's capacity to notice this and appreciate it.

Acts of compassion give rise to acts of compassion, just as acts of cruelty and neglect give rise to acts of cruelty and neglect. Acts of compassion are good cultural practice, just as the planting of grasses and trees to assure the health and stability of the soil and a rich and reliable layer of humus is good cultural practice. Compassion reduces fear. Where there is less fear, there is much less hostility. Where there is less hostility and more a spirit of human hospitality, there is less danger.

Compassion helps people feel safe in their minds and hearts, with themselves and with others. If we are not safe inside with our impulses and urges, we will not be able to find ways to make what surrounds us safe. This interior safety, which depends on interior acquaintance with ourselves, is the work of a lifetime. It is also the ongoing reward of that work. We cannot afford to let our excitements become incitements to do ill.

Part of the beauty of compassion is that there is no way to standardize it. It resists mechanization, because it is about people, not machines. The notion of a compassionate robot is a contradiction in terms. Compassion cannot be mass produced. There is no way to subject it to strict administrative control or to levy taxes on it. There is also no way to stamp it out. In the Nazi death camps, in the Gulag archipelago, amid the horrors of Cambodia, in Rwanda, inspired and ordinary individuals and small groups demonstrated their capacity for compassion. It is an expression of human freedom and feeling, a signature trait built as deeply into our natures as anything destructive or exploitative. If we forget this, we have lost sight of an inner beacon whose guidance we very much need.

The mother of a child of 19 months had just died, after a sudden, unexpected, and devastating illness. Just before the funeral was to take place, the child was sitting at the kitchen table having a snack. Her father's aunt was helping her with her snack. When, dressed for the funeral, her father came into the room, he could not help himself and burst into tears.

The little girl looked up at him. An expression of distress crossed her face. She lifted her glass of milk from the table and offered it to him. Smiling through his tears, he took a sip and returned it to her.

"I guess that is the milk of human kindness," the father's aunt said very quietly.

Unity in Diversity

Compassion flows from a practical intuition of the unity of
life and all living things. It rests on a sense of kinship that
goes far beyond ties of blood and nationality to embrace the
whole fragile earth, not as a theoretical construct, but as it
exists in all its intricate peculiarity right here under our feet
and noses. Humans and humus are not that far apart. This
is part of what makes for the pleasures of gardening. What
separates humans from decay and decomposition back to
humus is, after all, only a span of decades less than the number of fingers we each have on our two hands.

    This relationship is both elemental and fundamental.
We are literally the children of the earth. Without our ties
to it, we would make no sense. We cannot think about a figure without the ground that produced it. To take care of a
creature has no meaning without care for the environment
that holds that creature. Nor does the earth, this ancient
dependency of the sun, itself exist in isolation. It is part of a
large open system that confronts us with the mystery of its
presence. Our capacity to perceive and be challenged and
guided by the immensity of this mystery is part of what is
moving about our own presence. As we are present to ourselves, we are always changing. Our task is to find pleasure
and promise in this ongoing state of creation.

    Compassion is essential to our sense of identity. It is
essential to who we are and what we are for, where we come
from and where we are going. Without compassion, the vital
sense of a vital link, any inkling we have of our own identity,
of the difficult, dynamic, aggravating, and intriguing process
of being what we are, is bound to be negative. We will know
ourselves as *not* this or not *that*. We will find our knowing

always stopped by barriers. We will find both our reach and our grasp terribly cramped.

We will know ourselves always in opposition and estrangement. We will know ourselves through our enmities and envies. With this kind of knowing, there is always a sense of bleakness, of emptiness, even of desolation. Under these conditions, we dare not release the inner strain of all this friction for fear that without it we would be lost. As one man who felt particularly despairing and useless said, "I don't know what I'm for, but I sure do know what I'm against. It scares me to think of living any other way."

This negativism can be part of a subtle and pervasive paranoia, as the person feels surrounded by so much that he is *not*. He feels encircled by so much that seems to him to turn a cold shoulder on him. It is so hard for a person in this frame of mind to realize that the cold shoulder is his own, that, if it seems all frontiers are closed against him, it is because he in his insecurity has closed them off.

War begins in the human heart, and this rankling itch, this sense of being among enemies, is an important part of how it begins. We can and do require others to become our enemies, if we have no other way of making sense out of them and ourselves. To embrace the other, we need to find new resources in ourselves that free us from our dependency on enmities to help us know where we fit in. This conversion from a psychological economy based on defense needs is at least as difficult a process as the post-Cold War efforts to shrink our national military expenditures. In many cases, having enemies is a defense against confusion, the formlessness that underlies the need to draw the world in stark contrast.

"I started to think for a moment that I didn't hate my family, that actually I missed them, but I couldn't go on with that thought for too long. I didn't know how to do it. It was so different than the way that I am used to thinking," a young woman patient said. "If I stop hating my family, where does that leave me? I spend a lot of time hating my family, and that keeps us in touch. If I stop hating them, I'd have to find another way to stay in touch. I don't know if I can do that. I don't even know if I want to do that."

What the word *alien* means is "unlinked." Of course, opposition, envy, rivalry, antagonism make linkages. They have their developmental moments, as anyone who has ever watched or raised small children knows. But, if these far outlive their original and appropriate developmental moments, then these are troubled and troubling linkages. The spectacle of full-grown people behaving like 2-year-olds is both horrifying and frightening. These negativistic linkages are full of strain and dissonance.

For there to be opposition, there must be something in common. There must be a field on which to become engaged. Those with nothing in common cannot do battle. The bitterest quarrels often turn on the smallest differences. These differences would be insignificant were it not for a devastating lack of perspective that makes them seem worth killing and dying about.

Envy, rivalry, antagonism—all three presuppose communication. Communication would not be possible without an attunement that goes deeper, even if it is unrecognized. Where there is communication, there is in the depths a communion waiting to be known and appreciated. There is shared living. A certain security of organization is required to appreciate this communion just as an appreciation of this communion is essential to security of organization. In order to be secure in our appreciation of others, we must be secure in our appreciation of ourselves. We must be able to listen to the song of our own hearts and hear the notes changing and rearranging, registering the real joys and real pains of real life. We must be able to accept that we can both matter to ourselves and know how small we are.

Recognition—literally, a thinking again—is the double take that mind does that transforms the way it knows itself and others. This new knowing has the power to change actions and intentions. In the sphere of the negative, the deeper ground of unity is already implicit, but its message goes unheeded. The terror of engulfment by the other rules over any awareness of linkage in complementarity. Opposition puts us up against the other. It makes us rub shoulders with the other. This frictional knowledge brings back a great deal of information. Of course, we are different. No two persons, no two species, no two places, no two times are identical.

The intuition of compassion is that differences articulate and display an underlying unity that far transcends them. This intuition makes it possible to find harmony in the midst of all the practical dissonances of life. It makes it necessary to struggle practically to articulate this harmony in the midst of all the hurts and hopes of real daily life. When we have found our own center, we are in much less need of bristling along our frontiers. We find that we are much less edgy, with many more resources of calm and contentment within ourselves. When we have found our own center, we find that we are in much easier reach along shorter internal pathways of a much wider range of our experiences. So we are more available within ourselves for the intuitive attunement with others from which compassionate action arises.

An appreciation of unity and harmony is a call to action and engagement, not a justification for smug withdrawal. An appreciation of unity and harmony, of the common ground underneath even the most embittered differences, informs the refusal to despair. It supports the capacity to start small and to stay small, never allowing frustrated love to pass over to ravenous ambition, as it so often does. We hunger to stand for something. We hunger to stand with others whom we value, not simply on the lonely ground of the self-defined in abject opposition to others. We hunger not just for response but for responsibility. We hunger not just to feed ourselves but to see others able to feed themselves and go on with the creative and inventive tasks not just of outer life, but also of inner life. Just as we can all impoverish each other, so we can all enrich each other.

Compassion insists that there can be enough love to go around, because we have the means to make it. Our ownership of the means of compassionate production is inalienable. We can fail to use them, but we cannot get rid of them. Compassion knows that competition can return to its root meaning of trying together and being tried together, not a vain set of struggles for illusory superiority. Competition can mean striving together with each other to make enough for everyone. The lives we have we make together.

Ben Franklin's observation "If we don't all hang together, we'll all hang separately" has meaning in the larger human context. Compassion is about getting the hang of hanging together. In this sense, it is truly revolutionary. It can give the world a new twist and a new thrust.

Nurturing Compassion: A Collaboration

Like other human qualities, compassion can be taught, but it has to be taught in such a way that it can be caught. The teaching of compassion involves a transmission of spirit, not simply an initiation into the intricacies of another technology. So the teaching must be done in a spirit of compassionate respect for the spirit and freedom of the learner, the one who will have to find a unique compassionate way within him- or herself in accord with the dictates and complexities of his or her own nature and experience. If it is authentically the learner's, what the person finds will be both the same and different from what his or her teachers intended.

Compassion is best taught from the very beginning of life simply by being compassionate. When we act compassionately, we present a series of creative examples. These examples bear our impress, from which so much about us and our motives and our way of understanding and responding can be gleaned by a discerning observer. Reverse engineering was a central part of human learning long before it got a name. As parents, we often wonder how our children developed their stunning grasp of our characters. With astonishing thoroughness and concentration, our children take us apart in the course of everyday living in order to put themselves together. In so doing, they learn not just our physical postures but also our moral postures. They learn what makes us tick, what makes us blow up, and what helps us put ourselves back together again.

Compassion cannot be learned by rote because it is a *way* of being and acting, a set of ever-unfolding processes of practical and spirited invention. It goes on from moment to moment, producing different products. It changes from moment to moment as circumstances ask different questions of it and put new challenges to it. It gives shape to the flow of living. Compassion tinkers. It tries things out and on. If it can build a contraption that works out of the moral equivalent of spit and baling wire, it does not seek for grander materials. Rather, it takes pleasure in discovering sufficiency in a new combination of elements that would have seemed on the face of it inadequate to the task. It takes pleasure in discovering new ways to produce kindness and solace and pleasure.

Compassion is learned through watching and wondering. We do children a grievous injustice if we believe they are curious only about means of destruction and ways to be cruel. They are curious also about the ways of love and the intricacies of kindness. They are curious about understanding and the practical disposition to help. Thoughtfulness involves being able to think and feel at the same time. It involves an understanding every bit as rich and deep as any technology.

Compassion is learned by trying to imitate. Sometimes imitators fall short. Other times they succeed in ways that open up to them new prospects for trying. We never know when imitation will turn into innovation, which is nothing more than imitation with variation. Compassion may be the most distinctively human of art forms, producing the most useful of artifacts. These are not shown in museums but rather taken up and not only treasured in human hearts but used and reused. They are passed on from heart to heart through both words and deeds in a rich and enriching living tradition. Compassion is an attitude that conditions our aptitudes, what we are apt to feel and notice and know and do.

We all have experience of being treated compassionately. We all know the effect of compassion on us and in us. We have felt it resonate and known the relief and reprieve that it brought us. We have all experienced the liberating effects of compassion. We have all known occasions when compassion has released us to be ourselves. This experience of being treated compassionately is a major force in disposing us to act compassionately. We want to share with others what we have received. We want to have the pleasure of giving as well as the pleasure of getting. When we give, we also have the opportunity not only to relive the experience of getting but to explore and extend it.

Giving makes what we have received more meaningful. In fact, it may be that what is most convincing and contagious about a compassionate act is our sense of the doer's state. The quiet conviction, the pleasure far beyond any mere sensual indulgence, but in no way excluding sensory vitality, speak to us. Compassion suggests avenues of integration whose prospects beckon us. It shines a very special light on the human countenance, speaking to what is possible in us. It can be the spark that kindles a heart and hearth-warming blaze of love that produces more fuel even as it produces more heat and light. The compassionate act has a very special fit and feel both for the one who gives and the one who receives.

Actually, splitting the field of compassion into givers and receivers, those who do and those who are done for or to, introduces a dangerous confusion. Are not all compassionate acts really cooperative acts? Are not compassionate acts really performed conjointly and consensually by two or more persons? Compassionate acts depend on an agreement between persons, neither of whom is either totally active or totally passive, although one may be more active than the other, one more passive than the other at a particular moment in time. Compassionate acts depend on agreements that are so often far more intuitive than explicit.

A despairing patient complained that I was much too optimistic about her and her prospects in life. I found this difficult to take in and to take on, because I most often am used to thinking about myself as a pessimist. I told her that her view surprised me because it was so different. She replied that she thought I was wildly optimistic, even cruel, to believe that she could actually be present in any authentic way in a human relationship. She knew this was just too hard for her. I asked her whether she thought that I had come up with my

optimism all on my own. She said it often seemed that way
to her, even if what she herself wanted the most was to be
able to be in a relationship and to manage it and enjoy it. I
said I thought that perhaps she had to see the hope as all
mine because it was so frightening to her but that I very much
doubted my capacity to come up with it all on my own.

Compassion, like an embrace or a kiss, is not a matter
simply of haves and have nots. Rather, compassion is a creative process in which people join forces to make creative
products of decisive importance for the quality of their lives.
These products are not only materially but also emotionally
and spiritually tangible. They have a vital touch, a vital feel
that gives life and vigor and verve in a way that no merely
material wealth can. Compassion keeps us the best company
down through the years as we pass through joys and tears.
Compassion gives spirit to material acts of kindness. It helps
us with both change and continuity.

If we want to convince ourselves of the fact that compassion is a process of cooperation in the service of the ideal
of love, we need only consider the dynamic that obtains between a specially bitter and mistrustful person and the one
who tries to come to his or her aid. Both have their reasons.
The bitter and mistrustful person was not born that way. In
fact, many bitter and mistrustful people started out quite
open and hopeful and tender, sometimes unusually so. The
wounds they sustained, often before they could even tell
themselves the story of their hurt, closed them off. Their
bitterness and mistrust, which by long habit has come to seem
even to them a second nature indistinguishable from their first
natures, is a hard shell that covers what is underneath. It may
give them an illusion of power elaborated to ward off their
deeper and more compelling experience of helplessness.

Similarly, the one who tries to come to the aid of the
mistrustful and bitter person is, in all likelihood, not some-

one who has never felt the allure of bitterness and mistrust. Probably, even if he is mostly able to refuse their seductions, when he looks at the bitter and mistrustful person, there is a shock of recognition. After all, as the wise saying goes, it takes one to know one. The shock of recognition may be accompanied by a shudder, as he realizes just how close he came to choosing that road himself. He may even find himself wondering what it was that let him travel a gentler way. He may try to discern in what human form, inner or outer, this grace came cloaked to visit him.

Now, if the bitter and mistrustful person is simply unable to detach himself internally even a little bit from mistrust and bitterness, then the other will not be able to help. It is always possible that this will be the outcome but never certain. The only way to know is to try. Compassion in general knows by trying, learns by doing. Compassion is much more of a practical disposition than of a theoretical one. It is not that compassion does not think, does not have a disposition to make theories, but rather that it always tests its theories against the feelingful and fraught challenges of actual living. It remembers that theory is no substitute for experience, the mind no substitute for the heart.

Helping a bitter and mistrustful person is not likely to be easy. For one thing, bitterness serves as a probe for the other's capacity to understand and to forgive. Mistrust serves as a probe for the other's trustworthiness. Putting the worst foot forward immediately tests the other's capacity for forbearance. There can be a bitter pleasure in running these tests, a joy in turning the tables. How ingenious suffering people can be in turning succor and help from their doors, as if the help made the hurt. In a sense, of course, the help does make the hurt, because the help makes the hurt available to be experienced and struggled with by showing an alternative. Help-rejecting ingenuity can be indicative of a vitality that longs for a different employment, even as it gives itself over to its current twisted purpose. It may be indicative of a frustrated inner creative force that has turned to destruction in its search for the security that eludes it all the more for the way it goes about looking for it.

"I don't know why I've had to torture you for so long," said one patient. "In fact, I didn't really know that I was torturing you. But I had to test to see you if you really gave a damn. I had to test by trying to be just as awful as I could be, because it seems to me that that's how I really am. I didn't want you to be bothered with me if I had to pretend. I know that sounds mixed up, but I had to try to hurt you before I could even consider trusting you. I did a good job, too, didn't I? I'm sure there were many times when you hated me."

Compassion is not omnipotence. It meets rebuffs. It has to struggle. It even despairs and requires pity to restore its capacity to hope and to help. Sometimes it is most useful through its limitations. The person who takes on the task of reaching out to a bitter and mistrustful person will, in all probability, have occasion to wonder, perhaps even bitterly and mistrustfully, why he bothers.

The helper may ask himself, ruefully, to what extent his own vanity plays a part. Is he really out to help the other, or is he trying to impersonate an impressive figure of whom he has caught a glimpse in the distorting mirror of his own mixed-up imagination? Is the goal truly to bring solace to the other or to find ways to feel powerful at the other's expense? Most probably, it is a complex amalgam of these two families of motivations and still others as well. Love need not be pure still to be love, however trying this proposition may be to accept. It reminds us again of human limitation, our submission to life's fullness, richness, and complexity.

The one who tries to help may find himself becoming painfully and almost self-destructively mistrustful of his own motivations. He may experience a whole range of feelings that are new and that challenge cherished notions about who he is. The helper may wish fervently that he had had the good sense never to get involved in the first place, only to discover that something stubborn and mysterious inside holds him to the task. He may become intrigued in a very exasperating way with getting to know what inside holds him to it, as if there were an other concealed inside that was not yet quite integrated.

The one who sets out to help a bitter and mistrustful person will have the opportunity not just to get to know the other one better, but also the chance for more self-knowledge. Reaching out has two components, one that involves a reaching out to a real outside other and another that involves a reaching out toward some aspect of oneself that is as yet insufficiently realized and integrated. We reach out because we are not finished. We are not done but always works in progress who progress by working and risking. Often we do not know what we are risking when we set out on a particular path. What we meet of ourselves may surprise us not only unpleasantly but also pleasurably and not in a self-indulgent way.

Compassion is a road to self-knowledge. Sometimes we have to struggle hardest to know what is best about ourselves. We have to struggle to know what is best about ourselves apart from our vanity. In this struggle, effort is our best ally, because it reassures us of the validity of what we come to know about ourselves. Working hard to a decent end teaches us that our ferments are something else than fictions.

For his part, if things go well, the bitter and mistrustful person may find himself full of hopes and doubts, worries and fears, needs so new that he does not exactly know their names, even if they have a shadowy familiarity that suggests to him that he may have encountered their relatives and forebears at some murky point in the past. The interest of the other in him may start to call into question for him why he has kept others at such a distance for so long, refusing an intimacy that he now starts to recognize, and, with fear and trembling, he also craves desperately. Probably there is no real intimacy without fear and trembling.

Even if the bitter and mistrustful person can cite chapter and verse to himself of the hurts that have made him the way he is, he may start to ask himself whether he has not colluded with them to build a way of living that is at least as much prison as fortress. If he has colluded in a major way, so allowing his inner rage and hurt to fashion him in its own image, then, while on the one hand there is much to grieve in the form of myriad lost opportunities that will never come again, there is also new hope, for the present opportunity to know and be known by another need not be lost. There is a way out of the inner captivity and its despairing comfort. Life is bitter, but it is not only bitter.

The present opportunity to know and be known can serve as the gateway to a different kind of future, one that will make it possible to forgive, without needing to forget. In fact, realistic memory is essential to forgiveness. Nor is realistic memory synonymous with self-mortification. Realistic memory together with regret help make pathways to reparation and resiliency. We can even forgive those whom we have lost, so changing the relationship in our minds and hearts that is living and need not be lost unless we condemn it to inner death. When we forgive, we do not revise history but rather diffuse our investment in an old hurt and grudge across the whole space of living relatedness.

Compassion is a collaborative undertaking, one that is most likely to surprise both collaborators with a new slant on themselves and the other. Compassion couples suffering and succor. When we are treated compassionately, we learn to treat ourselves compassionately. If we did not have this capacity to take it in and to use it, to establish in ourselves a center of compassion that is truly our own, we would be utterly immune from the workings of compassion.

To be moved to be compassionate we must know what suffering is. To know what suffering is we must also have known joy. These are not matters for theoretical knowledge but rather matters of experience. They are matters of existential immersion. The fact is that across the span of a lifetime suffering spares no one. For so many, it starts so very near the dawn of life. Compassion comes to be in the encounter of uncertain persons who are at risk. Uncertainty, for all its fearfulness, makes a place for new invention and for the intervention of the new.

The example of the encounter between the bitter and mistrustful person and the one who tries to come to his or her aid is not a fanciful one. It happens between couples in and out of marriage. It happens between parents and children. In some cases, the parent is the bitter and mistrustful one; in others, it is the child. It happens at work and at school. It happens in hospitals and in places of worship. It happens wherever people meet and make commitments to each other, putting themselves at risk and seeking to elicit and provide responses that meet needs. It happens between strangers who find something arresting and intriguing in the particular strangeness of this particular other.

It is one of the basic dynamics in therapy. A gifted mental health worker at Sheppard Pratt who went on to train as a clinical psychologist described one of his first days on the unit. Illustrating his own particular patience and tenacity, he spent hours walking up and down the corridor with a young and despairing patient, trying to convince her that her suicidal project did not make sense because there was so much to live for. Her absolute immunity to his arguments and the futility of his efforts shocked him and set him thinking. When he came to summarize his work at Sheppard, he remarked that he thought so much of it, even most of it, was about what he called "that fragile trust issue. Do you care about me as I really am? Can I afford to take the risk of believing that you care?" This makes sense because trust influences our most basic orientation to life. We all have myriad reasons to mistrust not only others but ourselves. In the confrontation of this most basic of problems, neutrality has no meaning. We cannot stand on the sidelines.

Compassion as Exploration

Compassion is always an exploration of practical human possibility. It explores the inward and interpersonal frontiers of feeling and doing with which ordinary days and hours are honeycombed. Compassion creates a human sense of place and space, a deepened appreciation of the immense capacity and complexity of *here* and *now*. Compassion does not seek escape but encounter. It does not abhor or deny limits but rather recognizes that, even when they constrain, they give shape. It may seek to change or refine them, but not in the spirit of seeking perfection or of committing the violence so often associated with perfectionism. Compassion meets the *here* and *now* with a measure of confidence and trust, not with disdain and despair. It dares to embrace uncertainty and to see what can be made of it. It does not seek spurious security through the false assurance of premature closure. It does not seek security through the hard edges of cruelty. Compassion requires of us the sustained disciplines of both inner action and of interaction. Compassion is not utopian.

If compassion is exploratory, it is exploratory in a different sense and spirit than that of the conquistador or the colonialist in a pith helmet. It does not go with the sense of conquest. It does not go with any conviction of superiority. It accepts the necessity of undergoing in order to understand. It grasps that undergoing is often much more enriching than efforts to overcome. It knows that the world comes alive differently from different points of view. It knows that difference and variety have much to bring to life and that life is barren and devoid of spice without them. Compassion knows that it will have to change and rearrange itself to retain its basic shape and thrust. It knows in going that it will be different when it comes back. Compassion can tolerate perpetual transformation. It can even embrace it.

A patient remarked, "I don't really know what I've gotten here. I suppose it has something to do with sadness, with being able to get beyond anger to the sadness, and it has to do with limits, too, not that I like them, but that they're everywhere."

Compassion is attentive. It listens before it speaks, questions before it answers—not that it does not speak, not that it does not answer. Compassion revises its positions. It operates by trial and error, often relishing the acknowledgment of error, because such acknowledgment, far from representing only a loss, actually represents a much more important gain. By acknowledging error, compassion may see a new way forward, a new set of trials and errors on which to embark, a new chance of reconciling what before seemed irreparably split asunder.

There is a deeply human spirit of adventure at work in compassion, a spirit that can be quirky and troubled and troubling, but also full of the zest and peculiarities of human humor and vision. Although it is modest, compassion dares, not in a foolhardy way, but often in a way that is both hardy and robust. Compassion is often awkward, sometimes even embarrassing. It can get itself into terrible fixes, but it has the capacity to take a step back in order to find a way to take a step forward. Compassion can laugh to find a new perspective as well as cry in acknowledgment of the validity of an old one. It can use humor to tame and illuminate hurt, not to incite to cruelty.

The hallmark of compassion is appreciation. Compassion shines the light of sympathetic understanding on the human predicament. Compassion values what it finds. It recognizes that people have worked hard and struggled hard and thought hard and felt hard to become what they are. It recognizes the possibility, even the necessity of a whole host of serious and consequential mistakes in living. It recognizes helplessness and the fact of utterly undeserved misfortunes. It does not come with a full-blown plan of its own, a design to be imposed on the other. It does not see others as raw materials. Rather, it has sufficient inner creativity to try to note not just where the other's work in progress has been stymied, where it is deluded, where it is grandiose or self-contradictory, but also what was and is right in the originating intent. Compassion wants to learn as much or more than it wants to teach. It recognizes that there is often more to be taught by trying to learn. It is secure enough to let itself be changed by what it meets.

A paranoid schizophrenic, acutely psychotic at the time, was admitted to a Sheppard Pratt unit. He had a history of IV drug use and also of having served time in prison. The nursing staff dismissed him as a sociopathic type, feeling that he should be sent back to a public system of care for medication maintenance. However, medication had never succeeded in controlling his psychosis. Nor did it succeed when we tried. At one point the patient ran away from the hospital and threatened to jump off the balcony of his apartment, a jump that might well have proved fatal. As I discussed this possibility with him on the telephone in the nursing station, I got a clear sense of his helplessness and terror, because I felt them in myself.

I took him on as a private patient despite his lack of means. Over the next four years, as I got to know him, he was both exasperating and, in a certain way, inspiring. He had very little money, and, what little he had, he often spent unwisely on something he simply wanted without much view to the future. By the end of each month, he was broke and despondent again, severely castigating himself for his unwise ways with money. Yet, as he put it, sometimes "a person just needs what he wants." He stayed off drugs, although he often became delusionally afraid that others thought he was using drugs and so had only contempt for him. He kept on trying to go to school, although he often withdrew in panic before completing the class.

He sometimes called me three or four times a week at home to discuss with me what his voices were telling him. He went on and off his medications, alternately consenting to depot neuroleptics and becoming wary of them. As time went on and trust grew up between us, he started to talk to me about how wild he had been as a teenager, how remorseful he felt about how disrespectful he had been to his stepfather, how much it galled him to be still so dependent on his mother, and how hard it was for him to understand what had happened to him. He also started to talk with me about his joys and sorrows as a father of a young boy who did not live with him. As he spoke about his son, he also began to spend more time with him, enjoying this aspect of his life.

I found that I looked forward to seeing him each week, although sometimes he was very psychotic. On those occasions, it was as if a storm blowing out of control had invaded my office. Usually, he was a bit calmer by the time he left. However, for the most part, I found myself admiring him in his efforts to lead a decent life in face not only of limited means but of an illness that often brought him to total confusion and despair. What he wanted was simply a place in the human community, a sense of being able to contribute, and a few material comforts. He wanted to be a giver and not just a taker. He had a decency and, not infrequently, a sense of humorous perspective on life that I would have been delighted to help many of my other patients, not to say friends and family, acquire. Five or six times a year, he would call me up in a rage and inform me that I was fired, only to call again a few days later to say that he had not meant it and was truly sorry.

Compassion and Conscience

Compassion has to do with both conscience and consciousness, both of which are frequently misunderstood. Conscience is more a matter of attunement to our own larger purposes than it is a matter of an internal tyrant lording it cruelly over us in the name of harsh values that are alien to us. It is certainly a struggle to integrate a conscience that is new, raw, and primitive, but actually the guidance of a functioning conscience is essential to the work of integration that can help us find peace within ourselves and so make a genuine contribution to peace around us. Certainly, conscience can be perverted and put in the service of righteousness, rapaciousness, self-injury, or other corrupt ambitions, but there is nothing inevitable about this. Conscience can help us with both backbone and flexibility.

When it is functioning properly, our conscience goes along with us and knows along and grows along with us. If it questions our impulses and our intentions and sometimes questions them strongly, this questioning is like the questioning of a loyal and fearless friend, who finds it disrespectful to ask of us less than what we actually have to offer. Conscientious questioning is in the service of finding where our energies, impulses, and intentions truly fit and helping us to design ourselves in a capacious enough manner so that these energies, impulses, and intentions can find a proper place and proper application.

When we can confide in our consciences with confidence, then our consciences can confide in us, too. If we can admit errors, our consciences are likely to be able to admit their own errors and excesses, too. The resulting inner dialogue can be an important source of company, insight, consolation, and inspiration. We need all the help we can get in establishing a ground plan for ourselves.

When we act compassionately and feel with the discernment of compassion, we like ourselves better because we feel more like our real selves, more like the more realized selves that it is an essential function of conscience to help us seek and find. When, with the aid of conscience, we come to find real resources of compassion in ourselves, we can find in ourselves a human depth and dimension that helps us become less grasping. We are not so greedy, so angrily impressed by our own deficiencies, because we have realistic grounds for self-respect and -regard. We can bear to look ourselves, as the marvelous phrase goes, in the eye. While it is not the case that we are what we have, it is true that we have, inalienably, what we are.

Compassion and caring make us vulnerable in myriad ways that are at times awesomely painful. But compassion and caring also heal us, helping us break out of the confine-

ment of a meager self that is appalled to contemplate its own
poverty and seeks always to fulfill appetites that terrorize it.
Compassion and caring help us realize the links that cure our
alienation not only from others but from ourselves. Yes, we
are small, but we need not be small in our capacity to affirm
life and living, with all its attendant risks and sorrows as well
as joys. Yes, we are small, but through compassion we can
extend ourselves to all with which we connect. When we discover what is universal in ourselves this changes the universe
for us. Yes, we are small, but not without resonance. Good
conscience helps us live with ourselves and within ourselves
compassionately.

Compassion and Consciousness

Consciousness is as natural to human beings as leaves are to
trees. Consciousness is not something in which we are beside
ourselves. Consciousness is neither an embarrassment nor a
disease. It is an emergent capacity that is an integral part of
what we are and how we go about being and becoming. Consciousness cannot make us be what we are not any more than
leaves flapping in the breeze can uproot a tree from the
ground and make it fly. As leaves are essential for the receptive and transformative work of photosynthesis that begins
with the capture of photons from the sun and has both light
and dark phases, so consciousness is essential for the receptive and transformative work by which we nourish ourselves
in our becoming and realize our links to what surrounds us
and to our destinies as human beings. This work too has its
light phases and its dark phases.

Consciousness makes contemplation possible. It makes it possible for us to seek to map our essential connections. It makes it possible for us to engage in the creation of ethics. We might go so far as to say that compassion is the road contemplation takes in the direction of action.

To be human is to be designed to be exquisitely open to what surrounds us, to the environment, human, animal, vegetable, and mineral all interlinked and interdependent. It is to be designed to be open from the sensual to the symbolic. It is to be designed to be open in a symbolic way to the sensual and in a sensual way to the symbolic, so that imagination is a form of experience. In a thousand different ways we encapsulate our environments. For better and for worse we take the genius of what surrounds us into us, not that we need stop there without applying our own transformative bent to it. When we are truly conscious of what surrounds us, we find ourselves moved and challenged by it. We find that we care for it.

The sight of a landscape that has been, for example, brutally strip-mined is no more pleasing than the sight of a human being who has been stripped of the power to mind and care for him- or herself and what he or she does and becomes. Similar forms of brutal neglect are involved in both. Similarly enormous is the task of reclamation in both cases, but surely in both cases alike it is cowardice to shrink from the task just because it seems so large rather than to begin mindfully, step by small step. Whether a step seems small and insignificant or large and promising depends on how we are able to look at it. For a glass to get to be even half full, it must pass through the stage of containing only one drop, of containing only two drops and so forth. We must appreciate the fullness even in a single drop. We must be able to see its roundness as a promise of the possibility of plenty.

Denial, necessary as it often is, at least temporarily, in true emergencies of the heart and spirit, is opposed to compassion, for denial refuses to see, to know, to be implicated, and to be placed at risk. Denial represents a terrified form of acquiescence, because we cannot struggle successfully with problems we are unwilling to know we have. Compassion requires a consciousness of what is difficult, what is unfortunate, what is evil, without a righteous refusal of kinship with it. Compassion requires the capacity to articulate this consciousness so as to make it available to others who matter to us even though we may only be able to imagine them across the distances of space and time and circumstance.

Compassion is a joint undertaking across time and space. It helps us care for what surrounds us because what surrounds us is part of our own being and becoming. To become aware of all that really matters to us is a form of submission that gives us a foundation for refusing to submit to the neglect and brutal squandering of precious life and precious being.

A patient, a woman in her late thirties who had made serious suicide attempts, described her own circumstances and history with such a complex mixture of poignancy and terror that the psychiatric resident who was interviewing her was moved to tears. Upon seeing this, the patient became distressed and said, "Doctors don't cry. Doctors aren't human. You're not supposed to have feelings. If you have feelings that means that things hurt you. It means that I make a difference. It means that you care. When you cry like that, it really upsets me." This was a woman who could do terrible things to herself in a state of bland indifference.

Another patient, a young man in his twenties, had seriously contemplated hanging himself as a child. When he went for therapy, thinking that he "just had a problem with stress" that was making school hard for him, he happened to encounter a therapist who could feel with him. Years later, he talked about how, as he described his situation and how he felt, his therapist would cry silently. "I would get mad at her when she did that. It really bothered me. I wanted to say, 'Lady, will you just cut that out.' I didn't know enough to cry for myself at that time." In retrospect, he granted that this therapist's feelingful engagement with him, her unabashed wllingness to admit that she was troubled by what she heard from him, was probably life saving. Not only that, he showed a concern for the pain of others that seemed to be quite clearly modeled on hers.

Compassion Is a Passion

We can attempt to define compassion suggestively, not exhaustively. It is too large, too important, too variegated, too near for any claim to see it clearly and completely to issue in anything else but pretense. But in opening up the discussion of compassion, there is one central feature that we should not fail to remark, because without it the rest will make very little sense.

Compassion is a *passion*. It has the force, fervor, and ferment of passion. Like all passions, it remakes the one that it touches in its own image. In its case, the net effect is likely to be a combination of strengthening and refining, not of coarsening and debilitating. Nor is compassion always meek and mild. Its range is far greater than that. It dares to tell the truth to those in dire straits, if the truth is their best hope. As compassion is no stranger to joy and pleasure and fulfillment in living, it is also no stranger to rage, sorrow, envy, even treachery. Compassion also can hear when a person cannot bear a truth that seems clear.

Compassion can look being human in the eye and serve as a moral mirror, one that helps in finding not just the way to forgiveness of others and acceptance of circumstances but also the much more arduous route to genuine self-forgiveness. Compassion is a *passion* that has far more staying power, far more changing power, than a mere enthusiasm.

Compassion is not a matter of indulgence. Compassion has its own strictness. It expends effort and expects effort. Compassion is able to remember that, just because a person is damaged or compromised in one way or set of ways, that does not mean that the person does not have considerable resources in other areas. Compassion is passionate in defense of the liberty that is left a person in sore trouble, but compassion recognizes limitations, ones so basic as physical and mental energy when these are failing, as they regularly do as death comes near.

In a spirit of love and appreciation, not greed and ambition, compassion tries to make the most of what is and what can come to be. We need compassion and compassion needs us. Our silence about compassion is a silence about the central possibilities of our own natures. We need to allow compassion to speak to us and to speak through us. A way to begin is to speak of it, to question it, to go in quest of it, to let it elicit and renew our sense of wonder. We need to pay attention to compassion, because it will repay our attention with enrichment of the kind that really matters, not only in the long run but in the *here* and *now*, our true home.

3

Breaking the Silence

Compassion: A Neglected Virtue

We talk so much about growth, possessions, competition, efficiency, excellence, development, progress, discoveries, breakthroughs, conquests, and innovations. On so many of these topics, the words roll off our tongues with a numbing familiarity. The words we are accustomed to speak on these topics are like mantras that put us into the particular hypnotic states characteristic of our culture.

They produce mental states that help us go along with what is not so good for ourselves, our neighbors, or our world. While we go along to get along, we are all the while losing respect for ourselves. We are losing the capacity to look back at ourselves and our actions and to see more deeply into what we are and can become. It is not only the stocks of birds and fish and forests, the resources of earth and sky that are becoming depleted. Human potentials and the ecology of human relationships are also being dangerously depleted.

We participate in the illusion that our culture as we know it is somehow inevitable and complete. So we give in to the pervasive pessimism of a world without an open inward horizon, a world devoid of a sense of an inward frontier of human beckoning and spiritual reckoning. This is at once the most ancient of frontiers and the one that needs to be perpetually rediscovered, not to say reinvented.

If we ache, we may simply redouble our efforts in the wrong directions—to get more, to become more ingenious, to gain more complete "mastery" over nature quite apart from any deep understanding of our own nature and what the form of our relationship with nature might come to be. Our habits of thought and feeling put us in much more danger than we seem to be able to realize. We and the world we live in are both in danger because we refuse to understand the true nature of our vulnerability.

It should be a matter of wonder and consternation to us that we think and talk so little about compassion. Compassion, like any other virtue, suffers from social neglect, about which there is nothing benign. Why is it that the topic of compassion is so neglected in our culture? Even to ask this question is to pose a challenge to the prevailing cultural indifference. Perhaps if we could understand some of the reasons we think and talk so little about compassion, this understanding would put us in position to explore a different kind of awareness about our practical tasks in living.

Compassion Is Not a Thing

Compassion counts. It matters. But it cannot be counted. Compassion is not a thing. This is not to say that it is nothing. Ours is a very materialistic and quantitatively oriented culture. We regularly make the mistake of believing that if we cannot count something, it does not count. If a quality cannot be subjected to quantitative accounting practice so that it shows up in numerical form in a ledger book or on a spreadsheet, then this quality stands in real danger of disappearing from our cultural purview. Compassion is not the only quality that stands in danger this way. Something on which we count as fundamentally as mother love suffers a similar fate.

A psychotherapist is asked to send a treatment plan in to an insurance company for review so that benefits can be paid. The form asks for short-term objectives in behavioral and measurable terms. This demand for spurious quantitation is actually an attack on the whole notion of helping a patient by listening and understanding. It asks for a much more coercive and administrative approach, recasting therapy as something to be done to a patient in a specific technical manner to produce specific results defined in advance. What it neglects is how much in human relationship and in human development is neither quantifiable nor easily predictable.

Compassion is not a fungible commodity like sugar or salt or gasoline or brick or an automobile or air conditioner or personal computer. It is not homogenous, in the sense that one "unit" of compassion can be substituted for another. In fact, each act of compassion and the particular states of feeling and understanding and seeking from which it issues are as unique as any other work of art. The effect of the compassionate act, of compassionate caring, is subjective. It may have objective consequences, but these may be remote from the immediate compassionate act. Compassion depends so much on the mutual attunement that makes its cooperative creation possible. It depends on actions of human moment in particular human moments.

Certain interpersonal atmospheres dispose to kindness and compassion, but there is no obvious way to draw a detailed blueprint for these. Interpersonal atmospheres are the integral of so many different factors, much as the health of the earth's atmosphere depends on a whole host of activities and interactions in the seas and on land. Atmospheres, emotional and gaseous, require the most complex and integrated tending. We cannot simply take them for granted, as if we had no impact on them.

Compassion will not admit of management by objectives. It is much more a question of management by subjectives. Compassion depends upon subjective judgments of value, which in turn depend on complex series of highly individual acts of appreciation. The capacity for appreciation gives value. It asserts human creative freedom. It calls into being much in the way of experience that could not exist otherwise. When we begin to appreciate the role of subjective appreciation in the creation of the experience of satisfaction, we move out of the realm of the concrete, the material, and the external.

We must be comfortable with what is more abstract, less concrete, and more internal. We can start to discern the importance of making choices based on values. We can see the vital role of deciding many matters on the basis of general principles of an ethical and moral and aesthetic nature. We can only have confidence in ourselves if we are able to trust what we find in ourselves, using our own experiences as guarantors of trustworthiness.

Compassion illustrates what might be termed the paradox of value. Compassion, like education, like art, requires that money be spent in some ways and not in others, but it cannot be bought by money alone. These are all much more abstract and materially less tangible "goods." They are actually much more durable than so-called "durable goods." They are more durable because they endure in the human heart, nourishing its wisdom and its strength, its resilience and its creative intuition, its capacity to say yes and to say no based on human criteria.

These materially more intangible values are the true "big ticket" items in two important senses. First, they provide entry into realms that are at once extremely compact and very expansive. The pleasures of compassion, like the enjoyments and stimulations of music or art or understanding, expand our minds and hearts without taking up any room in our suitcases. They can have the force of revelation in our lives. Second, they are also big ticket items in the sense that they require real expenditures of intention, attention, and commitment. The crucial currency they require is real and ongoing presence of mind and heart.

A society with a deep interest in promoting compassion among its members will have a distinctive pattern of the use of resources. However, a budget line item of even ever so many billions devoted to promotion of compassionate behavior cannot by itself produce compassionate behavior. We should notice that we have spent an enormous amount on education at the same time that we have stopped believing in the crucial central value of education. We seem to have forgotten what there is to learn beyond technical skills, so also why learning is important. We should notice that we have spent enormous amounts of money on health care at the same time we seem to have lost sight of the essential value of caring. In both domains, the results have been dismaying.

Expenditures of money are part of the maintenance of values, but they are not enough in themselves. Less money with more human commitment and understanding will produce much more than more money with less human commitment and understanding. Social arrangements can be designed in a spirit of compassion only if the spirit of compassion has taken hold in diverse human spirits. Money without spirit produces results that are a sham and cause for shame.

The fate of a society depends on the quality of its vision and the pattern of its values as it actually enacts them. What we are able to value determines what is valuable to us. We must struggle to stay in touch with the abstract, the internal, the symbolic processes of human appreciation that infuse our purposes with meaning. We need to put *things* in a proper

human perspective, which is not to deny their real importance as instruments of human purposes. The fate of a society depends on its vision of the qualities it values. Quanti-
ties make no sense apart from a vision of qualities.

Acceptance of Dependence

We may be reluctant to think and talk about compassion
because, when we put ourselves in the way of thinking or
talking about compassion, we start to get in touch with our
own hurts. When we see the needs of others, we come face
to face with our own neediness. We realize that we are fundamentally and irreducibly vulnerable. We may be fortunate
today, but there is no guarantee that this good fortune can
be relied on to extend itself indefinitely into the future. The
Greeks, with their capacity for being particularly in touch with
what was grim in life, had the maxim, "Call no man fortunate until he is dead."

Certainly, we cannot maintain the belief that our good
fortune is exclusively the result of our intrinsic merit. To
think and talk about compassion is to recognize that we need
others, that we depend on them, that our dependence is both
deep and essential. We depend on others without any way
to know exactly what we will need in the way of help.

There is a primitive and persistent idea that misfortune
is contagious. If we avoid acknowledging what has befallen
others, we can delude ourselves into feeling a bit more safe.
If we embark on this path, then our fear is our master. We
cannot realistically help others unless we can bear the awareness that we too depend on others to help us in our own times
of need when (not if) they come. Helping others is more than

merely enlightened self-interest, but it is enlightened self-interest, too. It is the kind of self-interest that recognizes the self's genuine involvement in others. It is the kind of self-interest that follows from a deeper knowledge of what the self is and can become, a deeper knowledge both of the limits of the self and of its promise.

The temper of our culture is militantly and persistently, even phobically, counterdependent. We flee our needs at the same time we enact the most desperate searches for their fulfillment. Sometimes being dependent is so stigmatized as to be represented as a form of destruction. Our culture seems to hold to a perverse domino theory in which to depend a little is set equal to being totally helpless. Domino theories always propose the idea that the dominoes are set so close that a chain reaction will ensue if one is toppled. Often this is just not the case. We have trouble distinguishing between appropriate dependency on the one hand and the total loss of autonomy on the other hand. Dependency for so many carries with it an annihilation terror. "I can't bear to need anyone," said one middle-aged woman, "because what would I do without them? I refuse to let anyone have that kind of power over me. I think it's just a bad idea."

We can see the cultural aversion to the acknowledgment of dependency in many areas. There is a move under way to reduce all forms of care to as short a term as possible, as if caring was both a burden and an embarrassment. Shorter and shorter hospital stays are rationalized as financially necessary. Yet, what has really happened is that all the hospitality has gone out of the hospital. The hospital does not welcome guests. Health care is more and more bureaucratized and has less and less to do with human relationships. We take care of organs and organ systems, not whole people. Patients are blamed for being sick and exhausted, as if they were greedily and maliciously trying to use up scarce resources.

Fewer people die at home as we become less and less at home
with dying.

More and more young infants go to day care in the pitch
dark or in the gray haze of dawn. There seems to be no cultural awareness that a single sustaining relationship is the
essential underpinning of development, that the beginning
chooses the direction of the journey. More and more mothers
are expected to undertake the work of raising children with
only the most meager levels of support. More and more
mothers are expected to work full-time and be primarily
responsible for the care of small children at the same time.
Mothers without support, mothers who do not receive what
we might describe as ongoing social mothering themselves,
are much less likely to do an adequate job of mothering.

In the workplace, the bond between worker and em-
ployer is becoming more and more tenuous, as companies
seek to decrease costs by using more and more temporary
workers. This has tremendous social costs not only to communities but also to the sense of community. These social
costs do not appear on the books of any business enterprise,
but they are truly the business of us all. Work is an essential
part of human creativity. It is central to the making of our
lives.

At the same time that we scrutinize every social program
to see whether it may have the dread effect of "fostering
dependency," we have unprecedented epidemics of alcohol
and drug addiction. These have a serious impact on adoles-
cents and children. It is as if more and more people among
us were being rendered virtually soulless by being confined
to intimacy with substances, not persons, including themselves. Their dependent strivings are radically misplaced,
because there is no compassion in a bottle or drug. This "fos-
ter" dependency on toxic substances is infinitely inferior to
opportunity for real dependency on flesh-and-blood people

with real feeling. As one young addict put it, "I just can't stand to be alone without a fix."

These few examples provide only the briefest sketch of a vast domain of cultural trouble. It is no simple matter to try to explain the counterdependent trend in our culture. It has been explained in terms of the frontier experience. The assumption here was that frontier living required an extraordinary degree of self-reliance. However, it is also true that nowhere is cooperation and social connection of more importance than under frontier conditions, where there are so many threats to survival.

We have always been and continue to be a nation of immigrants. Nostalgia for the old country and great relief at being liberated from its social constraints are trends that regularly coexist in immigrant traditions. It is possible that the loss of old cultural ties and old forms of interaction serves to make satisfying dependency more difficult. Immigrants may long to get away from what they brought along at the same time that they long to go back to what they left behind. Satisfying dependency experiences, on the other hand, require a capacity to be here now, all the while recognizing that here and now are both imperfect and changing.

The industrial and postindustrial atomization of social life probably plays a part in the counterdependent trends. We are the most mobile society that has ever existed. Families and individuals move on the average every four or five years. Many families and individuals move as often as every year or every other year. This unprecedented degree of mobility makes, inevitably, for a weakening of the ties of familiarity and long association that are an essential nexus for satisfying dependency relationships. Mobility easily passes over into rootlessness. Instead of vitality and variety, it can produce monotony as the same superficial and stereotyped sequences of relationships are enacted over and over again.

High rates of divorce and disillusionment over the possibility of stable relationships also play into the counterdependent trends in our culture, just as the counterdependent trends make successful and stable marriages—indeed, any long-term committed relationships—difficult.

It may be true that we are never so well served as by ourselves in the sense that, if we do not do for ourselves what we can do for ourselves, nothing can compensate us for the loss of self-esteem we are bound to suffer. However, it is not true that we are well served by being only self-serving. Interdependency is the rule of life. Total dependence and total independence are limiting cases only. Compassion is about the acceptance of dependence and the responsibilities of being dependable. The fact is that in order to be dependable, we must know how to depend. We cannot depend successfully without being able to be dependable. Satisfying dependency experiences and satisfaction in taking responsibility go hand in hand.

Human maturation depends on the availability of a succession of appropriate opportunities for dependency. Dependency is necessary for the emergence of robust and reliable self-regulation. It is necessary for learning how to eat and sleep and walk and talk and feel and choose. It is necessary for the emergence of the capacity for secure and sustained involvement with others. Since imitation is such a basic form of learning, dependency is necessary to support deep and dynamic learning. Since dependency experiences are an important support for safe experimentation, they are essential to the nurturing of flexible characters. To the extent that we refuse to come to terms with the need for reliable dependency experiences, we insist on impoverishing ourselves. Compassion grows out of the mutuality of interdependence.

Engagement with Feelings

Our culture's curiosity concerning things outside our emotional selves is virtually infinite. Our curiosity concerning the intricacies of nature, matters biological as well as physical, neurological as well as cosmological, is seemingly without bound. No detail is too small for our attention. Even the tiniest particle may prove to be the rock under which a discovery of enormous consequence and value is concealed. We honor the scientist among us and look for him or her to bring us news, succor, the stuff that will make life more predictable, more bearable, more secure. We rejoice over the discovery of the top quark, as if physics could replace metaphysics.

Our curiosity is about mechanism much more than it is about meaning. It seems driven by a hunger for control. Currently, we even seem to believe that, if we chop enough DNA up into small enough pieces, we will be able to find out in some ultimate sense "what" life is. However, even when we know the design of the piano, we are a long long way from a glimpse of the possibility of a Bach, a Mozart, a Brahms, or a Beethoven. Scientists declare a "decade of the brain" and then advance claims to have figured the mind out by figuring out how the brain works. Of course, this will not answer the question of how to live. This question that concerns us most intimately exists in a different domain. We cannot escape the fact that our lives, in the most intimate sense, become what we make them and that we make them with others. We cannot escape the fact that outside and inside are inextricably linked, each playing a crucial role in the patterning of the other.

If we want truly to examine our lives and to ask "how" to live in a practical way, we must—together and apart—look thoughtfully and feelingfully inside ourselves. We must ask ourselves what is important to us and why it is important. We must find a foundation in experience for judgments of value and choices about how to invest ourselves in daily life. We are, alas, as avoidant about this engagement with our emotional selves as we are avid in the pursuit of knowledge outside ourselves. This avoidance is both cultural and individual.

Could it be that this capacity for inward knowing is itself an emergent capacity, a relatively new kind of possibility? What would a postscientific (not unscientific) culture look like? What would a culture explicitly and centrally concerned with inner human form more than external performance look like? The hallmark of such a culture might be the replacement of control as a supreme value with appreciation as a leading ethic.

Should we not be struck by our lack of curiosity about the near and practical ordinary intricacies of our emotional lives together as people who, for all the wonders promised us by scientific achievement, know better than to expect freedom from our vulnerability, our insecurity, our agonizing sense of limits, our peculiarly human capacity to hope and aspire beyond ourselves and then to be terribly disappointed in ourselves? Should we not be struck by how little informed attention we do give the emotional transactions of our everyday lives? Should we not wonder why we are not more curious about this? Should we not be intrigued at the ways in which we crave intimacy desperately and yet flee from it with what seems the very same desperation? Should we not wonder at the vicissitudes of our rages and our loves?

Are not the ordinary emotional transactions of our everyday lives, the way we interact with and imagine our fellows, the real substance of our lives, closer to us than our very skins? Are they not what compose our truest dwellings?

They are the stuff of us, and yet they are not "stuff" in the way that bricks or rocks or wood are. It might seem that they are intangible, abstract, and elusive. Yet, we all know that when we are sad or glad, hurt, jealous, furious, pleased, the feeling is immediately present to us. Nothing comes between us and these experiences. We all know that when we are numb, we are not available for joy or hope.

Why should we, then, be so shy about acknowledging and appreciating our feelings, making them the objects not only of our private attention but also intelligible to others in such a way as to let others know our concerns and invite them to show their concerns to us? Enormous cultural investment is required to sustain knowing about feelings and using them to inform choices, commitments, and actions. Just as young humans will not learn how to walk unless provided with the correct support at the appropriate developmental moment, learning to know and name and bear and explore and respond to feelings is not something that a child can do alone. It is instead an enterprise that requires a shared commitment among the generations, the child's developmental efforts supporting the parents' adult developmental efforts even as the parents devote themselves to supporting their children's developmental efforts.

Children learn to feel and love their feelings and to give these feelings symbolic representation that lets them become objects of thought, planning, and care by being felt for and felt with. They learn to feel and to name feelings in the back and forth of reliable relationship. Reliable relationship must provide not only closeness but also space to breathe freely and to become different and learn to appreciate differences. The ability to feel, to paint our reactions to the events of living with a rich and differentiated palette of affects, rests on a major set of achievements. It calls for a long and sociable voyage of inner self-discovery. No parent who has enjoyed raising a child can fail to remark the enormous maturational potential for him- or herself involved in this new journey of exploration of life.

One of the great virtues of real and variegated aware-ness of feeling is that it makes possible responses to one's own and others' needs that are in scale and that actually address the issues at hand in an economical way. For exam-ple, how much acquisitiveness, how much untrammeled ambition, how much aggression, is an effort to address un-acknowledged inner insecurities, inner sadnesses, inner shames and guilts, even inner hopes?

A doctor asked a woman in a full-body cast what had happened to her. "Doc," she said, "I don't rightly know. I just did what I always do when I get bothered. I went out driving on the highway to get myself calmed down. Some-times, when I've got the jitters like that I go fast, real fast. I don't rightly know what hit me."

This pattern of response is not good for people, and it is not good for the environment. Yet, it is a culturally sanc-tioned one that is common. So many people in their auto-mobiles are actually more driven than driving because of their own lack of knowledge of their own real motivations.

To be compassionate we must be able to feel. We must be able to use our own capacity to feel to listen to the other's feelings and to frame our responses. Compassion means feelingful contact. A culture that turns away from a practical day-to-day engagement with the possibilities and difficulties of human feeling deprives itself of the essential resources for compassionate mutual engagement. If we live in an avoidant way that declares that this engagement is too much for us, we are actually thinking much too little of ourselves.

A nursery school sent home a sheet that provided a means of assessing the language development of toddlers. What was most remarkable about this sheet was what it did not include. It did not include even a single word that referred to a feeling or to an interaction between people. It seemed implicitly to present language as simply a device for manipulating the outside world, not as a means for engaging the inner emotional world and the world of human relationships. Even more striking than the omission was the fact that none of the school staff and virtually none of the young and well-educated parents whose children were in the school were bothered by the omission. The language assessment tool expressed a consensus concerning the marginalization of feelings and the awareness of feeling. Nor was the school receptive to efforts to call this attitude into question.

Secure and Flexible Interpersonal Boundaries

When we talk of compassion, we are talking about getting close to others but not too close. We are talking about succoring without smothering. We are talking about finding the other without losing ourselves. We are talking about remembering and respecting the essential separateness and individuality of each person with whom we come in contact but not misusing this sense of separateness to allow yawning chasms to develop between ourselves and others. We are talking about respecting others' autonomy without using this ideal of respect for the autonomy of others to license acts of abandonment.

When we talk about compassion, we are talking about feeling with others, but not using the ideal of empathy to license our preempting the other's right to feel for himself as he actually does. Feeling with someone else must accept the other's creative sovereignty over his own states of feeling. Compassion has to do with knowing and accepting the other as he is and as he can come to be, not with a project for radical redesign of the other in accordance with our own plan.

When we talk about compassion, we are talking about being able to dip in and out. We are talking about becoming engaged with the situation of the other without becoming so overwhelmed by it that we lose a clear sense of where the border is between ourselves and the other. Sometimes we will be too involved. Other times we will be too little involved. We are likely to visit the extremes more than once in the course of any relationship. However, what is crucial is that we be able to observe our reactions and strive to move toward a more appropriate and sustainable middle ground, one that can accommodate not only the needs of the other but also our own.

Of course, we each have our own ghoulish aspects. We have parts that take active pleasure in the misfortunes of others, perhaps because of our own terrors or insecurities. We have parts that envy others their good fortune. We have parts that want to turn on our heels and leave others, shaking the dust of the encounter from our feet with the satisfaction of knowing that we have not stuck around long enough to be left ourselves. We have parts that fear intimacy, whether in good times or bad, because intimacy challenges a feeling of being special and unique and grand that we find essential to protect us against the chaos within. We have parts that want to know what others feel for the sake of the vicarious thrill, as if this form of eavesdropping might let us, finally, have our cake and eat it too, rob banks and remain honest people.

Compassion is as much about letting go as it is about taking hold. It has as much to do with knowing when and how to say good-bye as it does with knowing when and how to say hello. Neither of these domains is a small one. Compassion has to do with bearing witness and with grieving. Compassion is always about recognition. It is about thinking things over again and again and again. It is about recognizing what is inside ourselves and what is in others. It is about recognizing our effects on others and others' effects on us. It is about being able to ask questions and listen for answers in the midst of vital and challenging interactions with others. Compassion is about having the flexibility to revise our opinions not only of others but of ourselves as needs, circumstances, and possibilities change in the flow of life.

An elderly man, looking very frail and extremely emaciated, was brought to the hospital after collapsing at the train station, where he had just arrived from a distant city with his wife. The presumption on the part of the emergency workers who brought him to the hospital was that he had an advanced case of cancer. They said that it was hard to talk with him because his voice was so quiet. Any speech seemed to cost him a great effort. They were especially worried because his pulse was very quick and he seemed to have a slight fever. His wife seemed very distraught and as much at a loss as to what was going on as the man himself. He was admitted to the hospital with the fear that he was at death's door.

Within a day he had stabilized and become a diagnostic enigma. When one of the puzzled doctors came in to talk with him, he would turn his head away. Finally, after a great effort, one doctor succeeded in establishing some rapport with this man. He asked the man how he was. The man replied in a barely audible voice that he was hungry. This took the doctor aback, as everyone had assumed that this malnourished man was a very ill cancer patient with no appetite. The doctor went and got the patient a chocolate milk shake, which he polished off in good order through the straw that came with it. The doctor then got him another one, which he took in a bit more slowly.

With this beginning, a remarkable and sad human story came to light. The doctor was reasonably convinced simply on the evidence of the man's robust appetite that he was not a terminal cancer patient. Actually, the patient had a progressive neurological disease, whose first symptoms had begun to show just shortly after his retirement from a very successful career. As part of his work, he had been required to move very often, not only in the United States but also abroad. His wife had hated these moves but never complained. In fact, it was not clear to what extent she had been consciously aware of how much she resented all these dislocations. She had always felt that it was her duty to make a home for her family, wherever they went. In fact, she had been remarkably efficient and even creative at doing so.

However, she had always consoled herself with the thought that, when retirement came, they could settle in one place, someplace she found congenial, and stay there and enjoy themselves. She had hoped to be close to her own brothers and sisters. She had looked forward to retirement as a compensation for all that she had foregone throughout the course of her married life, probably also all that she had foregone before that. When she saw that her husband was in the early stages of what would become a disabling neurological disease, this was too much for her. She felt that she loved him so much that it was her responsibility to take care of him and make everything better. She felt she was doing what any loving and compassionate wife would do.

Still unable to acknowledge her own needs, she could not bear to know how disappointed she was or how betrayed she felt. She came to the conclusion that his condition could be treated through a very strict diet. He made no objection to this, following the regimen exactly as she prescribed it, even though he got steadily weaker and weaker. They led a more and more isolated existence. Eventually, he collapsed getting off the train and was brought to the hospital.

After a few days, she was able to tell the doctor the story of what had happened to them. She spoke bitterly of how no one had really taken an interest in their plight. She brought in a diary that she had kept throughout their ordeal. In it, she had tried to describe her struggle, her recurrent sense of doubt about what she was doing, followed by recurrent redoublings of her excessive and misguided efforts. Tearfully, she was able to acknowledge that she had made a serious mistake.

She apologized to her husband and very sadly talked about the fact that she had never known how to turn to others for help. She said she really felt like a murderer when she looked at what she had done. She was very grateful to her husband's caretakers for not judging her. As the two of them were in the process of making more realistic plans for his care and more realistic living arrangements, her husband said that he had never doubted that she meant well.

In this case, the blurring of the boundaries between a couple, a fusion fantasy that had given them both succor down through the years, went too far, producing dangerous confusion about reality and allowing rage to wear a mask of compassion that made it very nearly deadly. Real compassion calls for being able to remain separate, not aloof, but always aware that each person has an individual destiny and individual ways of finding meaning along that road.

A therapist struggled in supervision with the similarities between her own experience and her patient's experiences. She alternated between being shocked by the smilarities in the courses of their lives and being shocked by the differences. She felt alternatively too close to her patient and too far from her patient, neither position allowing for any comfort or assurance in response. She had trouble connecting this complex countertransference experience with the patient's own sense of not being allowed to be for her own sake and needing to assume a borrowed camouflage if she was to survive. She had trouble bringing into question her own use of her professional role to shore herself up against her own terrors of emptiness, insignificance, confusion, and unworthiness. Yet, she and the patient both stuck gamely to the treatment, as if they shared a commitment to sinking or swimming together.

This therapist struggled constantly to keep from imposing on herself and her patient tyrannical demands for swift and magical success. Much of supervision had to do with trying to bring these demands to light so that they could be questioned and an effort made to understand their function. In both the patient and the therapist there was a gap between the capacity to care and the capacity to relax and to enjoy caring. Caring and commitment kept taking on the character of an ordeal, a form of suffering designed to prove the value of the self, indeed, an ambitious martyrdom, as if to think well of oneself were so illicit that it could only be contemplated in extremis.

The involvement of the two was as moving as it was problematic for both of them. The opportunities were in the problems, even though these were experienced now and again by both patient and therapist as unbearable, so that even as they embraced each other, they longed to be rid of each other. This longing to be rid of each other, far from being a fault in the treatment, expressed the drive to individuate, to find a mode of freedom in which each was not so painfully compromised by the other. Because the treatment generated a dynamic in which they could not live without each other, it also generated new opportunities for each to explore innovations not only in being with an other but in being with one's own self.

Our Silence about Compassion

We talk and think so very little about compassion that we are most of the time unaware that we think and talk so little about it. We may even have stopped knowing what is missing. Should we not aspire to develop a sense of collective cultural shame about our silence on the topic of compassion? This need not be the kind of proud and envious shame that drives people into hiding. We already have quite enough of that. Rather this shame would be the kind of shame that produces a sense of needing to do better and being able to do better. This kind of shame brings people out of hiding and into the open.

George Bernard Shaw (1925), with a characteristic instinct for getting things ironically wrong, described compassion as "the fellow feeling of the unsound" (p. 264). In fact, it is the soundest of feelings of fellowship. The capacity to feel it is a central test of the soundness of a person. Compassion is unlikely to become a true occupation among us unless it retrieves its rightful place as a central cultural preoccupation, a topic on which we brood, one to which we return so often that after a while it can be truly said that it is as if we never left it. Our interpretations of our own lives, of our patients' problems, and of life in general cannot be "correct" in any meaningful human sense unless they are compassionate.

As we try to reorient ourselves to thinking and talking about compassion, we will be forced to contend with many of our culture's deeply engrained predilections. Compassion is not a thing. It asks of us that we learn to move more easily in the realm of the more abstract, the more internal, the qualitative. It asks that we appreciate the arts of appreciation.

Compassion calls for acceptance of dependency, because without dependency there can be no satisfying interdependency. So the struggle for compassion will require a major reevaluation of our cultural attitudes toward dependency. Compassion requires feelingful engagement. The quest for compassion will engage us in producing cultural practices that support much more awareness and attunement with feelings. This will mean a new look at child-rearing practices, educational practices, relations between the sexes, organization of work, and much more. This will mean the development of a new ideal of a feelingful, not sentimental, person. Compassion requires secure and flexible interpersonal boundaries. This implies much more active cultural support for self-examination and self-knowledge. It also implies much greater emphasis on communicative and interactive skills.

We need to recover our need to talk together about compassion because compassion is at once the most personal of issues and the most social and sociable issue. It lies between a person and his or her heart, between a person and his or her own conscience, between a person and his or her own deepest intuitions of what he or she is and what he or she might become. But the issue of compassion also informs the heart of the community and its real, practical, day-to-day communion. As we know only too well, communities as well as individuals can be large of heart, and communities as well as individuals can be stricken with awfully disheartening disease. They can have the courage to know their own fears, or they can channel their fears into cruel behaviors in a vain struggle against vulnerability.

Whenever we try to talk about the individual and the community, we come up with a paradox. The individual contains the community that contains him or her. The community depends for its existence on its presence as a life-giving idea and illusion in the mind and heart of the individual. It is because of the community's life-giving work that the individual, repository of information—living form—gained over many generations of exploration of the human condition, actually *has* a mind and heart in which to hold the image of the community. The graphic representation of this relationship of reverberating and reflexive containment would require the exquisite skills in making self-recursive conundrum visible of an M. C. Escher.

Compassion as a living value is not a matter to be restricted to homilies and sermons. It is a practical matter, as practical as shoes and bread and butter and electric lights. It has to be lived. So it is a matter for practical effort, for ingenuity and engineering. It has to be brought to bear across the whole range of situations that we encounter in daily life. Bringing it to bear does not depend primarily on the expenditure of money in the first instance but on the expenditure of attention and effort. Practice depends on practicing. The more we exercise compassion, the more we develop the capacity for compassion. In this regard, virtues are not so different than muscles. If we do not use them, then we lose them.

An Example

Let us consider for a moment a situation that is not particularly extreme but usefully illustrative because it is rather ordinary. It is the kind of situation that we hear about daily, both in and out of therapy. A young boy is being teased in school about a minor speech difficulty. The teasing has gone on day in and day out not just through this year but in years past. He is becoming more and more angry, more injured in his view of himself. He is struggling hard to keep up in school but finding it difficult to do so, even though he is quite intelligent.

What is the responsibility of the teacher? What is the responsibility of the school? The teacher, in fact, ignores the teasing. The school ignores the fact that the teacher ignores the teasing. It does not take place so much in class as on the playground, on the way back and forth to school. The teacher knows about it, but he does not seem to regard it as in any way central to his concerns as a teacher. It is not central to his concerns as a person.

When it is brought to his attention, he says that kids are kids and that they have to learn to get along with each other. He says that he feels that it is better for them if the adults do not meddle. He justifies this by saying that, if adults get involved in every little trouble that kids have, they do not teach kids to grow up but just to become big babies. For him, clearly, any form of dependency, especially in boys, is a weakness. When the boy's mother tries to bring the matter to the teacher's attention, he conveys the feeling that in talking with her he is tolerating a nuisance that he cannot avoid but that nonetheless irks him.

In fact, the school is enormously concerned with teaching children to read and write, to calculate, to reason in certain spheres. It carefully administers tests in all these areas to monitor the children's progress and holds itself accountable for the results. The teacher knows that he will be judged according to these results. This is a good school, certainly much better than average these days. It is not a school, for example, where children are bringing guns to class. Nor are they shooting each other (with guns) on the playground. The teacher holds strongly the conviction that the children's social and economic future depends on their performance in school. He does not ask himself how life will *feel* to the children he is teaching now thirty years hence. He assumes, if he thinks about it at all, that a good job makes for a good life because it provides a good income that makes it possible to buy good things, even "fine things."

The school does hold discussions of a residual category "citizenship." No one is quite clear exactly what this means or how it connects with the school's more central concerns. Good behavior is valued, but in certain children, a certain amount of difficult behavior is also valued as proof of some spunk and because it is interesting. The school is not especially concerned with the emotional life of children. It does not regard itself as particularly expert in this area. It might notice emotional difficulties if they produce the grossest interferences in functioning in school. It is more likely to notice them if they produce disruptive behavior disturbances, than if a child is overwhelmed and quiet and withdrawn. It certainly does not regard teaching kindness and compassion as a central part of its mission. A child who has not learned kindness is not an embarrassment to the school in the way that a child who has not learned to read is.

This teacher has not stopped to consider the fact that the teasing that is going on represents a real threat not only to this young boy's capacity to learn and function in school but also to the functioning of the other students. His understanding of the teasing and what it means to the teasers as well as to the one teased is, at the very best, superficial. It has not occurred to him that every student in his class has an area of vulnerability, a way in which he or she worries about being different or defective. Each student has something of which he or she is ashamed, as, of course, does this particular teacher.

The teacher's acquiescence in the boy's being teased sends a message that is silent and clear to every student in the class about how dangerous it is to be different, how dangerous it is to let any area of difficulty be shown. This message is all the more powerful for being off the record. This inhibiting effect will transfer to ideas and beliefs, too. It will act to oppose a climate of free and secure exploration of feelings and ideas. Nor will its harmful effects be easy to spot. They, too, will stay off the record unless an informed eye looks for them, in which case they will be only too clear. To start to explore in this area is to define the pattern of selective inattention that defines what the experience of school is for the children who go there as much as does the curriculum openly taught. It would lead to the exploration of massive learning and feeling interferences that are now virtually completely neglected. Among these is a pattern of using excitement to ward off anxiety, when in fact the excitement in the long run actually increases the anxiety and makes the pleasures of real mastery much harder to attain.

Children, not to mention adults, find differences, especially bodily differences, frightening. They are a challenge to the understanding. Perhaps, on investigation, it would turn out that some of the teasing had to do with an active pleasure in being cruel. Surely, it is a school's job to address such pleasure and actively to advocate that such pleasures need to be given up, so that other greater pleasures can be achieved. In all likelihood, it would also turn out to be the case that the other students were confused and frightened about this boy's speech difficulty, wondering what it really was, what caused it, and, perhaps most importantly, whether something like that could happen to them. The teasing and the cruelty in all likelihood have to do with all manner of unanswered questions and unaddressed worries.

With careful attention, they could be inflected in the direction of broader, deeper, and more decent human inquiry. A discussion of this small thing, once nurtured, would likely broaden to include other persons in the children's lives who also have differences. It would surely provide an opportunity to discuss the fact that, just because a person has one difficulty or difference—be it having a speech trouble, being unable to carry a tune, needing glasses or a hearing aid—this does not mean that other things about that person do not work. For example, he can run, jump, think, feel, and so forth, just like everyone else. In some areas, he may have special abilities, understanding, and sensitivity, possibly just because of the struggle he has gone through and is going through. Pleasure in diversity, including ethnic diversity and sexual difference, comes only if differences are addressed, understood, and put in a larger context. Responsible and feelingful relationship alone can provide this context. Otherwise scapegoating and the warding off of fears through hostile projections are likely to flourish.

To nurture a discussion of this kind, to nurture the capacity to nurture a discussion of this kind, requires an attitude that values this kind of discussion and understands that it is a not a work of an hour or a day or a month. It is an ongoing task. Children, like everyone else, know what is sham and what is for real. They know what is lip service. They know when teachers and other adults truly have put their heart into something. Compassion is a point of view. Because it is a point of view, it will help generate a way of looking at everything. This is as true outside of psychotherapy as it is within the boundary of the psychotherapeutic hour.

Compassion and Justice

Changing to the point where discussions of this kind are nurtured in schools and in the wider society schools serve and express is not principally a matter of money or law. It is a question of attitude, of a moral conviction that informs practice. This cannot be legislated or bought. It cannot be imposed from outside. It has to come from within by conviction. It has to come in by dialogue that is convincing and respectful. Compassion provides a grounds for resisting injustice and seeks means to do so without doing injustice. To attempt to cultivate justice without cultivating compassion is like trying to harvest fruit from a tree that has no roots.

Imagine for a moment what it would be like to live in a culture in which we thought and talked as much about compassion as we think and talk now about our incomes. Can we even pause for a moment to consider that compassion might be a form of income? Can we consider that it might be a form of coming into our own, at once emotionally and spiritually and biologically and practically, that goes beyond the power of numbers to measure?

If we pause to reflect on this possibility in the stillness of our hearts and minds and hopes, then we have already taken the first step to breaking our lamentable cultural silence about compassion. Once we start reflecting in this way, how are we to stop? The truth of compassion is that there is no deeper and more vital or more mysterious human pleasure than caring. This is not a truth about which we can afford to be silent. In a relationship like the one between the individual and compassion, after all, who is to say which is the host and which the guest? Can we do justice to ourselves and the possibilities of what we might become without a central concern with compassion?

4

On Hurting

What Must We Know to Be Kind?

If compassion is the knowing pursuit of kindness, what is it that we must know in order to be kind? This is no simple question but a way of referring to an enormous domain of experience. In fact, everything that we know can be put in the service of trying to be kind, and trying to be kind requires all sorts of knowing, from detailed practical knowledge about the world to the deepest and most detailed practical knowledge of the human heart. However, one essential thing that we need to know about is hurting.

Compassion arises both from the experience of feeling hurt and from the experience of knowing our own urges and capacity to do hurt. Compassion is a response to human vulnerability and destructiveness that admits and takes responsibility for both as essential features of our condition. It arises as a crucial transformation of these two kinds of experiences that opens up new frontiers of receptivity, vision, activity, and satisfaction.

"I think sometimes that I try to upset the people around me just so that they will have an idea how I feel. I know that this is really torture for them, but I have to do it, because it doesn't seem enough just to tell someone. They have to feel it the way that I feel it. Anything less just doesn't work for me. It's too lonely, because I've gone through everything all alone," said one patient. Both the experience of suffering and the experience of causing suffering are fundamental human experiences with endless ramifications. Both are terribly troubling. Both call forth our urges to fight and our urges to flee.

In order to make our way to compassion, we must learn to stay in the vicinity of what is difficult and disturbing and to be able to think and feel and act as we do so. How we use symbols internally is crucial for this capacity to stay in the vicinity. Of course, the way we use symbols internally is crucially dependent on the cultural use of symbols.

We suffer actually and we suffer in our imaginations. We cause suffering both actually and in our imaginations. We are, after all, the species one of whose identifying marks is its consummate skill in simulations. Our simulations can and do take on the force of reality for us. The reality we enact and the reality with which we interact are permeated with the fervors of our imaginings. In a basic sense, it is proper to say that we make ourselves up as we go along and that we go along the way that we make up for ourselves. We imagine our experience and experience our imaginings. One of the defensive purposes of trying to remain concrete and thing oriented in our thinking is to try to avoid knowing just how complex and fervent our imaginings are.

Our subjectivity, the richness of the trove of our inner experiencing, defines at once our freedom and our limitation. It is at once our means for exploring the wilderness of our lives and the constitutive element of the wilderness that we must explore. We might say that compassion was the practical discipline, both inner and outer, that grows out of a certain kind of imaginative understanding of the uses of imagination. With compassion we are able to know the situation of the other as meaningful and compelling at the same time that we do not lose the knowledge of our own separateness and limitation. With compassion we find a way to live in empathetic resonance with what surrounds us.

In other words, compassion represents a certain method for drawing active and practical conclusions from the integrated knowledge of the capacity both to suffer and to cause suffering. It makes a human response to human and natural suffering and human and natural destructive potential. Compassion uses a deep understanding of the capacity both to hurt and to be hurt, not as alien experiences but as intimate features of the human heart; to generate a resolve not to hurt but to succor; not to go from pain, anger, and bafflement to vengeance but from pain, anger, and bafflement to healing sorrow and reconstitutive and reconstructive hope. Compassion helps us let go of the very common strategy of trying to hold onto what we have lost by causing more losses.

In life we all lose and we all hurt. It makes a crucial difference whether we can hold onto what is good and generous and authentic in ourselves even through this enraging and humiliating process of losing and hurting. It makes *the* crucial difference if we can lose and hurt without needing to go over to losing and hurting ourselves. It makes *the* crucial difference if, in the midst of the pain of life, we can maintain our allegiance to loving and living rather than seeking to resolve our problems and our hurt through various forms of aggression that put others where we do not wish to be ourselves.

This allegiance to loving and living, to creating instead of destroying, is not always easy to maintain. It depends on remembering always that there is a dimension of inner freedom, that we always have at least a small degree of freedom in choosing our responses to our situations. If we remember that we have just a small degree of freedom, we can cultivate this so that we have more liberty in how we are present to ourselves and how we present ourselves to others. Our small degree of freedom can grow to become the portal to a much larger realm with much richer satisfactions. This sense of freedom is crucial to the sense of responsibility.

An art student carried a great deal of anger and resentment at his family around with him. His loyalty to his family was deep and fierce, so often instead of experiencing disappointment in his parents, he experienced himself as woefully inadequate. He was a very sensitive young man, very much attuned to the pain of others, particularly of his mother and father who had terrible troubles in communicating. Occasionally, he would get into black moods in which he would feel the need to destroy something. He collected old television sets for this purpose. On one occasion early in therapy, however, he turned his rage and disillusionment against sculpture that he, himself, had created.

I said to him that I understood that he was in pain and as angry as he could be but that I did not understand how destroying something, especially something that he had worked hard himself to make and that had been very important to him, could possibly help with that. I said that I imagined he found it very frightening to be so far out of control that he did something like that. He responded that he felt out of control and frightened a lot of the time. He agreed that destroying the sculpture, if it had helped at all, had not helped for long. Then he said in a very discouraged and sad tone that it was too late now to do anything about it.

I asked him whether he thought that he could do something to repair the sculpture, because, even if it was damaged, it might not be completely damaged. This idea struck him as so odd that it took him a while to realize that I was serious about it. I said that I thought he would find that he felt better if he tried to repair the sculpture that he had made and then broken. I went on to say that, just as his productions were worthy of compassion, so he was worthy of compassion. Repair, I said, was an honorable undertaking. After considerable vigorous and valuable discussion, he said he was not sure that it was possible to repair the sculpture but that he would think about it. We left the matter there for the time.

A few weeks later, he told me that he had taken my advice and made some repairs on the sculpture. He said that he had discovered that he was fond of the sculpture and liked it even in its bandaged state. Much of our work together focused after this time on his fear of his own destructive urges. In fact, he was a person of considerable tenderness who had many difficulties in communicating his feelings. Much of this had to do with struggles to feel autonomous. Most of our work together was done around his drawings, which showed a deep and clear grasp of many of the quandaries in human relationship. He would come and sit in my office and draw, proceeding then to explain his drawings to me and to comment on them. As he became less depressed, a marvelous sense of humor, the kind that is tinged with a deep sadness, showed in his drawings.

Compassion depends on being able to face up to our fear and insecurity, our tininess in the vast scale of things, without going over to vain posturing or destructive protest. If we turn to hating as a way to repair the wounds to our illusions of ourselves, this is much like trying to use a sword to get a scab on a wound. This strategy will only cause more bleeding and extend the wound because the sword is so sharp.

Compassion involves being intimate with our fear and insecurity, knowing them up close and personally. It involves keeping faith and hope without becoming grandiose or vindictive. It involves being able to accommodate the urge to hurt inside, knowing about it without having to enact it. It involves taking good care of rage and vengefulness and jealousy and terror. It involves knowing how to regret without regressing to be not simply primitive but barbaric. It involves being able to bear feelings of disillusionment and futility, of defeat and doubt, without losing sight of the human countenance of hope and possibility, not so much on a grand scale but on an intimate scale.

Our creativity can be put in the service of destruction just as our anger and sense of how to take things apart, to unmake them, can be put in the service of construction and reconciliation. The drama of our actual freedom can be alternately awesome and awful, so much so that we may wish to flee knowledge of it.

Barbarism is not something of which only others are capable. Not only are we all in part susceptible to this spell, but there are parts of all of us that long to be susceptible to it as a way of escape from the uncertainties of our freedom, from the need to be perpetually alert and in doubt, from the need to bear our own experience. Acting in a barbaric manner can be very enjoyable in the short run. It can produce what seems like a pure thrill. It is even possible to become addicted to this debased form of pleasure.

An extremely judicious and careful business executive described how he felt the morning after a church vestry meeting at which he had assented to the firing of a church employee: "It was like waking up after a three-day drunk. I rubbed my eyes and thought, 'We fired someone for absolutely no reason at all.' My God, I don't know what got going in that room. I was part of it, too. I haven't yet come to grips with how I could have gotten caught up in that. I'm shocked. I really didn't know I was capable of that."

A Hutu youth who had killed a number of his Tutsi friends in Rwanda spoke in much the same terms. The difference is one of degree more than of kind. Differences of degree make a big and decisive differences in human life, but if we recognize the kinship in situations, we may be fortunate enough to feel a protective discomfort.

We may be fortunate enough not to try to escape our conflicts through smugness or righteousness but rather to struggle through them to live better with ourselves and our fellows. Many internal conflicts are not so much curses as blessings, calls to further development that, while difficult, may be very rewarding in the long run, more rewarding in fact than we can imagine when we are in the midst of the struggle. Along these lines, compassion is not easily won but calls for real and practical day-to-day, minute-to-minute engagement with what is dauntingly difficult in human life. Compassion, as is so often so clear in psychotherapy, often involves helping people have conflicts rather than avoid them in inner fragmentation and impulsive action. In this way, compassion is not simply soothing but also animating and inspiring.

Why Is Life So Full of Suffering?

Why is life so full of pain and hurt and sorrow? Why is suffering so ubiquitous? Anyone who has lived a bit and considered a bit is only too well aware that while pain, suffering, and loss may come in forms that are incidental or accidental, there is nothing incidental or accidental about the place of pain, suffering, and loss in life. They are built into the ground plan of our existence. They are essential features of life without which our lives would not be our lives. They are built in deeper than where any social engineering can reach.

They are built in as deep as DNA, possibly deeper. No amount of mapping, snipping, rearranging, and recombining of the elements of life—DNA or otherwise—can serve to excise them. They are here to stay, every bit as much as the breeze in the trees, the sound of waves against the beach, or the twinned miracles of sunrise and sunset. To accept life is to accept them. To try to exclude them from awareness is to live in a delusion that is also an exile from any real intimacy with ourselves or others. Life is a taxing and entrancing marriage with what mars us, not simply with a set of pleasurable and easy marvels. Even at its very best, this marriage is bound to be full of lovers' quarrels.

Sometimes, on a bright spring day, as we watch a group of young children at play, this knowledge can bring us great sadness. We see their joy and vitality, and we know only too well that sorrow and travail wait for them. We know only too well that they will not only feel hurt but do hurt. We know also that childhood is full of sorrows and hurts. If we look around, we are aware that not even the brightest of spring days is without shadows. More than that, the shadows are an integral part of the beauty, the depth, the resonance, the mystery not only of the spring day but of the children's play and of our observation of it. After all, we, too, were once children and took in so much of the complexity of life's patterns with the fervent immediacy of childhood. We knew so much without knowing either what it was that we knew or that we knew it, just as do these children whom we now watch.

As life goes on, we can become both more articulated and more articulate. We can enjoy the pleasure of children playing on a bright spring day without closing our eyes either to the shadows or to the sadness that comes with our own extended acquaintance with these shadows. The children are rich in possibilities, but we are rich in memories, none simple, but dappled with delights and sorrows, joys and pains, remorse and a measure of satisfaction, even wonder at what we have done and known and lived through.

Asking why life is so full of pain and sorrow is different than asking why a certain house has termites. Asking why life is so full of pain and sorrow is not an instrumental question. When we ask why a certain house has termites, we can then search to find the damp and rotten wood on which they are feeding. We know that if we remove the rotten wood, then we can make the house free of termites. We might have to inquire what is making the wood wet so that it rots, but we can have some confidence that we will be effective. We will be able to do something to combat the termites. They are, after all, only termites, little insects with special bacterial gut symbionts that make it possible for them to digest cellulose, a very useful property in the right place.

We can, to be sure, inquire about certain causes of human suffering in a way that is analogous to how we ask about the termites in the house. We can be effective in removing certain causes of suffering and in mitigating certain kinds of situations that cause suffering. Smallpox is, for all practical purposes, no more. The polio vaccines have made an enormous difference in the lives of children and families. Modern sewage facilities have made huge differences, as has vastly increased agricultural productivity. Changes in lifestyle, as well as changes in treatment, have moderated the toll of the heart disease epidemic.

Nor is it only past accomplishments that can be thought of as making a difference. Corrections in the vastly unequal distribution of wealth in the world would be of enormous benefit not only to so many of the poor but also to so many of the rich. Environmental reforms have the same capacity to mitigate suffering, not just now but in the future. They are essential to the possibility of a peaceful world order based on a stable population and sustainable use of resources. The alternative is a world marred by savage fighting for limited resources, many of which will be diverted to support the savage fighting.

At another and more profound level, we should pause with a sense of wonder to notice how much the formulation of the golden rule has done to improve the human lot. Charity as a quality of heart and a set of practical initiatives is, in the vast scale of time, a very tender green shoot that has already made a noticeable difference.

But, even if we were much wiser and more charitable than we are, even if we were much better at perceiving our essential needs and, therefore, compromising about our differences of interest, even if our technologies and political and ecological understanding were much more advanced, pain and suffering would still be an integral part of human life, even a central defining part. There is no escaping human limitation. There is no escaping mortality. We may combat particular sources of pain and suffering, but pain and suffering will remain. With pain and suffering, if it is not one thing, then it is another. If it does not come today, then it will come some other day.

In that they are always present as possibilities, pain and suffering are part of every breath we take, part of inspiration as well as of expiration. Vulnerability means that we are born endowed with the ability to be wounded. We have the gift for trauma and suffering, the gift also for response to and responsibility for trauma and suffering. These gifts make both for our access to hope and our access to despair.

To put it this way is not to advocate a dour and pessimistic approach to life. It is not to devalue love and pleasure and attachment and zest and hope and intelligence. Quite to the contrary, the fact of the essential role of pain and suffering in human life only adds to the luster of these. It helps us appreciate them, because they too are central, essential, and irreducible facts of life. When we speak of the essential role of pain and suffering in human life, we are simply trying to put matters in perspective, to see what is real and reliable in our life here on earth. We are trying to make a reasonably truthful, comprehensive, and comprehensible picture of what we are and what we can expect. We are trying to make a truthful picture of what we will have to respond to, of what we will have to be responsible for.

When we ask why human life is so full of pain and suffering, we may ask it with an instrumental edge, as if we were to say, "Let's get to the root of this and do something about it." Certainly much good has been done by people who bore a grudge against human suffering, who went about attacking particular sufferings almost in a spirit of vengeance. However, this kind of approach, this kind of edge, is problematic as well. It is problematic precisely because human pain and suffering are not incidental and accidental. They are essential parts of human life, which cannot be, as it were, refined or distilled away. They cannot be made to go away. This kind of edge is problematic because it stops short of wisdom.

If we are ruled by the urge to get rid of pain and suffering, then there will be so many situations in which we just do not get it. We will find ourselves estranged and alienated from so many people who suffer and are in pain. There is so much in life that can be ameliorated only by learning to *live* with it, that is by changes in the meanings and significance that we give to it and to ourselves within ourselves. Learning to live with something does not mean being passive, resigned, and indifferent. It means being active and engaged in ways that are creative and considered. It means being responsive and responsible rather than grandiose and vengeful. It means being able to let go and take hold, to gauge when is the time for letting go and when is the time for taking hold.

When we try to avoid knowing that human pain and suffering are essential experiences, built into life, however apparently well intentioned our activist zeal may be, we make a serious mistake concerning our own nature and place in the larger scheme of things. This kind of fundamental mistake is never without consequences. When we take on an impossible task that is impossible just because it is based on a fundamental misconception, we are bound to squander our resources. We are bound to encounter a level of frustration that may easily lead to our becoming embittered.

When we seek to overreach ourselves, we invariably meet defeat, just because life is so very much bigger than we are. Efforts at impossible feats lead to inevitable and crushing defeats. Millenial utopianism so often prepares the way for barbarism. When we refuse to recognize suffering's essential place in life, we end up increasing our suffering, because there is so much from which we have to turn away. The ambition to achieve final solutions, purity, definitive answers is itself one of the prime dangers to the human spirit, for, as we have seen so clearly in this century, it can unleash orgies of destructiveness that justifiably stagger our imagination. The urge to final solutions is a regressive urge but one that we all feel and need to resist.

The best answer to the question "Why is life so full of pain and suffering?" is probably "Because. . . ." We all remember from childhood the mixed feelings of bafflement, irritation, and embarrassment we felt when we managed to elicit this sort of an answer from our parents, a "Because . . ." that at once explained nothing and told us that we were up against something bigger than our little selves, with which we would have nonetheless to learn to come to an accommodation.

When we ask ourselves, "Why is life so full of pain and suffering?" and then, after long struggle and thought and much difficulty, receive from our very own selves the answer "Because . . . ," which quickly extends to the tautology "Life is so full of pain and suffering *because* life is so full of suffering," we feel once more those old familiar childlike feelings of frustration, irritation, and not a little embarrassment that we are not capable of taking the matter any further. We have met an edge. We have found one of the limiting conditions of our existence that can help give it shape and meaning, provided, of course, that our petulance does not drive us into an exaggerated, embittered, and hopeless rebellion.

The fact is that the question "Why is life so full of pain and suffering?" with its hint of rebellion at the basic parameters of the human condition, is, for all that it recurs in each one of us over and over again, neither a very practical nor a very useful question. A more useful and more practical question is "How are we to accommodate ourselves to the fact that human life is so full of suffering and pain?" Should we pretend that it is not so? That requires an enormous piece of pretending. Should we try to run and hide from it? Where could we run and hide? Where could we go that pain and suffering would not be able to find us?

Can we even conceive of a way to leave our vulnerability behind? Should we amass wealth or knowledge or take refuge in a haze of alcohol or heroin? Should we try to grab as much sensual pleasure as we can get, no matter how tedious that might be? Should we become as numb and vicious as possible, trying to disguise our fear as fearlessness and to toughen ourselves beyond feeling?

None of these approaches, despite the fact that each one is very common, is very promising. They are all dead ends that lead to particular kinds of death-in-life, states that are worse than suffering, because they exclude fellowship, make loving impossible, and generally cramp the spirit. An accommodation with the facts of human pain and suffering is no simple accommodation. It is not a theoretical issue but a practical one, one that must take its shape with each breath, with each action, intention, and feeling of everyday life. We all meet different pains and sufferings along the different ways of our lives. What is common to all of us is precisely that we do encounter pain and suffering in different guises.

What sort of inner attitudes are we to take up? How are we to act? How are we to go about understanding ourselves and others who hurt and suffer? How are we to manage our rage and hurt, our disillusionment and dread? A Philippine headhunter explained to an anthropologist, as if this were the most obvious thing in the world, that he went on head-hunting raids because he had no other way to carry his grief and rage (Rosaldo 1993). Surely, the spirit of this Philippine headhunter is not alien to us, even if we do not wish to go in for head-hunting or its symbolic and practical modern equivalents. We all have trouble carrying our grief and rage.

We hear now a tremendous number of complaints from patients about doctors who, for all their technological zeal, for all their years of demanding training and hard work, somehow do not seem to get what is at issue for their patients in facing their illnesses and their sufferings. The patients' experience of these doctors is that, for all that they can do, they turn away from their patients at the crucial moment when the patients' heart and spirit, not only their bodies, are on the line. The patients feel, with great sorrow and rage and shame, that they cannot rely on their physicians for something crucial to them.

These patients often do not know even exactly how to phrase their complaints. For one thing, their real gratitude for their doctors' efforts and their appreciation of these efforts gets in the way. What they are missing, though, seems to be the compassionate wisdom of a physician who knows where the limits are and can remain present with a suffering person at the limit. They are missing physicianly guidance at the threshold where the physical problems must be taken on in terms of their individual and infinitely varied meanings. They are missing help at the point where what is at risk is not *a* body but *my* body, not *a* life but *my one and only body*.

Part of the trouble here is the overzealous urge to cure not care, which has become a defining part of the identity not only of physicians but also of a culture that has trouble knowing deeply about the real limits and foundations of the human experience. There is a confessional quality to our declarations of war on drugs, war on cancer, war on aging, and so forth. We are hoping that some sort of violent and drastic means can produce something so simple as victory.

The implicit notion in this dramatizing rhetoric of violence and breakthrough is the foolish one that there is nothing we cannot overcome if we only we set our minds to the task and bring our full forces to bear on it. This is simply not so. When our efforts misfire or prove not to be as effective as we had hoped, we do not look into what it is that made us need to hope in these strangely distorted ways. Instead, we seem to experience an insult that embitters us, makes us feel badly about ourselves, and so withdraw to plot new and vengeful strategies against our enemies.

Not only individuals but cultures, too, can mature in the direction of deeper and more realistic assessments of their situations. To mature in this way is to mature in the direction of compassion and appreciation. This kind of maturity does not bring a decrease in effectiveness but rather a decrease in vanity. This, so experience teaches us, often heralds being able to make differences differently but no less effectively. It leads to being able to use and enjoy what we do have differently.

Understanding Our Own Impact

Just as we cannot deny that human life is full of pain and suffering, we also cannot deny our own capacity to cause pain and suffering, both deliberately and inadvertently. We cannot deny our capacity to take pleasure in causing pain and suffering. We cannot deny our capacity to cause pain and suffering as a way to avoid knowing about our own vulnerability.

Following Aristotle in his "Rhetoric" (Book II, Chapter 2 [Aristotle 1941]), we can define anger as the desire to return hurt for hurt. One of the many virtues of this definition is that it immediately suggests the possibility of escalating cycles of angry exchanges. If anger is the desire to return hurt for hurt, then this return, this new causing of hurt, will stimulate the desire to return another hurt for this new one, thus leading to a cascade of hurting that all too easily gets out of control. The power of this cycle and the difficulty of containing it are matters of daily experience for all of us. We can come to rely on cycles of anger and seeking to hurt and their resulting hurts to define our identities. This is a truly tragic outcome, representing as it does ostracism from whole gentle and beautiful domains of human possibility. We see this happen in families, in communities, between nations, all to tragic effect.

The desire to return hurt for hurt is immediate and comes always with a set of action plans, some more elaborate and some less elaborate. These action plans are no less premeditated than is any other impulse. They may seem impulsive, but in reality they draw on a vast storehouse of urges and imaginings, inner explorations and inventions that in turn have drawn on real experiences in feeling and in action in the world. This desire to return hurt for hurt, so essential to protection and preservation of the species over the long evolutionary haul leading to the now in which we live, bypasses gentling reason and logic, including the logic of the loving heart. It has, as it were, a mind of its very own.

That is, it is not a matter of presenting a bill of facts to an internal grand jury and then obtaining an indictment before we proceed to being angry. We simply react. We feel first and ask questions, if ever, later on. When we wish to return hurt for hurt, we bear within ourselves a set of hurtful intentions as well as a set of hurtful inventions. We are activated in a way that gives us a very special and selective experience not only of ourselves but also of the world around us and the other people in it.

Anger is a desire. It need not take control of our musculature. It need not seize control of the major planning apparatus inside ourselves. It need not seize control of our families, our streets, our communities, our nations, our world. It can be released and redeemed inside and between people through symbolic communication before it does either anyone else or ourselves harm. This releasing and redeeming is an essential personal and cultural task. It is psychological and interpersonal all at once. It takes a lot of work with feelings, not simply with things. Its product is difficult to account for because it shows as havoc *not* produced, peace not just in the streets but also in human homes and hearts.

A statement to the effect that anger is the desire to return hurt for hurt raises so many more questions than it answers. It has the philosophical virtue of defining an enormous area for inquiry. The human capacity to be hurt is nearly infinite. Our bodies get hurt. Our sense of self gets injured. Our hopes are dashed. Our illusions are punctured. In our imaginations we suffer hurts.

In every case, we are moved to anger, moved to try to return the hurt, to find some effective way to communicate our hurt and to redress it. Nor is there always just measure between the hurt and the desire to return hurt for hurt. We may select for the target of wrath someone who reminds us of the hurt, a situation that has a similarity perhaps evident to no one but ourselves, perhaps even obscure to our conscious selves. But the immediacy and vividity of human anger, its force and its fervor, as well as its capacity to endure and assume a thousand different disguises, its capacity to permeate and influence the course not only of the lives of individuals but of groups, cannot be denied. So much of vengefulness, even at its most bitter, expresses communicative failure. The failure is both in communicating with others and in communicating with ourselves.

Communicating with others depends on our capacity to communicate with ourselves just as communicating with ourselves depends on our capacity for communicating with others. Communication makes possible not only the sharing and storing of information but also the search for form, for new shapes that have consequences for how we shape our understanding and our behavior. When we feel hurt, we will be quicker to let our anger drive us to action if we experience the hurt more globally; in other words, if our hurt leaves us unaware that, in many ways, we are still whole. Inner communication allows us to keep a perspective on what hurts that lets us be more abiding and seek less to hurt.

There is no one among us who has not been in his or her mind a murderer many times over. There is, of course, a vital difference between an actual murderer and a person who has been a murderer only in his or her mind. In fact, the murderer may have been confined to being only or mostly an enraged person in his or her mind or even to a situation in which the mind, as he or she knew it, was mostly barren of urges and promptings that could be examined and addressed, subjected to scrutiny and taming. In this latter case, the violent urge leading to murder would have been only too easily able to have the person instead of the person's being able to hold it.

Nor is there anyone who is not gifted with a substantial endowment of greed, of jealousy, of unease over differences. We all have the capacity to want much more than our own share until such time that we stop and contemplate what this means for the kind of life and living conditions that we will all have to share. But how are we to reach this "Stop!" sign that actually opens the way to a wider realm of contemplation and to a different sense of ourselves and our lives?

How are we to reach this stop that signals a new start? To give ourselves shape, we must have a capacity for both inhibition and for understanding. We must have the capacity to tolerate frustration in order to achieve understanding. We must have understanding in order to learn to accept the frustration of inhibiting ourselves so that we can come to have a wider range of choice as to how we exhibit ourselves not only to others but also to ourselves.

We all long for simple solutions, for black-and-white delineations of complex situations, for a clear sense of right as against the claims of others. We all have acted on our baser impulses in a variety of situations, public and private. Compassion involves being honest about what we have done and what we are capable of doing. It requires being honest about who we are and about our inner tensions. Compassion calls for the capacity to regret and to take responsibility for trying to make reparation, if not in the situation in which we did the hurt, then in other situations that have similar features. It is part of the tragedy of life that we often cannot make reparation exactly where we have done injury but must take what we have learned from the ill that we have done and let it sensitize us to the possibilities for doing good in other situations, all of which will reawaken our sorrow over the original ills we did.

A young man on the verge of getting married found himself feeling very sad and disoriented. He related these feelings to his deep regrets over his family of origin and the misfortunes and estrangements that had befallen it. He was surprised to find himself so sad and so full of regrets. He talked as if he still held the notion that had originally brought him to therapy: that it was unacceptable to feel sad. I suggested to him that, as he faced getting married, there was a need to say good-bye to what had happened before and to accept it in a new way, which was what made him feel so much regret. I said that I thought that his capacity to feel regrets, without having to grow enraged and seek to punish himself, was an important new strength. We spoke about how hard it was to accept how little we can change and influence in life.

We need not be shamed by our destructive potentials and so seek to hide them, any more than we need to be shamed by our capacity to suffer and be injured and seek to hide it behind masks of omnipotence, invulnerability, or indifference. We must take the measure of these destructive potentials not merely individually but also collectively. We must learn to look into the mirror and to see what is actually there. We cannot manage or bring into creative collaboration what we do not acknowledge. If we try to think in terms of "mastering" our anger, we are already a bit off the track, because the tensions of a master–subject relationship within ourselves are already so dangerous. If we try to "master" our anger so that we stop knowing about the depths of our capacity to be hurt, the rebellion of anger inside us is apt to be not far off.

We need to mix with our capacity for anger more deeply than that. Anger is not simply bad and dangerous. Anger indicates an inner mobilization against a threat to the self. Anger also brings energy. Anger is a starting place. It brings promptings to activity and invention, to initiatives in thought and feeling as well that go beyond its own narrow precincts. Anger mixed with love creates alloys that open up new possibilities, much as the mixing of tin and copper to make bronze produced the possibilities of a whole new age. However, the possibilities that are opened up when love and anger

mix their energies are at once more extensive and more intimate than any a metallurgic technological innovation can
release. They are more intimate because they are located in
our minds and hearts, nearer than any things. They are more
extensive because they can reach transformatively to the very
wellsprings of our motivations, of our sense of what we are,
why we are, and what we are for.

This topic of the mixing and melding of the energies of
love and anger is a vast and fateful one. It is an evolutionary
frontier with revolutionary potentials. It defines, perhaps,
even a frontier that, should humans falter at it, will be explored again and again by other species and forms of life
almost unimaginably removed from us and these local circumstances to which our fates are irrevocably tethered. The
work of striving to mix and meld the energies of love and
anger may help us sink down roots into intuitions of essential attributes of being quite independent of the specificity
of our own place, time, and shape.

Mixing love and rage, anger and constructive urges is a
matter of the discipline of everyday living. The work of blend-
ing angry and loving feelings starts very early in life. It is a
matter of transitions and linkages. The child who is hurt and
angry at her mother, who is driven by need to protest, then
who is able to find succor from a mother who is attuned to
her pain and protest and limitation is already at work on the
set of skills involved. The child who breaks something that
he loves in a fit of anger and then is helped to repair it is at
work on this set of skills. So is the child who makes the discovery that not only is it possible to hurt someone else's feelings, but it is also possible to become aware of this and to
seek to assuage the hurt.

No child makes these discoveries in isolation. It always
is a matter of a cultural surround providing the crucial signals, the crucial cues, the modulating and bridging that helps

the child along the way. Nurturing the capacity to meld loving and angry feeling is an important cultural undertaking,
one from which the cultivation of compassion is inseparable.

The capacity to blend angry and loving feelings depends
on deepening abilities to understand sequences, one's own
reactions, the reactions of others, the possibility for change
and growth not only in one's own ways of perceiving and
reacting but the possibilities for and constraints on others'
capacities to change. The struggle to blend loving and angry
feelings is not one that is ever done. It is joined and rejoined
at new levels in each different phase of life. It is one of those
problems that is not solved but rather serves to define what
it is to be a person. Its outcome for each one of us depends
on our capacity to relate in depth not only to others but to
ourselves, to pursue ourselves and others down alternative
pathways without losing sight either of the possibilities for
choice or of the limitations on choosing.

A young woman said, "When I'm angry, there's nothing but anger. It's as if the whole world is at war, and the
only possibilities are destructive ones. I have to destroy before
I get destroyed. And I have to do it fast, because if I think
about it, it only gets worse." This woman was providing an
honest account of her state of mind, one in which she was
confined in a very narrow domain of feeling and response,
as if anything more complex would have been simply too
confusing. This kind of totalistic anger is a confession of lack
of inner repertoire, an inability to see farther in time and
space and more deeply inside into possibilities. It is, of course,
common in very young children and becomes modified only
in relationship, in a steady and abiding back and forth. The
experiencing of the feeling without dire consequences allows
it to pass and so to be revealed as a state of intention that is
only temporary and partial, therefore subject to modification.

The expansion of inner horizons requires outer support. It is always a cooperative undertaking. A young man became so angry in a confrontation over a woman that he was ready to kill his rival. The rival backed off, avoiding a situation in which the young man feared that his rage would get out of control and be expressed as murderousness. He found himself feeling very grateful to his rival, actually affectionate toward him because of the superior judgment and restraint that he had shown. Of course, in this affection toward his rival, there could be detected the love for his father that he had always denied, focusing instead on his disappointment in him.

This young man was profoundly frightened afterward, saying that he had discovered a part of himself that he had not known. He said that it was strange that this discovery made him feel more real and like he mattered more than he thought. He felt that it conferred a responsibility on him that he could never turn away from. "Once you know that you could really get angry enough to kill someone so that they would really be dead, that it's not a game but real, then you just can't back away from the fact that it's your job to watch how angry you get and why and what else you could do about it." He said he thought he had always been too angry to know how angry he was, but it struck him that he really had not known that he was angry at all.

Just before the advent of effective antibiotic therapy for tuberculosis, a young man was confined to a sanitorium for an extended period. His experience in the sanitorium marked him for life. He hated the institutional attitude toward him as a patient. He experienced a loss of autonomy and dignity and scope of initiative that he found both profoundly humiliating and enraging. Later he became a doctor who worked with patients with serious injuries that severely limited their ability to function. He campaigned throughout his career for the treatment of such persons as just that, namely persons who were entitled to as large a scope of autonomy as possible and steady respect for their freedom and dignity.

His work put him in the role of one of those people who participated in running an institution of the kind that he had hated so much, but, rather than giving in to the temptations of an identification with those whom he felt had misunderstood and oppressed him, he kept an identification with those who were hurt and threatened that guided him in trying to help an institution achieve a different perspective.

He was, needless to say, often in frustrating and painful conflict with other authorities in the institution, so that he reexperienced the old hurts enough to provide him with ample opportunity for making progress in understanding them better. One of the achievements that pleased him the most was his part in supporting the development of an art studio for paraplegics and quadriplegics that was staffed by instructors in wheelchairs. With a passion that bordered on rage, he insisted that this be known, although it was in a hospital, as an art studio rather than an art therapy studio. He had used his own trauma to provide a beacon to light the way to addressing the hurts of others.

The question of how we make a reliable break with our own sadistic and vengeful urges so that, when we are hurt, we try to take care of our own hurt and of the hurts of others without increasing the hurt, is no simple one. It is a matter of developing a conscience, an agency of our own egos with real and detailed and deep knowledge of ourselves and also with a moral and ethical vision of the future in which we are at once separate and attuned to others as being fundamentally kin. It is a question of knowing how to tolerate a great deal of frustration and seeing alternatives that are very complex clearly in our minds. To break with sadism and vengefulness, we must both appreciate our own pain and hurt and appreciate the pain of others and their hurt. We must feel ample enough to undertake the struggle to assuage pain.

We must appreciate both what we have lost and what we have not lost, as well as what we stand to lose if we let sadism and our vengefulness take us over. We must see the complexity of situations and the possibilities that they hold over long periods of time. We must understand and accept the futility of trying to effect repairs by destructive means. This is a developmental question that requires a profound appreciation of and reconciliation with our own scale and limitations.

To break with sadism and vengefulness, we must resonate deeply enough with ourselves to be a kindly other to ourselves and deeply enough with others to accept the burden of being kind to them as a road to rewards that have real value for us. This means that we must have a deep and practical grasp of what matters to us and why it matters, of what we value and why we value it, of what gives us pleasure, why we care for it, and where it fits in our approach to living. When we talk of a deep and practical grasp, this does not mean that it needs to be made explicit in words. It may not even have to be conscious. But it has to be articulated in how we live and how we choose.

The marriage of love and anger is an act of practical imagination or, rather, a set of acts of practical imagination that have not only craft elements but also an artistic and creative dimension that is nowhere nearly enough appreciated. The art is to make the energy of anger available for helping, recognizing all the while that helping, too, is limited and brings with it no sense of omnipotence or omniscience, but rather the satisfaction of shared efforts in human time and scale, producing shared results that fill out the creative definition of what it is to be human. To do this, we must be able to abstract from our own situations at the same time that we remain deeply rooted in them. We must find new styles for saying new things about what is oldest about our condition.

Stewardship of Destructive Potentials

We are creatures with enormous powers to understand and shape the environment around us. We can imagine complex sequences of cause and effect. We can plan and scheme and sequence and delay and disguise and persevere. We can invent and improvise and revise. This is what makes us so dangerous, not only to others of our species and to other species but to ourselves.

These capacities are at once our promise and our peril. We can endanger ourselves precisely through our efforts to protect ourselves. We can bring destruction on ourselves through our efforts at self-preservation. In seeking to thrive, we can eliminate the conditions that are essential for our very existence, because we fail to understand that what surrounds us is also part of us. We can engage in all sorts of projects for vengeance and empire that boomerang and makes us subject to conditions worse than when we started out.

There is nothing new about the idea that the depth of our understanding is limited by our understanding of ourselves and of our own motivations and intentions. Without this, we are not apt to know what we do. Sustainable human development depends on deep human understanding of what we are, how our needs shape us and we shape our needs, what we can live with and what we can live better without. It is a perfectly commonplace observation that very often when we display the most zeal for what we are undertaking, we understand the least about its real meanings for us or its likely consequences for ourselves and others. Our zeal expresses as much an enthusiasm for what we can keep from knowing as for what we know.

Our current infatuation with science and technology, with instrumental control based on a certain kind of understanding of the world around us, is certainly an example of such a blind passion. This understanding is limited and proud, because it misconstrues what we are and our place in the world. Does not the air have rights, the ground, too, have rights? What about the water, not to mention plants and animals? Are we really as different, as special, as we like to think we are, or does this way of looking at ourselves in nature not make us in many ways strangers to ourselves? Is it possible that it is not just the voice of nature that is drowned out by the noise of our ill-considered activity but our own authentic voices? Surely, we, too, are an endangered species. We are part of what surrounds us, even as we are parted from it.

Our sense of our smallness goads us on to understand, to control and to conquer. Our vulnerability makes us vow over and over again deep in the secrecy of the darkness and the light of our hearts, "Never again, never again." We strive with a wild zeal for mastery of what disturbs us. We want always to push back the border of mystery, the area of natural caprice that always encircles us. We feel that these projects for security that issue forth from the wilderness of our hurt hearts are self-evidently good.

Who could be against warmth in winter, the capacity for extensive travel, sufficiency, and even superabundance of food, enough to feed not only ourselves but perhaps the whole planet? Who can challenge the wonder of our myriad devices for linking ourselves together through voices that travel, pictures, and music that resounds all over the globe? No generation on earth has ever heard so much music. All this and so much more takes energy. The hunger for energy has all sorts of unintended consequences. For one example among many, consider the image of the Exxon *Valdez* split open like a soup can on the rocks of Prudhoe Bay pouring out its cargo into a sea that it poisons, destroying salmon and seals and herring and birds in enormous numbers, not to mention the way of life of people who were in no way consulted about its mission.

We can respond to disasters like this one on a case-by-case basis. We can build tankers that are harder to split apart, decrease the number of pilots who have too much alcohol on board, just as we can make cars that burn fuel more cleanly or homes that lose less heat in winter. We can try to clean up the Love Canals, the sites where nuclear waste has accumulated during the Cold War, the lead imbued soils of our old harbor sites where industrial facilities once stood. Certainly, all this is important, none of these innovations to be ignored. But is all this enough?

Do we not need to ask more general questions? Do we not need to question our way of living, to debate general principles in a lively and vigorous way? Do we not need to ask questions about scale, about how much is enough, about how to take into account the fact that our actions always have unintended consequences and that perhaps one of the most dangerous and destructive human characteristics is our capacity to introduce turmoil into large-scale systems, biological, social, and physical, without any clear idea of the implications of this? Just because we can explore one or another initiative, should we? Just because we can make a device with some apparently promising features, should we? Can we afford to leave all these choices to markets and act like innocent bystanders? Do we even begin to grasp what it means that we make 50,000 exotic new chemical compounds a year? Do we have any clear sense of what a whole new transgenic flora and fauna means? If we are posing these questions actively to ourselves, we may find we hear the doubts and difficulties of some of our young patients differently.

Do we not need to learn to be more troubled by our capacity to remain untroubled about remote consequences of current actions, consequences that are remote not only in time but in terms of their connection with the immediate concerns of our day-to-day lives? How do we rein in the zeal of our human enterprise, direct it, use it to explore ourselves, not simply to control and also devestate the world around us? How do we strike a balance between change and familiarity?

How can we make progress in taking a more critical view of claims to external material progress, in grasping more clearly the claims of the internal, the personal, the interpersonal? Consider the following very troubling ordinary anecdote. At a birthday party not so long ago, a 2-year-old was given a play stove. She was also given molded plastic toy food shapes: a hot dog, a hamburger, a loaf of bread. She was also given a plastic steak and told that, if she scratched it, then she would smell the steak cooking. The children at the party and their parents became involved in a discussion of what other plastic simulated foods could be gotten. The list went on and on.

The discussion had already an acquisitive flavor. Surely, all this represents a most destructive form of waste. Not only are resources devoted to tasks that are really of no importance, but this kind of toy production is a massive onslaught on the imaginations of small children, an attack of no small moment. It is of extreme consequence because it is part of a cultural education that teaches that satisfaction lies outside yourself, not in your capacity to appreciate but in your ability to *possess*. The imaginative cooking that small children do with leaves, pebbles, mud, sticks, and dandelions has such a more vibrant flavor. It is simpler, nobler, more real in the ways of the imagination. It is better for the inner environment as well as the outer environment. How have we lost our trust in it?

We are more than devices for making devices to control and upset the external environment around us. Neither our intelligence nor our feeling is artificial, that is, unrooted in the ancient experience of the earth that surrounds us. Do we not need a change in our consciousness, a move to a consciousness that is less instrumental, more disposed toward inner knowledge and less toward environmental manipulation, more disposed toward being and less toward having? We need to be able to ask ourselves whether we cannot grow best by changing the aims of our growth, by thinking more about how to fit in with our surroundings than to break their constraints. Do we not need to ask ourselves whether we are in the process of destroying ourselves because of our failure to understand ourselves and the deeper layers of our inner natures, because of the unintended consequences of our currently limited way of viewing consequences?

Do we not need new ways to look more deeply and more closely at ourselves and at our neighbors? Do we not need exit routes from our current enchantments with projects of material invulnerability, our enchantment with matter and lack of understanding of how we matter not only to each other but each one to ourselves within ourselves? Do we not need to find a way to more inner activity and less pushing around of the material world around us? Is not the environment a part of us as much as we are part of it, so that we need to enter into a constructive dialogue with it every bit as much as we do with ourselves? What of the pleasures of contemplation? How many of us have even an inkling of the practical experience to which such a phrase refers?

Compassion is not without a deeply critical dimension. Profit is not the only promise, increase not the only reward.

When we make judgments about our actions and about our projects, we need to be able to apply some general principles. These may be ethical and aesthetic. For example, we might try to build a city where everyone could walk to work for aesthetic and ethical reasons, because we felt that it was immoral and aesthetically repugnant to have the environmental degradation involved in superhighways and the fragmentation in family life involved in such long-distance commuting. We might decide that walking was good for thinking and feeling and for interacting with others and so be willing to invest a great deal in it. The general principles may have to do with using simulations in place of real actions with more concrete risks. They may have to do with deliberately turning away from certain areas of potential promise because there is no way to assess their risks adequately.

General principles of this kind are not simply utilitarian. They have religious and spiritual overtones in that they must be based on a set of answers concerning what it is to be human and how we conceive the relationship between ourselves and the cosmos. Our capacity inadvertently to produce destructive consequences that we have not consciously intended is not one that we can manage using only thinking and feeling that are concrete and tied to specific instances. To be disturbed about it requires not only a grasp of history but a large capacity for abstraction and an intuitive grasp of high orders of complexity. Yet, recognizing the complexity of consequences beyond the horizon of what is readily visible today is an essential part of the stewardship of our destructive potentials. Today we might think of the essential political document as a declaration of interdependence.

Compassion depends on an internal mental poise, a vividity and vitality of feeling that, in their turn, depend on the availability of the energy of the whole range of human responsiveness. A deep awareness of our vulnerability, of our urge to respond by controlling, by hurting where and when we are hurt, gives us a set of choices about what *not* to do, how *not* to channel our being. We come to a certain point of arousal in the face of life's difficulty, its pains and sufferings and sorrows, and then, by reason of having closed off the menu of destructive possibilities, we can use the energy of our arousal to look for new channnels and opportunities with a more constructive twist.

The Bridge of Understanding

An 80-year-old lady with a terrible temper and a lifelong history of enormous enterprise and determination formed a program to enlist retirees in the job of teaching criminals awaiting trial how to read in a jail in a large metropolitan area. She said she knew many of the people she taught had murdered others, had done truly terrible things, but it was not her lot to judge, not her lot to exact vengeance, but rather to go forward and to try to help these people have more means for understanding what they are doing, what they have done, and how they might make amends.

What remained unspoken—and crucial—was her sense of kinship, a fresh wondering after long experience of life about what she might have done with her energy had she not known how to read, not only words and music but also herself and other people. Some scoffed at her efforts as quixotic, but despite this scoffing they grew. Many of the retirees were surprised to find themselves in the jail, shocked at the pathos they encountered there, surprised to find themselves coming back again and again, surprised at how compelling the work was, how it seemed to make them feel less isolated.

Our sufferings and sorrows, our awareness of how these are not incidental but inevitable, can make possible a liberating inner surrender. We not only see but feel the truth that it is no use to rage against the basic ground plan of life as if we could revise or overthrow it. It is not that we are not moved to rage but rather that our rage coupled with our loyalty to love and life can move us beyond the terrain of simple unalloyed rage to richer landscapes. "But man is born unto trouble, as the sparks fly upward," says the wise Eliphaz in the Book of Job (Job 5:7). Being that it is so, the question we must answer in our living is how to be troubled by our troubles, how to be troubled by the troubles of our fellows.

The way to compassion involves accepting limits, knowing the difference between our wishes and desires and what is possible, given that we are mortal humans. It involves discovering the liberty of finding in one's own sufferings the urge to bring balm to others who suffer, turning aside from the urge to assign blame for suffering, as if each particular suffering were a kind of cast-out child to be returned to its guilty mother to be made good. It involves a form of inner awareness in which others' sufferings concern us and speak to us, talking a human language of love and longing and limitation that we, too, understand and speak. In this dialogue of concern there is always learning and teaching flowing in both directions across the bridge of understanding.

A young woman was dying alone of AIDS in the bleak surroundings of a ward of a public hospital. She was withdrawn, in that peculiar twilight where people sometimes linger between life and death, waiting the moment to pass beyond, struggling because it is in the nature of living beings to cling to life, sometimes angry, sometimes too inaccessible for anger, even. Her family, including her two young children, had stopped coming to visit her, unable to bear the burden of the experience of visiting someone who was in so many ways no longer either accessible to or recognizable to them.

A social worker, moved by this woman's isolation, her position just at the boundary of the circle of life, went out into the garden in front of the hospital and picked a yellow daffodil. The social worker was someone who had herself contended all her life with the pains of loneliness and helplessness. She placed the daffodil in a vase on the tray beside the woman's bed. She slid the vase across the tray until the daffodil was illuminated bright gold by the stripe of sunshine that came from a window at the far end of the room.

The young woman focused her attention on the daffodil and then looked at the social worker, bestowing on her a smile of presence without any words, one that served to sustain the social worker as she went on with the difficult work of being with the mortally ill and their families. We can be present in the face of human suffering and hurt without adding to the hurt, but this requires courage and creativity. In this creative work, we will discover that we find many different kinds of closeness, many forms of encounter not only with others but with ourselves that show living to us in a new light, so enrich us.

5

Compassion and Joy

Joy and the Case for Life

A middle-aged woman had had a very difficult time in life, starting with her pressed and depressed mother's failure to welcome her into life. She had never had a period of happiness and security, despite her enormous tenacity and inborn vitality. She had experienced a variety of calamities that started early and made her very fearful of others, for she knew only too well what could befall her at the hands of other people. She had so little trust that she had enormous difficulties speaking, and many, many sessions were spent in long and painful silences. In more than ten years of intensive therapy, her history and the lasting wounds that she had sustained became plainer to her as well as to me.

Almost the entire time was very stormy. She was continually in doubt and despair, always questioning whether life was worth living. Yet from time to time, there would be a period of some accord in therapy, a time when, looking back on it, it would seem to me that we both had found a way not only to communicate but to enjoy being together. These moments came and went. There was no counting on this kind of atmosphere to last a whole session, let alone beyond that. Yet, as I thought about this woman's treatment, about her attachment to me and my attachment to her, it came to seem to me that these moments of pleasure, these moments of mutual attunement, these moments when between us in the sessions life seemed good, were of the utmost importance.

I have found in supervising psychotherapists that many are very shy about admitting the pleasure they find with their patients and the moments of accord that they find with their patients, as if to do so would be either immodest or improper. Partly, this may have to do with the natural tendency to use supervision to highlight and to work on what is most difficult and disturbing in a treatment. But also it has to do with a difficulty in appreciating the importance of the pleasure in therapy and the pleasure in the relationship as an essential developmental supply for the difficult work that is undertaken in therapy. When a patient is unable to take any pleasure in this process of psychotherapy, when the therapist and the patient do not find moments that they enjoy together at however great intervals, then the prognosis for the therapy is not likely to be good.

When it appears before our mind's eye, compassion most often wears a watchful, worried expression. There are good reasons for us to associate compassion with what is hard and full of hurt. Our compassion is most sorely tested in the face of the pain of life. The pity and the sorrow of life call for the exercise of our compassion in the most anguishing and uncomfortable circumstances. They test and temper our compassion. Life is not easy and spares no one. Trouble visits every human heart and tests the depths of every human heart. Human suffering is ordinary, which is not to say that it does not have profound meaning.

The relationships between compassion and joy, between compassion and pleasure, between compassion and satisfaction, are every bit as important as the relationships between compassion and pain and sorrow. Would compassion even be possible were we not sensible of what was good in life? Could we be moved to attend to the sufferings of others, to give ourselves to the task in a wholehearted way, were we not intimately acquainted with what is appealing about life, with what is right in life, not exclusively with what is wrong? Do not our joys, our pleasures, our moments of fullness and quiet gratitude play an essential role in the development of our compassion?

If we are to defend life and the possibilities of living, we must first of all be able to enjoy life and the opportunities it offers us. We must have realized some of these possibilities. We must be able to appreciate and value what we have. Otherwise the case we make for life and living in difficult and even dire straits will be weak and unappealing, without the staying power of real conviction. Nothing convinces like pleasure. We need our pleasures, our joys, our intimacies, including the pleasures and joys and intimacies of memory, to sustain us in our search for compassionate responses.

Compassion involves a knowing, an understanding, a giving, a witnessing, an abiding, a doing, and an abstaining from doing that test the integration of our personalities, our resiliency, our consistency, our practical creativity. Pleasure and joys are essential to the development and maintaining of integrated personalities. Our pleasures and our joys change with us as we change through the entire cycle of our lives, but we are never without their accompaniment. A pleasure in learning about ourselves and about other people is an important support for the development of compassion.

The compassionate person has a knack for finding him- or herself in the presence of the good, however relative, however damaged, however limited. This is a hard-won knack, with nothing magical to it. The compassionate person knows that, even when so much is so difficult, even when so much is so painful, pain, hurt and fear are not the whole story of life. The compassionate person neither denies the hurt, nor allows it entirely to dominate the field of his or her inner vision. In fact, the compassionate person needs more than a little stubbornness in the defense of what is good in life. The defense of what is to be loved and cherished in life is not a matter for the faint of heart. Sometimes it requires stubbornness and obstinacy, even ferocity, an abiding sense of the possibility of the seemingly improbable.

Life's pains and sorrows and sufferings threaten to make us forget that there is good in life, past, present, or future. This is a serious threat. The hurt that gnaws so near our center threatens to make us forget that we are capable of closeness and pleasure and zest and humor. It threatens to make us forget all about beauty and harmony. When it is clear that things are not all right, it is always a temptation to experience them as all wrong. This urgent sense that things are all wrong can have a comforting aspect, too, protecting us against the confusing work of trying to weave together disparate strands of emotion that ask different kinds of response from us. We can find ourselves wishing in pain that everything was all wrong. We can even find ourselves wishing for a death imagined as peace, surcease, and tranquility.

Job himself cries out, "Why died I not from the womb? Why did I not perish at birth? Why did the knees receive me? And wherefore the breast, that I should suck? For now should I have lain still and been quiet; I should have slept; then had I been at rest" (Job, 3:12–13).

Much of the torment of Job's suffering comes from his memory of the goodness of the life that has been his beforehand. The conflict for all its pain has a hopeful side, too, for Job can only wish for the peace of death, not entirely accede to the simplification of his experience that this peace can seem to offer him. Despair's inventiveness stands as a token of its secret connection with hope.

Under the press of pain, of sorrow and loss and disappointment, of sickness and its attendant insecurities and uncertainties, we may be tempted to start spinning the gold of our lives back into straw. Compassion must always stay in touch with the possibility of what is good in life, however restricted the scope is that circumstances seem to allow pleasure and enjoyment and the feeling of being whole enough and well enough. Without being sentimental, compassion must always keep in mind the fact that people in trouble may have or come to discover surprising degrees of inner freedom. When so much is not working, it is vital to keep in mind that this does not mean that nothing at all works, even if what works requires extensive assistance in order to work.

An elderly man had been very sick in the hospital. He had had lung troubles that sapped his strength and made it very difficult for him to breathe. He lay for many days at the edge of awareness. The turn back from death's door was characterized by an increase in his energy, so that he actually became mean, disagreeable. This phase tried the nurses' patience, but it passed. It so happened that his wife, too, was sick and in the hospital on the same hospital floor, a fact of which he became once more aware as his strength came back.

One morning, still very weak on his feet, this old gentleman in a white hospital gown that flapped behind him set sail down the hall to see his wife who was sitting in a wheelchair out in the hall in front of her room. When he got to her, there was a moment of hesitation. Then he leaned over and kissed her full on the lips. What was most remarkable about this scene was not only the man's action, but the reaction of the other people standing about in the hall who witnessed it. Their faces warmed. The nurses smiled. The other patients smiled. The visitors on the unit smiled. It was as if every one recognized him- or herself and his or her own capacity to love in this spontaneous gesture between two older people whose perils had almost been mortal. This kiss was a kiss in which everyone participated.

Bearing Pleasure

It may seem odd to say so, but, if we are truly to be compassionate, we must show compassion for the pleasures and joys of others. We must show our compassion not only in our willingness to share and be moved painfully by the sufferings of others but, equally importantly, in our willingness to share and be moved by the pleasures and joys of others. We must be able to be glad that they are glad just as we are sad that they are sad. When there is a lack of compassion, there is so often present not only the wish to flee and ignore the sufferings of the other person but also the wish to flee and ignore the pleasures of the other person, as if these, too, represented a threat to the self. Compassion means being able to take pleasure in the joys of others even when they have not suffered.

Far from pleasing us, when we lack compassion, the pleasures, the health, the youth, the prosperity, the wholeness and beauty of others, their sexual force, upset us and rouse in us the sense of envy. Others show us a lack in ourselves, or so it seems to us. The other makes us feel that we have failed ourselves or been failed by life. We may wish to spoil the pleasure of the other, not to get near it. We may want to ignore it, to deny it, if not to destroy it. Because we want it for ourselves, there is larceny in our hearts. If we cannot have it, our wish goes, then no one should have it. We cannot stay separate enough and active enough within ourselves to participate in the other's pleasure and so find our way to an enjoyment of our own capacities. We can be just as greedy about experiences as about possessions, to similar detrimental effect.

Envy is an exceedingly subtle, powerful, and complex passion. None of us is without it, any more than we are without more than a tinge of base pleasure in the misfortunes of others, as if there were a limited supply, so that the misfortunes of others conduced to our own increased chance of safety. Envy has to do with desire. There is no health or vigor in life without desire of a variety of kinds. But envy unmastered is desire gone sour, desire that despairs and becomes destructive in proportion as it feels helpless and hopeless. At the root of envy is a difficulty in appreciating ourselves. We are consumed by desire for something external to ourselves because we have turned a profoundly cold shoulder to what is inside ourselves. We become destructive because we are out of touch with our own creativity.

La Rochefoucauld (1977) observed more than three centuries ago that our envy of others' good fortune often lasts longer than does the good fortune that we envy them. His observation highlights the fact that envy has to do much more with our own inner situations and predicaments than with what we see in the outside world. Envy can produce a stabilizing structure of desire, whose price is closing off internal possibilities of dynamic rearrangements. Envy makes a structure, but one based on painful notions of limitation and on blame. Often we envy in others what we have secretly closed off and made unavailable to ourselves. We long for a solution in the outside world of what is really a problem within ourselves. We protect ourselves against chaos with defective inner form.

Envy may wear the disguise of its opposite. The noisiest cheerleader for the pleasures of others, the most conspicuous and apparently generous appreciator of the joys and good fortunes of others, may be the one who is secretly most envious. Not only do such persons not wish to have their own shameful secret known; they also use the show of their sympathetic appreciation to make a claim on the attentions of others. Actually, they may be competing with the one they seem to be appreciating. Underneath the show of appreciation, they may be suffering terribly, feeling wronged, becoming more and more enraged over their own lack. Their appreciation may actually be invasive, a project for a form of psychological colonialism.

To enjoy the pleasures of others requires active imaginative participation, not with the goal in mind of any kind of usurpation but more the way that we take pleasure in singing along with an attractive melody. We enjoy ourselves as we sing along. We hear the melody in our minds. Active imaginative participation requires an inner flexibility and mobility of feeling and conception. We have to be able to find pleasure in ourselves, in a space of simulations that draw not only on our past experience but on recombinations of their elements and improvisations based on their themes and themes suggested by their themes.

This taking pleasure in others' pleasures can open up new avenues of pleasure for us, providing that we can accommodate the inner exploration involved without feeling that we are losing ourselves. In fact, the pleasures of others can provide us with an enormous source of variety and interest, a series of royal roads to travels in hitherto unexplored regions of ourselves. Enjoying the pleasures of others can be as full of surprise and syncopation as the best jazz.

Enjoying ourselves takes skill, practice, thought, experience, imagination, creativity, poise, and perseverance. When we enjoy ourselves, we have to be able to let ourselves go, without losing ourselves. We have to be able to let the experience flow within ourselves, changing us as we go along. We have to be able to go along with ourselves as we change. Real pleasure involves giving ourselves over to an inner transformation without losing our capacity for self-recognition, for secure management of our boundaries and modulation of our urges. Real pleasure involves being able to maintain our integration under diverse conditions of inner and external exploration, because real pleasure is not stereotyped but inventive and innovative, musical in its capacity for progression, harmony, rhythmicity, and plasticity. In fact, when we see repetitive, stereotyped behavior, repetitive, stereotyped approaches to life, we know that the urge to play and pleasure has been confined by defensive needs, constricted by shame and anxiety. The loss of the capacity for play is one of the great losses that an individual can sustain in life.

A middle-aged man driving down the street on a beautiful spring day noticed, with some puzzlement, that just as his enjoyment of his surroundings peaked, he began to worry that a spate of drive-by shootings that had been going on in another city about an hour's drive away might easily extend itself to his own city. He imagined that, suddenly, without any warning, he himself might become a victim of a drive-by shooting. Then, catching hold of himself, he reminded himself that the prospect was exceedingly remote. He wondered what function this arresting fantasy served for him. He wondered what wish might be mother to his fear. He wondered if, in fact, he found that enjoying the beauty of the day disturbed him, or made him feel very insecure, or threatened him with a kind of inner disorganization, so that he had to find a worrisome thought with which to interrupt it.

He asked himself whether he had to find a circuit breaker to restore some form of inner control to protect him against a surge of feeling that threatened him with inner overload. Joy, after all, can bring its own terror, as if there might be no way back from it and its buoyancy might free not only what is best in us but also what is worst.

Much of the trouble in life may derive from our tendency to flee the joy, the simple superabundance of deep pleasure that can fill ordinary moments of human presence. It is hard to describe the secret, voluptuous, deadly security of a simple refusal to be pleased. The power to please can often seem the power to destroy, because it demands such flexibility of us.

Joy, pleasure, intimacy all are essential to our integration, and integration is essential to being able to attain, sustain, and explore them all. To find peace in life, a peace that is vivid and zestful, not simply the peace of a numbed and defeated withdrawal, we must be able to locate all our pieces with their diverse interests and strivings. We must be able to locate our pieces with respect to each other, so that we do not become unbalanced and lose our bearings. Real peace and real pleasure depend on the inner orchestration of many different instruments of experience, each with its own particular timbre and set of available tonalities. The sound of each particular inner instrument, of the striving of each piece of ourselves, each interest, each curiosity, each allegiance, contributes to the soundness of the whole. Not only that, but the full characteristics of each part, of each instrument, can be appreciated only with regard to the whole, that is, with regard to the ensemble.

Perhaps music, that most particular of human ways to give voice to the depths of specifically human experience, brings such consolation, pleasure even in the depths of pain, because it speaks directly to the architecture of our emotions and intuitions. It helps us along the way to compose inner ensembles that show us more universal aspects of our own resemblance. Consolation has the feature always of moving from the isolated particular to the place of the particular in the universal. It helps us move to the universal through the particular, so that *this* bud, *this* flower, *this* leaf, *this* loss, *this* longing become portals through which we pass to grasp the connection of budding, flowering, losing, and longing in more articulated and resonant patterns. Consolation is the opposite of isolation.

A patient presented his therapist with the news of a significant accomplishment with what seemed to be considerable enthusiasm. To his chagrin, the therapist found that he was having difficulty taking pleasure in the good news he had been told by his patient. Instead, he found himself feeling jealous. This was a patient who often presented himself as having limitless possibilities and appealed to the therapist for support of this notion. As the therapist felt himself envying his patient, he was ashamed of this feeling. He had to struggle hard to admit it even to himself. As he listened to the patient discussing his accomplishment, he had the idea that the patient was having trouble enjoying it, too. It occurred to him that often the patient asked him to feel something the patient felt incapable of experiencing for himself.

He wondered whether the patient had not aroused his envy in order to communicate to him just what a trouble the patient had inside himself with his own urges to spoil his own pleasures. Did the patient, he wondered, have to remain immune to pleasure for fear of losing any sense of who he was and any sense of inner control? When the therapist wondered about this, the patient was able to discuss how conflicted he was about his accomplishment and how frightened he was of what it would cost him in his intimate relationships. The theme emerged that he felt whatever he got had to come at the expense of others.

Range and Resilience

We perform our pleasures and our joys in our minds and in our hearts. In this era when we are all agog with the possibilities of information superhighways, of knowing so much in such stupefying detail about the world outside us, have we not become more and more remote from the world of inner form that is so much more inalienably ours? The wealth of possibility for experience, for enjoyment, for pleasure, for intimacy and mystery that lies within us is the most neglected natural resource on the planet. The performance of pleasure and joy in our minds and hearts depends on our inner forms. We are much freer in the shaping of our experience than we are often aware. This is not the freedom of wishing but the freedom of understanding, of undergoing, of accommodating. It does not overturn the rules of reality but explores the realm of inner reality, the inner contexts in which we can situate our experience. It makes an inner place where we can live, one that can be quite roomy enough to accommodate all we know of ourselves or can come to know.

A young man in his early twenties had to undergo an extensive surgical resection of his large bowel in an Air Force hospital because he had familial polyposis, a precancerous condition of the large intestine that, untreated, progresses to life-threatening malignancy. Before the operation, he seemed quite anxious and talked about being worried about his future because everything seemed so unknown. He wondered what he would feel like after the operation and whether he would still be able to act like himself.

Within a few days after the surgery, his mood had considerably brightened. He had given his colostomy a name. He called it "The Roadrunner," after the cartoon character of the same name. He talked about liking that particular cartoon character because it was always getting into such terrible scrapes and then getting out of them again. He did not make the analogy explicit, but it seemed clear that he was grateful to the colostomy, "The Roadrunner," for helping him escape the clutches of death at such a young age. There was a twinkle in his eye.

He rather enjoyed displaying his colostomy, deriving some mischievous pleasure from the discomfort of others in observing this intimate revision of his anatomy. He presented the operation as more triumph than loss, at once a tour de farce and a tour de force. He refused to tolerate anyone feeling in the least bit sorry for him, as if this was what was humiliating. While it was a worry that he had to be so active and so insistent in warding off any feelings of pity or loss, still his adaptation was impressive.

The noted physicist and cosmologist Stephen Hawking has been confined to a wheelchair and unable to undertake any but the most restricted movements for many years because of his amyotrophic lateral sclerosis, more popularly known as Lou Gehrig's disease after the great Yankee first baseman whom it laid low after he had set the major league record for most consecutive games played. It has been said of Hawking that his amyotrophic lateral sclerosis has been in some ways a stroke of professional good fortune for him because it has made it impossible for him to do calculations because of the burden of physical work involved in them. As a result he has been free to reflect more deeply on the topics in physics that interest him and bring him pleasure (Gribbin and White 1992).

While we can speculate on what his deep motivations may be for taking on ultimate problems of cosmology, such as the meaning of time, the fact remains that Hawking's is a remarkable adaptation to what to most of us seems a terrifyingly restrictive condition. How admirable to be able to find freedom in such a constraint, to experience life as more spacious, containing more mental room, to turn to what does work for succor when so much does not work.

A doctor who had always been interested in art but too busy to pursue his interest had a stroke that left him partially paralyzed and with serious difficulties in speech. He was able to communicate to his wife that he wanted to be taken to the art museum. Once there, he would indicate which paintings he wanted to look at. He managed to work out for himself a routine that left him many hours to gaze upon and enjoy the paintings that interested and pleased him, even though he was unable to communicate in any verbal form what the experience of looking at the paintings was. Even with the loss of what had been a vital function for him, he was able to go on enjoying himself, the actual self that was his following the stroke.

All three of these adaptations are remarkable because of the person's ability to find freedom in constraint. In each case, rather than responding with bitterness and disillusionment as the predominant emotional elements, a person in difficulty was able to find a way to make his situation habitable, to draw pleasure and meaning from the particular circumstances in which he found himself. The fact is that we cannot deny hurt and suffering, disappointment and vulnerability. Even what is most precious to us about ourselves is fragile and temporary.

Where we do have a margin of potential freedom, of not easily eradicable liberty, is in how we accommodate our hurts, how we are able to remodel our dwellings so that there is a place for hurt but also a place for joy and pleasure, for meaning and continuity of being. Remodeling can be a chaotic process in which our house at certain phases seems more like a wreckage than a home, but these three anecdotes make it clear that remodeling is possible and worthwhile. We are who we are, and what we have all in common is that we are each one irrevocably bound to the particular circumstances that happen, apparently quite capriciously, to happen to us.

Pleasure and pain, joy and hurt have in common their capacity to dominate the present, to rule our awareness with their sheer immediacy. Perhaps, though, the immediacy is sheer in the other sense, too, namely that it is possible under certain circumstances, in certain forms of inner light, to see through it. The older we get, the more experience we have the opportunity to accommodate within us. As we accommodate more experience within ourselves, we may find that our ways of accommodating experience change. We may not, for example, be so interested in details of external interaction but rather in the feeling tones that weave together our experience of ourselves over the years. We may find ourselves able to listen more deeply to the music of our lives, to discern themes with broad resonance beyond ourselves. As we deepen, we may find that we can simplify, achieving economies of design and scale both.

The pleasures of memory, the vivaciousness of memory, the power of memory to turn situations over in mind and examine them from many different angles, all open up new avenues of pleasure as life goes on. It is an irony that so many people wish to travel literally to, as they put it, see the world, when they remain so stationary in their interior points of view, as if they were stuck in rock from which they could not quite extract themselves. To see the world within us can provide the most thrilling and engaging voyages.

In fact, the pleasures of memory can be extraordinary and provide a sense of internal companionship and interest that provides a buffer against so much hurt, a creative counterpoint to inevitable losses and disappointments. To remember need not be only to repeat but to appreciate differently in new relationships with other experiences, also more deeply. Memory is not simply about repeating the past but about transforming it as part of the ongoing transformation of presence that is life. Memory is recollection *and* invention, neither one alone.

Memory is internal presence. It is not so much about the declaration of so-called facts but about the continued creation of meanings. As such, it is not principally about the past but about an inner dimension of *now*, a dimension in which we live every bit as much as we live in action, in the accustomed rituals of everyday life or in our hopes concerning the future. Of course, our sense of the future is always modeled on our acquaintance with the past. Even the most rueful memories can have a sensory power and grace that wakens us, stirs us, and animates us. Our memories make a psychological skin. Touch along this more subtle skin can give us great pleasure and comfort, too, as well as bring us pain. We have in our memories both the pleasure of a special kind of privacy—our memories are so unequivocally our own—and the pleasures of a deep sociability, keeping company with ourselves and with the others with whom our lives have become mingled.

A person in great pain and in great desperation often turns to memory for solace, for internal justification and reinforcement, for a sphere of initiative in a time when his surface circumstances give him great trouble. People in great pain and desperation turn to memory also as to an enormous collection of previous technical knowledge that may bear on the present circumstances, reliving so much that they need to relive to support their current initiatives in living.

Compassion can never ignore either the pleasures of memory or the presence of memory. When memory is painful, there is also the chance of some resolution through a current internal initiative. It is never too late for a person to experience genuine contrition, to seek to make amends, to find the balm and pleasure of self-forgiveness. Self-forgiveness involves a release from an internal prison that we have constructed for ourselves, often as intricately and cunningly as also unwittingly. Self-forgiveness can make a great deal not only new but unfamiliar, so that when we forgive ourselves we need compassionate help in seeking to settle ourselves in new inner circumstances. We need help also in grieving why we have kept ourselves out of these precincts so very long. Memory is a creative process that involves taking hold and letting go in cycles of inner action and inner passion and inner interpretation.

Compassion does not insist that others enjoy themselves. Enjoyment and pleasure, immense in their variety, are only part of life—pain, hurt, and suffering, also immense in their variety, being also part of that same life. Compassion does not wish to make itself more comfortable by requiring of those in dire straits that they seem more pleased than they actually are. What compassion does, though, is remember that life is a vast potential space, in which there must also be room for pleasure and enjoyment, not according to any pre-set formula but as we happen to be able to find them or create them. Compassion maintains a receptive attitude toward enjoyment and pleasure just as it does toward hurt, sorrow, and suffering. Compassion knows that receiving what is, accepting it as it actually is, is the crucial initiating step in seeking what may come to be better.

A young woman described how her neurological illness had caused her such a severe tremor that she was unable to untie her shoes. This had made her feel helpless and desperate. In the course of struggling for a solution, she had remembered how her dentist-father, with whom she had had a very stormy and difficult relationship, had used a piece of dental floss to jury-rig a solution to a mechanical problem at home. She laughed as she described how complicated his solution had been, how intently he had pursued building what was essentially a Rube Goldberg contraption. She still had a picture in her mind of the dental floss attached to the bannister on the stairs. She had had the thought that, if her father could do that, then surely she could find a way to deal with her own predicament concerning her shoelaces.

After much tinkering, she found that, if she used a fork, then she could manage to pry at the laces in such a way that she could untie them. The fork helped her damp out the effects of the tremor and apply the kind of forces needed at precise spots. Her face lit up as she told this story, which brought her the memory of a pleasurable internal contact with her father, a way in which she could be like him and so feel liked by him, even if he was otherwise so remote, hostile, and demeaning. The current appreciation of an interested listener helped her get more pleasure out of her creativity. It helped her use the story to remind herself of her own ingenuity and capacity to cope in the current dire circumstances.

Receptivity and Integration

Compassion depends on being able to keep in mind an image of possible ways of being whole while meeting parts. This is diffferent than imposing a particular synthetic scheme. Receptivity helps provide a way for the finding of a way, a form for finding a form to suit a particular set of exigencies as well as an individual can. With compassion comes an understanding that the other has sustained or is subject to a threat of loss or hurt that in turn endangers the other's integration, usual way of going about being a person, if not actual existence. It endangers the other's pleasures and possibilities.

Compassion comes into play often when there is a serious hurt and the outcome is in doubt, with more than a small likelihood that it will be occasion more for grief than for joy. Of course, under such circumstances, it is not only or even principally the threatened person's best qualities that are

likely to be highlighted. In the presence of great hurt, each
joy, each pleasure takes on an even greater importance.
Sometimes it is in dire straits that we most come to appreciate the pleasures of being pleased, so effecting real changes
in our inner organization.

Often, the compassionate person has to function as a
trustee for the past and eclipsed or lost self of the suffering
person, while helping the sufferer maintain at least a partially
open mind about future possibilities. The compassionate
person, we might say, has to act as a trustee for the sufferer's
once and future self, all the while sustaining the burden of
current uncertainty and the load of fearfulness and rage that
comes with it. Compassion is able to put what is happening
into a situational perspective that takes account of the impact
on the other of the hurt the other is sustaining. It is able to
remember the possibilities of pleasure and meaning even
when they seem very unavailable. It is able to remember that
the road of life has many twists and turns and that what lies
around the next bend is often very hard to see. It is able to
remember that a little pleasure, a little joy can take us a long
way.

Compassion comes to the aid of the integration, the
personhood of the other, the other's threatened or compromised sense of ongoingness. It comes to the aid of the other
as a person who can feel good and be pleased and experience life as having meaning. Compassion must most often
bear witness to and assist processes of strategic retreat and
regrouping. What these will eventually make possible is not
known at the time they are undertaken. They can issue in
surprises that are dreadful as well as very fulfilling. Compassion understands that where there is life, there is not only
hope but also risk and dread. Human possibilities cannot be
prejudged.

A fundamental and hopeful dynamic of childhood is a

growing capacity to do for oneself, to take pleasure in doing for oneself. The child and young person enjoys progressively increased self-esteem as they are more and more able to do for themselves. This pleasure in doing for oneself starts very early, is a core driving dynamic in the toddler years, and is a foundation of self-regard and feeling good about oneself throughout life. Under conditions of threat, duress, injury, and illness, it is common for persons to be forced to travel this road in reverse. They find they are less and less able to do for themselves. This is a source of anguish. It is a source of rage and despair. The burden of this rage and despair can make it very difficult for a person to arrive at sorrow, even if such grief is essential to finding a new way of looking at the self.

A crucial element in a compassionate effort to assist others in a strategic retreat and regrouping is recognizing the importance of helping others do what they can for themselves, participate actively in the assistance they receive, and allow what they need to have done for them to be done without sabotaging it. It is commonly, if not invariably, the case that no one knows better how to conceive the help a person needs than that person him- or herself. An essential aspect of any compassionate caring is a sustained effort to enlist others in the project of realistically assessing what they can and cannot do for themselves, what they can and cannot assist helpers in helping them with, and what kind of cues they can give for what they need simply to have done for them. It is important that the helpers take a pleasure in helping that is not a flight from an awareness of the common human vulnerability. It is vital that the helpers have the capacity to appreciate and value the help they get from the ones they are helping. Helping helpers help us can be an authentic, even thrilling application of our creativity. It can be a pleasure in the midst of great suffering.

Part of a compassionate defense of an other's integration and personhood is to help the other retain as much of the pleasure in doing for and feeling proud of him- or herself for doing for him- or herself as is possible. This is no small undertaking, for under conditions of threat and duress, it is an unusual person who does not go too far in the direction of insisting on doing for him- or herself or too far in the direction of wanting things done for him or her. Finding the right place in this sequence usually involves a series of repetitive approximations, missing sometimes on one side and sometimes on the other. There can be considerable conflict and strain in searching for the correct approximations, for ways not to be cripplingly helpful or cruelly demanding.

Of course, part of this effort involves helping people understand what is happening as it affects their inner form and sense of themselves. This means clear communication about what is known in the outside world about the process taking place and what is not known. Illness and loss are both very difficult to understand, very difficult to accept. The person in duress needs help in assimilating this set of experiences to other ones, bringing to bear both feelingful and cognitive understanding from previous experiences. No two persons' hurts and hurdles or reservoirs of ways to manage are the same, a fact we are often tempted to neglect for the sake of finding broader categories and smoother-appearing ways. We must take account of the threatened person's particular ways of knowing and feeling, the inner dimensions of his ways of experiencing, his style of being pleased and coming to joy.

Compassion involves remembering what others have been, even when others have lost their grip on what they once were able to do and to be, what they were able to enjoy and organize. This is not to say that the compassionate person insists that sufferers return to being what they used to be or to enjoying what they used to enjoy in just the way that they used to enjoy it. No, compassion recognizes and explores realistic limits. To be driven from a position of more ability to do for yourself to one that involves less ability to do for yourself is a serious loss, not only practically and operationally but in the dimensions of relationship, self-esteem, and meaning. It calls up both the difficulties of childhood dependence and the fears of that decrease in powers and prospects that inevitably attends the last phases of life. It places on suffering people an enormous demand for flexibility just at the time when they are most likely to seek security in accustomed ways of doing and being, to want to enjoy just what they used to enjoy just the way they used to enjoy it.

A woman with a complex psychiatric illness had once been a very competent weaver. In her current situation, she could not even remember how to set up a loom. This occasioned her enormous despair, as the weaving had been her most prized and pleasurable accomplishment in life. She still thought of herself as an artist but was unable to practice her art. It was a significant moment when she brought into therapy a beautiful small basket that she had made with naturally dyed reeds. She had done the dyeing and the weaving all on her own and was shocked that she had been able to do it. She said that one thing the basket meant to her was that the weaving skills were still in her, somewhere, even if she could not now find them. This gave her hope that she could find them again one day. What was most striking was her pleasure in the basket.

Compassion strives to takes account of the complexity of others' task in trying to find a new place and new pleasures, with as much in the way of links to the old as is possible and helpful. This calls for great patience in listening to others' efforts to explore where they now find themselves and the memories and fears and hopes that they find in the course of the exploration. Compassion involves an imaginative participation in others' search for pleasure and meaning in the changed circumstances of the evolving present. Often, listening empowers speech.

In times of trouble, a sense of humor can be an enormous help in breaking the frame of reference and allowing new ideas and inspirations. Sometimes the most bitter and rueful humor, that kind that drives us to laugh so hard we cry, can be especially helpful in releasing the inner hold of an enormously powerful affect that has become a roadblock to more mobility and vivacity of inner composition of feeling. The kind of humor that is funny precisely because there is nothing funny about it sometimes acknowledges a trouble in a way that allows us to find a place for the trouble and to move around its edges. Hobbes referred to laughter as "sudden glory," an apt description because it so often releases us just where we have felt most bound, most painfully captive (Kay 1988, p. 33). We take such pleasure in humor because it gives us back our spontaneity, restores our perspective, reminds us that no human vision is ever complete or definitive. Humor can help us take pride and pleasure in the modesty of our circumstances.

The dimensions of pleasure in relationship, in self-esteem, and in meaning are crucially interlinked and interactive. A leading quality of compassion is its exploratory interest in diverse ways to take pleasure in relationship, in self-esteem, and in meaning. Compassion recognizes that the ways are infinite and that preexisting templates may be inadequate to the task at hand. It allows for trial and error, without the punitive excesses of despair. To find a new template, to modify an old one, we must be willing to tinker, often like a frustrated and patient mechanic with limited resources and knowledge under a shade tree. Compassion holds the other always as a person, that is, as a fellow who, for all the appearance of difference and peculiarity can be both reached and appreciated. A genuine smile is a genuine success.

Self-esteem is crucially linked to pleasure in relationships with others and is especially vulnerable when these have been sources of large hurts in the past. Sometimes there are enormous loyalty conflicts in letting go of past hurts enough to sustain current healing, as if the hurt had to be cherished because the person's sense of him- or herself was rooted in it, so that to give it up would be to encounter a chaos that was unbearable. Sometimes people will choose the pleasure of a familiar hurt simply because of its familiarity. It can be very frustrating to appreciate how seriously the need for the security of familiarity can compromise initiative in directions that might bring much more in the way of satisfaction. Compassion has to be able to acknowledge, too, the degree of pleasure there can be in what seems from outside a bleak familiarity, an apparently cold prison. Compassion must resist the temptations of a revolutionary liberating fervor just as it must resist the temptations of other forms of aggression against people in relatively helpless and exposed positions. It must sometimes be able to accept that life in the most cramped inner and outer circumstances is what suits a particular person and brings him or her known pleasure.

The capacity to relate to others is crucially linked to self-esteem, because relating to others presupposes elements of a fulfilling relationship within oneself with oneself that makes one feel like a person among persons. Sometimes it is excruciatingly difficult to recognize and even respect the limitations in people's capacity to relate to others and to esteem themselves. Compassion can bear to recognize when the prospects even for these essential pleasures are limited. This involves accepting the difference between the ideal and real, a major frustration for all of us. Compassion recognizes limits of energy, too, whether physiological or psychological.

The quests for meaning and for meetings with the self and the other, the pleasures of true encounter, go hand in hand. Suffering people seek a structure of sustaining meaning both within themselves and around them. Whether they discover this or create it is a question that pales in significance before the question of whether they are actually able to experience it, even partially and fitfully. Compassion recognizes the claims of practical immanence over theoretical or ideological transcendence. Pleasure and enjoyment are natural facts of embodied life.

We are such social animals. Our sociability is built into our souls and bodies. Companionship, the variegated sense of the presence of others in whom we find ourselves reflected and whose reflections we can hold in ourselves, is one of our chief and abiding joys. Often the prime compassionate act is simply being there for and with another person, taking and offering the pleasures of human company.

A middle-aged man went each day for a number of weeks to the intensive care unit to visit his wife who lay there in a coma following a sudden, devastating, and entirely unanticipated heart attack. His wife eventually died. As he looked back on this shattering experience, one of the real comforts was the presence of a nun in her seventies, who would come almost every day he was there in the ICU. She would look the situation over and listen, offering no false hope, only a calm and calming steadfastness. Her tranquility seemed to contain within it both appreciation and acceptance of the stormy feelings it was his lot to pass through at the time.

She had known the family of one of his friends over the years. Although he did not share her religious faith, there was something about this nun's presence, her bearing, the twinkle in her eye that was enormously comforting to him. She expressed her sympathy not so much in words but in the way that she was. When this man was very upset by how difficult it was to communicate with the doctors, she agreed that it was hard to deal with the doctors because they were in such a hurry. They could not easily slow down because they seemed so nervous. She said she had tried some years back to get a few of them to notice the impact they were having in this way, how it was tantamount to a form of human cruelty, but had noticed that instead of making things better, it had made them worse, so she had stopped.

One day she told a few stories about the obstetrician-father, now deceased, of one of this man's friends. He had liked to tease her in front of her nursing students. She remembered how embarrassed she had been once during a delivery when he had turned to her and asked her whether she realized what she had missed by turning down his repeated offers to take her out on a date. She said she had turned beet red and that her students had absolutely loved it. She did not take his teasing amiss but understood the affection and respect that underlay it. She blushed even now as she told the story. The story had the flavor of life lived and enjoyed and appreciated.

This was a woman in her seventies who was vital, engaged, and full of feeling. Her presence served as a beacon for a man in severe distress. When she appeared at the memorial service for his wife, a trip that represented no small inconvenience for her, he was delighted to see her. He found himself thinking about her years later, grateful to her for being there so fully and frankly and matter-of-factly during a time when he had such great pain and need. She had offered in her own person a defense of the goodness of life, one that stayed with him and represented a pleasant memory from a time of deep woe, doubt, and even despair.

Of course, he was aware that in his memories of her at this time, he encapsulated so much, not only of the remarkable kindnesses of other friends and relatives but also of those others who had been able to be present at previous times of need. In time, too, he became aware that he had had a part in eliciting and enjoying her consolation, that he had been present there as well as she and that his own presence had had a measure of richness and goodness, even if this was obscure to him because of his great pain. When we can be pleased, we find in ourselves new resources of life and love, reminding ourselves that we can create both.

6

Grief

Emotional Recycling

It takes love to get the knack of grief. Love represents not just a heartland but also a frontier always in the process of being mapped for the first time. Tears can be a crucial part of this mapping process. It takes love to get the knack of missing, of being able to live without someone or something lost and yet remaining in contact within ourselves with what we have lost. If we cannot grieve, we are condemned to emptiness and bitterness.

Grief is an essential part of the emotional recycling process that makes us available to new experience and keeps us vital within ourselves. Is it that we mourn those we have lost all our lives? Or is it equally that those we have lost give shape to our mourning, that perpetual turning over of the inward soil so that it can bear new crops of experience to be harvested in their turn? Mourning keeps our imaginations, our feelings, our sympathies, our ideas, and our ideals fertile. It is a recycling process in which those we have lost give shape to a vital inner function.

If we cannot miss, then we are likely to be condemned to an inner bleakness and blankness that goes far beyond the relative vividity of loneliness to a numbness that forfeits most of the potential of human living. When our missing is missing, we have very little access to ourselves. We are shut up by what we shut out. What we shut out shuts us out, so that we live in a relationship of excruciating constriction with ourselves.

If we cannot mourn, we may be in the horrible predicament of staying in touch with those we have lost through hatred. Is it not conceivable that so much ethnic hatred is based on a mechanism where the hatred represents a secret link to what has been lost and loved? A man whose entire family has been killed in one of the horrors of this century goes for years without mentioning them, but he is instead consumed by hatred for the other side, the ones he blames. He cannot let go of his hatred or in anyway modify it because it represents his only access route to what he has lost. He cannot progress to sadness and so reclaim what is left of himself and the treasures of his own memory.

We should be extremely hesitant about trying to describe normal or normative patterns of grieving. Grieving depends on the broadest features of personality, on the nature of the actual relationship to be grieved, on the way the loss occurred, on the time of life of the person doing the grieving and the real hopes and opportunities presented not just by the external world but also by the inner world of the one doing the grieving. Grieving depends not just on what a person has been but on what that person is in the process of becoming, not just on where the person comes from but also on where the person has set out to go. Grieving is a complicated mixture of creation and renunciation, enjoyment, confirmation, and disillusionment of the most radical kind.

The love we need in order to get the knack of grieving is not only the love we get from others but the love we have for others. It is not only the love we have for and get from those who are living and present but also the love we have for and got from those we have lost. It is also the love we have for ourselves that we get from ourselves. This is not a selfish love but a love that nourishes the self and its capacity to care both for and about itself and also for and about others. As with compassion, when it comes to love, we own the means of production. Nor is there any way definitvely to give the deed away. Certainly such ownership entails responsibilities.

Change and Continuity

The knack of grief is essential to the knack of changing, of growing. Of course, the major issue in changing and growing is how, in the midst of all the challenges of inner turbulence, to maintain continuity of feeling and form. It is to find ways to recognize oneself in the mirror of new times and new trusts more or less as one was able to do in the mirrors of former times and former trusts. We change in the course of our lives and have to look at both ourselves and the world around us from different inner vantage points as we know more and have experienced more, as we have learned to set different values on our knowing and our experiencing.

In the course of life, the nature of our attachment and investment of ourselves changes. In life, we must grieve the successive stages of ourselves as we pass through them, no less than we must grieve all that we lose outside ourselves. We are less and less only the body of our physical capacities and more and more the body of our experience. We must come to be able to look back on the way we were without rancor, with remorse and regret, but also with appreciation. As life goes on, we may become less and less concrete in our outlook, less and less literal minded, as more and more of what we meet reminds us of so much else. Life is a project that changes as we realize it.

To be able to grieve, we must have compassion for ourselves. We must be able to feel the sorrow and the pity of the loss, without denying them or denigrating life because of them. We must be able to bind the hurt and rage with loving feelings toward ourselves. We must be able to interpose loving feelings between ourselves and our vengefulness. There is no such thing as grief without a significant admixture of fury, because every loss is an insult, a reminder of how small we are and how little influence we have on the course of the events that most touch us, of how life lies beyond the frontier of our imagining of it. This job of binding the rage is a huge undertaking. The river Styx, across which in Greek myth the souls of the departed made their way to Hades, gets its name from the same root that gives us the word for hatred. In grieving we must bear our hurt and our hatred, lest it sweep us away, too.

Many people keep their grieving shallow in order to avoid the inner turmoil that comes with the working through of the rage and hurt. They seal off large sectors of themselves so that the net effect is that they suffer a loss of vital capacity. Sometimes many decades can pass in a person's life before the person is willing to know what a loss has really meant. These sealed-off griefs can be passed on from generation to generation. No one is more sensitive to the hurts and losses parents have suffered than children, who often take on what their parents have put off, who often are aware of the parents' hurts more keenly than the parents themselves just because, as children, they do not have the same means of psychological anesthesia available to them.

I have observed over and over again how helpful young children can be to a parent in grieving major losses, if only the parent will attend to the child's feelings and questions. In fact, it can be a helpful psychotherapeutic strategy in assisting a patient who has trouble letting him- or herself grieve simply to help the patient notice how much the patient's young child feels and cares and wonders about the parent's loss and its effects on the parent.

In order to grieve, we need the compassionate support of others. We need a concern that is at once attentive, sustaining, and relatively but not wholly abstinent in terms of action or making demands on us. Grief is at once a most private and most social undertaking. In times of grief, we are very self-absorbed. We are so much invested in the inner world that we may have very little left over for the world around us. We need that world to be ongoing and to be able to wait as we dive deep in ourselves. We need for the others who care about us and about whom we care to trust us to go deep within ourselves and then come back up from the dive. We need for them to trust us to be able to change and rearrange ourselves. We need to be able to trust them to accommodate our changes, even if this means some changing and rearranging within them, too.

When we are grieving, our self-absorption is not only absorption in ourselves. We dive deep in ourselves for the sake of finding what we have left of the other, a whole host of memories and urges, meanings, patterns of interaction that have their special cadences and melodies, their special ways of linking with all that we are and do. We grieve to preserve the inner impressions of the one that we have lost and so also the range of expressiveness that we formed and used with the one that we lost. Grief is an important means for holding onto life. Grief is as much about a reunion with parts of ourselves that were dedicated to the one we have lost as it is about a separation from the real lost other. Sadness can be such a soothing and comforting feeling, provided, of course, that we can accept the helplessness involved in it, because in sadness we find ourselves again joined to feelingful parts of ourselves from which we had become estranged because the hurt was too great.

"A good cry," said one grieving patient, "can tell me much more about myself than two weeks' worth of thinking."

When we are grieving, we are engaged in tasks of inner viewing and reviewing. While we may seem very sad and self-absorbed, this self-absorption is a crucial kind of relatedness to others. It expresses not only how important the lost other has been to us, but also how important others can come to be to us again under changed conditions of the self. Our grieving has to do not only with the past but also with the possibilities of the future. By mourning the past and giving it its due, we ready ourselves for the future that will resonate in all sorts of different ways with the past, acquiring some of its luster and meaning from just these resonances, even as future experience will change our past, sometimes enriching it and deepening it for us.

An elderly man said, "I think I've enjoyed my childhood much more thinking back on it and looking back on it, than I did at the time. It's really become much more interesting and rich. Now, who is to say which childhood is the real one? I think each one is real in its own way. My childhood has sort of grown up along with me. It's not as young as it used to be, for better and for worse."

Complexity of Grief

Grief is such a complicated and creative human experience, having to do at once with the continuation of past relationships under changed circumstances, liberation from the past, and preparation for the as yet undefined possibilities of future living and losing. Grief comes from roots that also give rise to "grave," the place where we bury the dead; "gravity," as in the force that gives weight to mass; and "gravid," implying being pregnant, heavy with child, with life to come. Grief is a somber and grave experience, one that puts us in mind of the ultimate perspective of death. Grief has to do with giving due weight to what we have lost, with valuing it in all the many contexts that exist within us. Grief also has to do with achieving the inner fecundity to give birth to a renewed self that has been changed by the loss.

Often when we are grieving, we feel so heavy in our bodies. Grief is an embodied experience that affects all our physical functioning. It affects how we walk, how we talk, how we eat, how we digest, how we see, how we hear, how we touch, how we sleep, and so on. It is an embodied experience through which we live. It is one of our species' major instruments for living, playing perhaps the central role in the creation of culture, the way we have of becoming and being human together, of passing on prospects for humanity to our progeny. Grief gives the weight of inner presence to what is absent and bound to continue in absence. In so doing, it establishes the category of the ancestral. Culture depends on the memory of what went before being sustained in a transgenerational representational space that does not depend on the literal presence of what was and is no more.

Grief, too, is an essential part of establishing an inner culture within the space of a lifetime by bringing disparate elements into new forms of relationship with each other. Grief and culture agree in making a cardinal virtue of the virtual. We can find treasures in our grief provided we can bear the press of it and remember all the while that we struggle that not only are we still alive but that others like ourselves and those we lost will live on after us.

A woman in her forties lost her mother after a prolonged and difficult illness. She said that she knew her mother's death was coming and that she thought she had prepared herself well for it. She felt a certain relief that her mother had died, because her mother had already suffered enough and there was really no purpose to more suffering. She was stunned that, when her mother died, it came as a great shock to her, a surprise, as if she had not known it was coming at all. She said she thought about her mother all the time, even though four months had passed since her death. She sometimes even felt guilty that she thought so much about her mother. She wondered whether it was normal or whether she was ill in some way. She said she had not even thought this much about someone else when she had been in love.

She noted what so many other grieving people notice, that it seemed to her that no one was particularly interested in listening to her talk about her mother. She felt that the people around her, family, friends, co-workers just wanted her to get on with it. This, she said, was one of the most painful aspects of the grieving process, namely, that she felt increasingly isolated in it. She was concerned with things that seemed to have no meaning for others, as if she lived in one world and they in another. She felt other people just wanted her to be the way they were used to her being. She said there was a part of her that wanted to do this, too, to go on without skipping a beat, providing what she always had provided for others. This, she knew, was unrealistic. It was something she could not do while being true to herself and her own experience.

She felt that others were a bit frightened of her and her grief, as if it might bring them news they really did not want to hear. She found herself sometimes feeling embarrassed at being grieved. She went on to say that her mother's death made her feel much closer to death than before, as if somehow her mother had always stood between her and death. Now there was nothing between her and death, so that everything around her seemed different, too, more fragile, more precious. She was less inclined to be critical because she was struck with how remarkable it was that anyone was alive at all. She noticed that it was odd now that sometimes she felt closer to her mother than when her mother was alive because she felt better able to imagine her mother and her mother's circumstances. Her mother's responses made more sense to her now.

She said that when she felt close to her mother in this way, it just made her ache, because she could not tell her mother about it. She felt bad that there was so much about her mother that she had not noticed when her mother was alive. She felt a certain kind of shame that she could talk to her mother more clearly and deeply now that her mother was gone, or at least gone in the outside world. She said it made her feel very shy even to try to talk about this sort of thing. She imagined that others would not understand, but then wondered whether perhaps her experience was really so very different, after all, from the experience of other people who had grieved. Sometimes she saw her mother in her dreams and when she woke up found it impossible to believe that her mother was dead and gone. Nothing in the world seemed to make sense without her mother, yet she knew that it was a normal experience to lose one's mother. It was an experience her children would go through one day as well.

A compassionate response to grief involves understanding that grief is not vain or idle. The grieving person is not doing nothing. Rather, he or she is hard at work in the workshop of the human soul, where the person is all at once material, tool, and artisan. The grieving person is the stuff being worked on, the tool doing the work, and the artisan responsible for both the design and the craft of fulfilling it. When we see grief in this way, we find it easy to understand why it is so tiring and why it does not only occupy the attention of the grieving person but also preoccupies the person. We find it easy to understand why grief is so draining, why it can be draining not only to the one who is grieving but also to those who watch, knowing that loss has been and will be their lot again, too, and that what challenges the mourner now has challenged them in the past and will challenge them again. Compassion means grieving our losses again and anew as we accompany other mourners on the journey of loss and inner renunciation and creation.

Grief, after all, is everywhere around us, not only as reminder of loss and injury and of our own inevitable transience but also as a stimulus to new creation, new appreciation, deepening understanding and engagement. Grief can both fill us up and help us make more room within ourselves, vastly increasing our capacity. Grief can help us know what is central and what is peripheral, what matters to us and how it matters. Grief can help us understand the mystery that we have most truly what we are able to let go and enjoy. Grief can help us realize that the pleasure of love is quite different than possession, which can bring us to the brink of despair. Grief can help us understand that possessiveness as part of an intransigent pattern of control can rob us more surely than death. Grief can even help us better understand our own capacity to hate and hurt and be cruel.

Accompanying Grief

Compassion for those who are grieving involves being at once attentive, sustaining, and relatively abstinent in terms of actions and making demands on them. This is a complex mix that requires numerous acts of judgment and discretion on our part. These judgments depend on intuition as well as on information. We need to honor the attachment of the grieved person to what has been lost. We need to try to find a way to be present with the person while we also leave him or her alone, so that he or she can explore deeply what has happened and what is happening within. Grief does not involve simply withdrawing from the lost other. It does not mean consigning that lost other to a gray world of emotional half-tones. Grief is not about liquidating relationships but rather about finding how to carry them on in changed ways appropriate to changed circumstances.

To be compassionately with a grieving person is to bear witness, often silently, to this process. If we remember and reminisce along with the person in grief, we often provide more comfort by the simple fact of doing so than we realize. How precious to a grieving person the mere mention of the lost one can be, signaling that there is another real other, gloriously and inconveniently external, who can move alongside him or her at least for a moment in the world of loss. How many grieving people hunger just to hear the name of the one they have lost spoken aloud! They hunger to hear another human voice with the special range and splendor and infinite variety of the human voice give life again to that name that meant so much to them and still means so much to them.

"I feel ashamed of myself for going on talking about this all the time," said a bereaved patient. "I know it can't be very interesting for you that I come in here and say the same thing day after day. I know I'm boring you, yet I can't help myself. I keep telling myself that I should find something else to talk about. But for me there isn't anything else, at least not right now."

I responded to this patient that she was not boring me. Nor did I feel that she was saying the same thing over and over, because each time the context was ever so slightly different. What she was complaining about was her own sense of the monotony. What she found abhorrent was that no matter what she did, no matter what inner maneuvers she tried, there was no way around the simultaneously inescapable and unacceptable fact of her loss. She felt all at once the urge to overthrow the order of the world and the futility of this urge to revolt.

The change in circumstances brought on by loss, especially through death, is of the most fateful kind, for there is no longer an external presence corresponding to the internal presence of the lost other. We must now turn to relating to the lost other within ourselves, as a part of the inner world, not the outer world. We miss sorely the corrective dissonance and extending harmony of the other's external presence. We miss sorely the way in which the real external lost other always stood free of our simulation of that other, enriching us and challenging us precisely by this failure to come under the sway of our inner version of the other. We miss the other as an original, someone unimaginable, whom, in a painful paradox that is one of the most awesome twists of fate, we can now know only by imagining. We miss the precious inconvenience of the other's external presence, the series of small surprises and inspirations that jolted us as we lived alongside the one who is lost. We never get free of our awareness of this missing, either. We may find new realms of freedom in it, but we never get free of it.

We often continue our relationships with those we have lost in how we relate to those who are still with us and with those who come to be with us. Our past loves live in our current loves, even as the seeds of our current loves stirred in our past loves, even though we knew nothing of what life held in store for us. This is certainly not to say that the present and the past are identical, nor that the past rules the present as with a dead hand. This is far from the actual case because the relationships between what we have been and what we now are, between different moments in our becoming, are far richer and more dynamic than that. Part of compassion for a person who is grieving is to remember just how vast life and its possibilities can be. Grieving is about the creation of new meaning.

Presence always contains not only elements of freedom but an elemental freedom, all the more powerful and capacious if we are able to explore the past. Reliving need not be barren repetition but can be a new living that brings to fruition possibilities that were previously neglected and left in abeyance. In reliving we can taste a great deal of bitterness, but we also can find our way toward a forgiveness not only of the other and of ourselves but of fate. We can find our way toward a more practical and profound embrace of the framework of our existence.

The task of sustaining the grieving person is an immensely practical one. It starts with respecting the process of grieving, both as it is bitter and stormy and as it is sweet and consoling, because there is pleasure as well as pain in grieving. There is a second grief, sometimes even more poignant than the first, that comes when the grieving person realizes that the grief is moderating. He or she has to separate from it, too, or at least to take up a new inner perspective with regard to it. It cannot be as important as it once was but has to take its place as one among many concerns. The grieving person needs sustenance and respect as he or she deals with this pain, this resignation, this healing submission to life that yet hurts. He or she needs help in not feeling too guilty that the grief is abating.

The grieving person often needs concrete practical help of a host of different kinds, for the loss means that he or she has to come to grips with new external circumstances. Compassion does not confine itself to feeling kindly or mouthing kind words. It also involves practical and active support where that is indicated. It can mean help with taking care of children, help with work, help with making difficult decisions, help with taking care of the mourning person's own body. It does not mean taking over for the other what the other can do for him- or herself. It does not mean helping the other avoid stretching to meet the exacting demands of a new difficult situation.

A man in deep grief looked out the window of his house at twilight on a late fall day shortly after his difficult bereavement and saw his ill and frail old father sweeping the leaves off the steps of the sidewalks to make certain that no one coming into or going out of the house would fall and become injured. This small physical act of caring spoke so eloquently of a father's concern that the fully grown son, himself middle-aged and a father as well, found himself carrying the picture of it around in his mind for many difficult months as a significant solace. So much feeling did he have that it was more than two years before he could acknowledge to his father that he had seen him out there sweeping the leaves and try to tell him how much it meant to him.

When it comes to compassionate support of the grieving, we must remember that small acts can stand for large feelings and take on a communicative, embracing, and warming meaning far beyond what we imagine possible. Sometimes we are diffident in offering what we can to those who are grieving not because we are indifferent at all but rather because we are almost paralytically aware that we cannot provide what the bereaved person most wants, namely, the restoration of the world and its possibilities the way they were before the loss. We feel that whatever we have to offer must disappoint, as indeed it will. However, this is another one of those classes of situations in life in which we can be best only by being second best. We must be able to sustain the awareness of the lack we can never repair without despairing of what we can and should do and its usefulness in helping the grieving person come to terms with massive disappointment. We must be able to reach out our actual, small, warm human hands, even at the edge of the abyss. We must be able to bear the knowledge that our help *hurts,* that the tug back to present life may make the mourner gasp in pain like a hooked fish that has been pulled out of its element, but that the lack of help hurts even more.

Unfortunately, even the most basic respect for the process of grieving cannot always be taken for granted. A young and very responsible hospital worker's father died suddenly in a far-off foreign country. This young man's position in the hospital hierarchy was very low. When he requested two weeks' emergency leave so that he could travel to his native land to be with his mother and to attend his father's funeral, he was told this was just out of the question because leave schedules for the holidays had already been made months ahead of time and there was simply not sufficient staff to make a change at this late date.

In this particular case, the young hospital worker, after discussing the matter not only with his co-workers, who were absolutely furious over the way he was being treated, but with his family, including his mother, decided to postpone his trip home. He reasoned that his father was already dead and that his mother seemed to be getting along as well as could be expected and might need company even more a few weeks later. The residual hurt of this situation was still being felt many years later, as not only this young man but many of his co-workers took it very hard and felt very alienated from the organization for which they worked.

Perhaps the idea that such an incident can occur even in a hospital, where the rhetoric of kindness and compassion is widely espoused and kindness and compassion are often even practiced, can serve as a useful caution. Nor was it simply a matter of callousness on the part of the administrative hierarchy, although there was certainly that, too. It had also to do with a failure to understand and respect the process of grieving, as if grieving were a "doing nothing" rather than a task that has a central constructive role in the development and sustaining of persons. Grieving, just because it is so taxing and so profound a task, can seem inordinately inconvenient, not only to those who must deal with the grieving person but to that person him- or herself. If we turn away from grieving's demands, then we have sacrificed much more than we realize to the claims of a short-run expediency. If we do this, we cannot help but feel ourselves diminished in our own eyes. Then, of course, our shame will make it even harder to get back to grieving and its difficult opportunities. Our shame can lead to pride that refuses to let us admit how much our losses mean to us.

Attentiveness, sustaining, abstaining from doing too much but not neglecting to do what manifestly needs to be done, respecting the meaning of grieving without needing to insist that it be different than it is—all these have the quality of accompanying without intruding. Of course, we will err. No matter how practiced we are, compassionate action and feeling are perpetual approximations, without the comfort of any mathematical formulations to guide us. We err. We regret. We wonder. We wander. We try and try again. However, we should not forget that the grieving person also errs, regrets, questions, wonders, wanders. One of the most difficult parts of loss and grieving is one we all too readily forget, probably just because it is so disturbing.

Disorientation

Our losses are disorienting. They render what seemed definite and clear to us anything but definite and clear. They wreak havoc with our habits, both in the external world and internally. We may look in the mirror without feeling any particular sense of acquaintance or accord with the reflection that looks back at us. We may find ourselves unable to sing even the tune we thought of as our own special signature. Our losses bring into suddenly sharp focus aspects of life that we had worked hard to keep blurred and fuzzy. In the face of loss, we are propelled back sometimes to the edge of chaos. Grief is a mixed state that is normally very confusing, hard to articulate. Even as we describe it, we are already emerging from it. We are giving form to what was formless, teeming with complexity and contradiction. It takes a steady effort to remember the confusion, which approximates in some instances a state of being inchoate before creation.

A woman in her late thirties was extremely upset after a mastectomy. She did not feel like herself. She had no clear idea how to go forward in life. She had ordered a prosthesis, which did not come for what seemed to her an agonizingly long time. In fact, the order had gotten misplaced. Until it came, she had told herself that she would not go out of the house. She did not talk about any of this but was simply mortified at the loss of a part of herself that was essential to her feeling like herself. She began to get depressed and irritable. One morning, a friend came to visit her. This friend, a few years older than she, had also had a mastectomy, but some four or five years previously. The friend, although she had found it quite difficult, had made a good adaptation.

When finally this woman was able, tearfully, to tell her friend how things were for her, how terrified she was about her future, how she was not feeling at all like herself no matter how hard she tried, the friend asked her whether she could have one of her bras. The friend took the bra and said it did not matter what she stuffed in there. She tried tissues and paper towels and then stuffed a cloth diaper in it. The friend said that a breast was important but not as important as she, herself, was. To her great astonishment, this woman found herself able to go out to lunch with her friend, wearing a bunched-up cloth diaper instead of a breast. She said that it was the kind of thing she, herself, would never have thought of doing in a thousand years. In fact, feeling as she did, she never would have thought of doing anything. She had somehow stopped feeling she could take any initiative, could choose, could adapt. In fact, she enjoyed lunch. She said she had felt a little bit the way she had when she sneaked off to the bathroom to have a smoke in junior high school just to see whether she was brave enough to do it.

The friend helped her find her way back to herself with a stroke that was at once very daring and very practical. This woman went on struggling with her loss, but the crucial gain made possible by her friend's compassion was that she was able to struggle. Now, of course, this kind of initiative would not work for everyone. Some women might find it the height of crude meddling. That it worked in this case was a tribute to the attunement of the two women in a particular situation of peril. It was a tribute to their capacity to confide and trust in each other. The point, though, is that a compassionate response to loss and to the needs of a grieving person requires creativity, sometimes even daring. It may mean taking risks. As in most situations of human difficulty, there are no guarantees.

A woman in her early forties who had suffered a number of devastating blows, including the loss of both her parents, described her experience of a holiday. "You sit there and all you can think of is who is not there. Certain moments come and you know just what this one or that one would have said. And they don't say it. That's when you feel the holes. I say it in my mind and I try to pretend they're there, but it doesn't work." For this woman, the holes were in herself, a normal experience in grief.

A recently bereaved middle-aged man was actually much comforted when, shortly after his return to work, a co-worker said to him with a particularly grim set of his face, "You know what you look like? You look like a man walking around who has just had his arm amputated." This, in fact, was what he felt like. His co-worker's capacity to see and accept his pain and talk about it with him helped him establish a sense of his own self-continuity. His co-worker helped him bridge before and after by having the compassion not to act as if nothing had changed.

A very active and self-reliant woman in her early eighties described the feeling of disorientation after a major loss very well to a nephew of hers who had driven her home from a family dinner. He had happened to ask her how she was managing since the death of her husband of more than fifty years. He asked in such a way as to make clear that he was not merely inquiring, as people so often do, out of a sense of social obligation, but because he really wanted to know how it was for her to go on. "Well, you know, I do everything I've always done, maybe even more. I smile and I tell everyone that I'm doing fine. Why not? Why shouldn't I? It's all a charade, playacting, pretend. I don't want to make anyone unhappy. But everything that was real for me died when your uncle died. Now what's there to do, but to go on?"

Two years later she was still going strong, but a note of pleasure had returned. She did not remember making these statements, probably because, as the disorientation of grieving had passed, they were no longer true. It was not that they had not been true when she made them. Rather, it was that she had lived past the point where everything she did seemed false, so that it seemed to her at the time more that she was impersonating herself than that she was living as herself.

Disorientation, the loss of the accustomed shape and differentiation of the self, brings with it exposure to profound feelings of helplessness. It is very hard to remain still in the midst of feelings of helplessness because to do so we must overcome the urge to flee and the urge to fight, both built into the core of our very bodies. If we can remain still in the face of feelings of helplessness, we may discover the annihilation threat is not so great as we thought it was. Remaining still requires organization and an advanced capacity to evaluate a difficult and amorphous situation. Remaining still *and* organized is an *activity* that breaks new ground, extending the evolutionary horizon beyond flight and fight. It reflects an increased maintenance capacity. It opens up an entire new horizon of inner possibilities.

Helplessness is one of the cardinal aspects of grief, and we often see that a loss unleashes a storm of activity that, far from bringing consolation, does a great deal of damage. Panic, incompatible with survival, is intense activity without adequate organization. Part of compassion toward the grieving is to recognize how close they often find themselves to panic. Grieving involves an at least partial mastery of the fight/flight dilemma. Often, it is of enormous help to a grieving person to suggest that the person slow down and trust the process of grieving.

Grieving people who experience the inner disorientation of serious loss need, as part of a compassionate response, help in feeling like themselves and help in being able to accept not only the change in the world around them but the changes that are coming to be within themselves. Sometimes people who have experienced a loss will start changing everything in their lives without being able to stop and think or, what is even more difficult, to stop and feel. The underlying impulse, paradoxically, is conservative. By changing everything, they are trying to set their worlds right, that is, back in some more accustomed order. They are trying to transform their passivity in the face of loss into activity to gain some measure of control. The harder they try, the more they change, the more baffled they feel. In a vicious cycle, they redouble their efforts, until there is very little left that is familiar. They are in a panic where everything seems topsy-turvy and nothing about themselves seems familiar enough to let them settle down.

They are, literally, missing in action. They are alienated from themselves and their feelings in their actions. When people are acting this way, the compassionate response may be to try to challenge quite directly what they are doing, so as to help them settle down. This may generate a great deal of friction. But as long as they go on blindly acting, furiously acting, compulsively acting, they will be missing in their actions and unable to get to the more rewarding job of missing in feeling and so finding order and some measure of peace.

A man whose wife had died suddenly and unexpectedly, leaving him with three small children, reported that, for two and a half years after the event, he had no idea what he was doing. He could not bear to go home and went from bar to bar to bar, drinking sometimes, sometimes not. He said the only way he could understand it was that he was looking for his wife in the bars but could not bear even to let himself think that. He said he wished someone had just sat him down and told him that he was out of his mind.

Shadowed Grief

What of the grief of a person who loses someone he or she has longed to be rid of for many years? What of compassion for this kind of grief? Certainly, there is triumph and a sense of pleasure, a sense of having been at last delivered when a person "loses" in this way. However, very rarely are these feelings the only ones. To be sure, there is a triumph in having outlived and outlasted the other, this most intimate adversary. Yet, this lost other, however awful, was part of the experience of the now bereaved person. He participated in giving that experience shape and meaning. If the bereaved person chose the one of whom he longed to be rid, how much more complicated is the process of mourning. The bereaved person may have many and complicated reproaches against himself, for choosing as he did, for remaining bound so long by his choice, for not being honest with himself, and more courageous about his situation. If this is the case, then the course of mourning will have even more twists and turns in it. The loss is not just an answer but the overture to a thousand questions.

The mourner is presented with a stimulus to look at his or her own complicity in creating just the circumstances so long complained about. There is an opportunity for the mourner to look at his or her dependency on the hated one, the despised one, the one who is now gone. There is a challenge to face up to and own the need to be involved with someone for whom the mourner had little or no respect. There is a chance to confront the need for someone to hate and look down upon and to try to understand its roots. The person in this predicament needs our compassionate honesty, our willingness to look at what is hard and convoluted in life.

The mourner needs something other than sentimental reassurance. He or she needs our understanding that we can fail ourselves seriously in life and that part of life is feeling and facing our own failures, including the ways we have failed ourselves, as squarely as we can. Contrition and repentance always have an important part to play in grieving that renews us. Nor is it ever too late for contrition and repentance. It is part of inner liberty that deep and far-reaching changes in a person's way of being can take place very late in life and be full of meaning not only for that person but for all who know him or her. Of course, contrition and repentance demand a realistic facing of how we have erred, not a sham that is as spurious as that form of seeming apology whose real goal is to create the conditions for renewing the offense. Sometimes people become arrested in very complicated states in which they struggle to resolve their mourning but, for a very long time, are unable to go either forward or backward.

A woman in her early fifties had hated her mother-in-law for almost three decades. She felt that her mother-in-law always regarded her as an interloper and that her husband and mother-in-law were often in collusion with each other to devalue her. She had often looked forward to the time when her mother-in-law would die. She resented bitterly taking care of her mother-in-law during her terminal illness. She felt that she had gotten stuck with this task, just as she had gotten stuck with so much else in her life. She felt also that no one appreciated what it cost her to take care of her mother-in-law, not her mother-in-law herself or her husband.

When her mother-in-law finally died, she was relieved and pleased but also discomfited. For one thing, she felt very much alone and very worried about the future. Her three children were grown and out of the house. Her husband was ill with a condition that was not life threatening but one that the doctors said was chronic. Her mother-in-law had directed that she be cremated, although this was not the custom of her church. The problem of disposing of the ashes became a vexing one. There were no ritual requirements to guide the family as to what to do, so they did not do anything at all. The ashes came to rest in the closet of what had been the mother-in-law's room. That they were there was never mentioned. Yet, this woman never went into that room without thinking about it. She did not bring it up because she felt her husband would be distraught if she mentioned it. She said he had enough worries without that.

One day she remarked that she knew what her husband thought, although she also knew that he would never have the courage to say it. She went on that, if he spoke his mind, he would most certainly say that he thought she was just like his mother, every bit as demanding and jealous, in short, a kindred spirit. She said that she did not think that this was fair, that, although she could see how he might form this idea, if he only listened to how bitterly she complained about his mother, she was really very different. She said she knew that she actually got in trouble because she was so desperate to please everyone and so frightened of what might happen if she did not try her very hardest to please them. She said she thought her major problem was that she had never found a way to be fair to herself in life. She had just left herself out.

Conspicuously, she stopped short of wondering whether, in fact, her mother-in-law had not suffered from a similar difficulty. I simply remarked that sometimes it was an awful lot to expect of oneself that one find a way to be fair to oneself, because that could mean giving up so much. The mother-in-law's ashes stayed in the closet of the bedroom she had once occupied, which was not refurnished for any other purpose. Life went on in many ways as if she were still there, still a central part of this woman's life, a kindred spirit still available to be resented, still available to be leaned on. This woman could not face the confusion and inner disorientation that would have been involved in going a step farther in grieving, in letting her own pain and perplexity at once out and in. She knew and did not know what she was doing, was able to make an inventory of her own feelings and failings, but was also unable to face up to that inventory.

An Intimate Visit

A doctor in his late fifties who knew he was dying of cancer went one dark and cold winter evening to pay a consolation call on a younger colleague who had recently lost his wife. The two men had been on terms that were a mixture of cordiality and guardedness. As they settled themselves in front of the fire, the younger man was acutely aware that something was different between them. In the course of their long conversation, the older man told the younger man much about his life that the younger one had not previously known. He recounted how his father had died when he was 4 years old, and his mother had become despondent and inaccessible. As he told this story, the pain of it across the whole span of a lifetime was present and palpable.

He said, clearly thinking about the younger man's child who was now quite suddenly motherless, that he found it very hard to understand exactly what the effect of losing his father so early had been on his life and his view of himself. He admonished the younger man that it was not enough to live for the sake of his child, that this would not be good either for him or for her. He told the younger man that he had to find a way to go on and live for himself, too. The younger man was a bit disconcerted, feeling at once lectured and that the motivation behind the lecture was both terribly sincere and terribly decent. The older man was clearly trying to give him the benefit of his own experience, trying to help him find a way other than that the older man's bereaved mother had traveled.

The older man then proceeded to tell a remarkable story. One sunny morning when he was 16, he had happened to be walking past a drugstore. As he looked through the window, he saw the face of a man whom he immediately took to be his father. Seized by the excitement of the moment, he went rushing into the drugstore, his heart pounding in his chest, convinced that the man he had seen through the window was his father. In this state, he got within three or four feet of the man, who looked up at him with a surprised expression on his face. It was a terrible moment, for the man was clearly not his father but a total stranger. In total disarray, near panic, the 16-year-old boy went running out of the store, kept running down the street, trying to dull the pain.

This story of the never-ending search for those we have lost, of its sudden twists and turns, its capacity to bring fresh dismay and disappointment, stayed with the younger man long after that night's talk in front of the fire, in fact long after the older man had died of his cancer. Our griefs are never entirely done but always available to be stimulated anew by turns in our life's experiences, changes in the interior landscapes of our wishes and needs. We keep on looking for those we have lost. The younger man found himself reflecting how different it was when this older colleague could speak to him from his heart and wondering what had stood in the way of this happening before. What had kept him from making himself available to the older man? Had he been too competitive, too judgmental? Had the older man been too envious, too bitter, too angry, too frightened, too lonely to acknowledge being lonely?

The younger man was very touched by the older one's frankness, his willingness to be open, to be vulnerable, to tell what he knew of the realm of life in which the younger man found himself voyaging largely without the guidance of a compass. This, after all, is the essence of compassion, namely, the willingness to share ourselves as we actually are with others in the course of life, recognizing that we are all limited in what we can encompass but that we may have much more to offer than we suspect. The younger man found his regard for his colleague growing over the years after the older man's death as he thought back on that winter evening's encounter, the privilege of intimacy in grief that it had brought along with it.

He felt also ashamed that he had not previously appreciated his older colleague properly and vowed within himself to try to be more open, himself, in the future. He valued the gift his colleague had given him, the gift of compassionate presence, a presence that was not aloof but itself engaged and at risk. He resolved to try to make amends for what he saw in his own mind as his own aloofness in the years that had gone before. Of course, there was no way to make amends to his departed colleague, but he did feel that he could make reparation through his future behavior, by working hard to adopt a more welcoming and appreciative posture, being slower to know, and showing himself to be more vulnerable rather than trying always to disguise his hurts for fear that others would deepen them. He found himself wondering whether, in some sense, his older colleague had related to him that night as the father he had lost so young. But he was also aware that he might have seemed a more accessible version of the older man's mother.

He also thought back to the story that this older colleague had told him about his own psychotherapy, one that had taken place in an era when the technical sway of the rule of neutrality had been unchallenged. At a period in his treatment when he was in great pain and turmoil, the older man had threatened to leave treatment. His therapist had remained neutral and abstinent, making no move to oppose him or to say that he would miss him if he left. He had, in fact, left treatment feeling bitterly hurt and disillusioned. He could not understand why his therapist had not spoken up, why his therapist had not been able or willing even to say that he would miss him and that their relationship meant something to the therapist. Here again the dynamics of his early loss of his father, without a chance to say good-bye, seemed very much to be at work.

Certainly, the therapist missed a chance to engage more deeply and compassionately. Of course, this is one of the griefs of all therapists, that surely each one of us has missed many opportunities, often without knowing quite what is it that we have missed. If this grief stays fresh in our minds and hearts, it will move us toward a posture in treatment that is more open and collaborative, more willing to take risks, more willing to ask our patients for their guidance in treating them, more willing to be present. We will want to hear their grievances so that we can try to understand them and find ways to respond that meet the tests of practicality and presence. Grief frustrated is one of the leading producers of grievances.

Grief as a Human Achievement

When we think of a compassionate response to grief, we must be aware that grief is common human property, a signally human achievement, an ever-changing and demanding task, not a problem that can be solved but one of the shaping and creative processes that give form to our lives. It is a process that is practical in its challenge and that demands an embodied response in action and feeling. We must grieve along with those who grieve, commingle our stories, our knowledge and our bafflement, our achievements and our failures with theirs, striving always not to do harm but rather to provide what succor we can. Grief is as human as knowing that we all must one day perish, a knowledge that is always with us and colors all our perceptions.

We must grieve along with those who grieve, all the while respecting their privacy and autonomy, just as we would wish for others to respect ours. We must be willing to expend effort and thought and feeling. We must be willing to work and wonder and worry and communicate. We must be willing to accept that life is as full of losses as of gains. We must be willing to accept that the variety of griefs is as enormous as the variety of joys, so that each new grief is a new occasion for wonderment and learning as well as for sadness and resignation, an occasion for meetings as well as for partings. To grieve together is to be alive together.

7

Homelessness

What Do We Mean by "Home"?

When we set out to discuss the vast and agonizing problems of homelessness and our responsibility for them, that is, our possible responses to them, we must come to grips with what we mean by "home." Home has to do with shelter, but we can take shelter at more or less concrete levels. Certainly, it has to do physically and concretely with shelter from the unkindness of the elements, from cold, heat, flood, and storm.

However, since we live even more intimately in our feelings than we do in our material dealings with the outside world, home also has to do with shelter from the elements of unkindness, both within ourselves and around ourselves. These elements can destroy any brick-and-mortar structure ever built, as is perpetually being demonstrated in diverse parts of the world, now in Bosnia, Rwanda, Haiti; now also in the inner cities of the United States, not to mention in any family where violence breaks out.

Home has to do with the continuity of our experience not only with other people but with ourselves. Home has to do with meeting and meaning as well as with eating and sleeping. Home has to do with the creation of bonds of kinship and concern based not only on lineage but on love. Home has to do with all the linkages that make for reliability.

Our physical needs are basic, but so are our emotional needs. To try to ask which is more basic so as to try to assign priority to one or the other is in some respects not so very different than seeking to discover which is more important in the making of water, hydrogen or oxygen. This latter question is obviously absurd because water is a particular and distinct substance that arises from a specific combination of hydrogen and oxygen. It is not so much more than the sum of its parts as it is quite other than the sum of its parts.

Perhaps, though, our physical and emotional needs are even more closely related than this analogy to the combination of hydrogen and oxygen to make water suggests. Our physical needs *are* emotional, and our emotional needs *are* physical. Our experience is embodied, and the separations we make between our minds and our bodies always leave something out. We can die of the human bleakness of homelessness as well as of the exposure. To live we need not just walls but connections. Connections call for both collaboration and maintenance. Connections are what keep the walls of houses standing and their roofs intact. Connections make the foundations for our houses. Connections depend on our ability both to share and to differentiate.

A young man who had experienced tragic and sudden losses as a very small child was leaving the hospital where he had been treated for more than two years. His doctor asked him whether he might not feel a little bit homeless on leaving. With no hesitation, the young man answered, "Doc, if we live in our minds, your neighbor may be homeless." This statement probably distilled years of silent and painful consideration of the world from the point of view of his losses. His point, made with breathtaking directness and clarity, was that homelessness is always very near. It may actually be located between our ears, inside, in the way that we are unable to hold, contain, and comfort ourselves.

If we cannot get a grip on ourselves, we may be condemned to a nomadic form of existence, one in which we have no fixed abode within ourselves, no inner peace or space that we can call "home." We can feel deserted without any awareness that we have created the desert ourselves. We can feel empty without having any sense of space or capacity. We can feel homeless because we cannot give our lives any meaning.

This is a predicament that can be culturewide as well as individual. Certainly, reliance on greed, compulsive sex, and violence to provide an edge, a buzz that substitutes for a deeper and more variegated vitality, is symptomatic of a culture adrift without a satisfying cosmology to relate it to the stars that make the roof over our heads. Meaning is a matter of finding inner shelter that is both individual and available to be shared. In a culture like ours, sex as a human splendor and attachment as a genuine recognition of another both so very often seem homeless.

Our capacity to be "at home" within ourselves—that is, to experience ourselves as providing an environment of security, tranquility, animation, and satisfaction for ourselves —is the foundation for our finding adequate housing in the world. Our external shelters, the actual physical houses we live in, as well as the actual external surroundings—physical, social, and cultural—in which they are situated, are likewise important foundations for our capacity to be "at home" within ourselves. "Home" is no simple thing but a most complex process of accommodation involving ourselves, others, and a whole host of habits and circumstances. "Home" is not principally the place to and from which we commute but rather the place where we seek communion.

"Home" is not simply "the place where," as one of Robert Frost's (1949) voices puts it in "The Death of a Hired Man," "when you have to go there, /They have to take you in." It is not where we get taken in or deceived, sold a bill of goods, or required to subscribe to arbitrary creeds or swear allegiances at gunpoint. Rather, it is a place, a situation in which we can be attached both to ourselves and to others, a place that we can make habitable and find habitable. It is a space with potentials. It is a dynamic human living space. If we think deeply enough, we will come to such notions as that home is at once our starting place and our destination, what we have lost and what we seek to find. Home has to do with the truth of our natures. So to find a home means appreciating who we actually are, not so much in theoretical terms as in practical terms that can be lived. To put a roof over our heads we need to have foundations, floors, walls, and a roof *in* our heads and hearts.

We may name a process in a way that makes it seem a thing, more external and concrete than any process could be, because we derive comfort from the illusion of solidity that we achieve this way. We may feel that we can possess a thing, where we can never possess a changing, developing process but only make room for it within ourselves. When we find ourselves feeling nostalgic, that so typically human pining for a return home, it is not the concrete that we are missing but a whole surround, sensory and social, that gave a particular sense to our lives at a particular time. We are missing the external correlates of something that was happening in ourselves. Of course, the resolution of the sometimes bittersweet, sometimes agonizing pain of nostalgia does not lie outside ourselves but within ourselves, in a new transformation of ourselves and our living conditions that does justice to the old. Especially as we get older, being who we are and being where we are means making a place within ourselves for who we were and where we have been.

We can never go home again in the sense of returning externally to another time in our lives. However, we can resolve much of the pain by, once again and not for the last time, finding a way to house our feelings, including our sense of having failed and been failed in the passage of time, within ourselves within the current surroundings and circumstances of our lives. We need to accept bitterness and disappointment as parts of our lives. We need to be able to use our own bitterness and disappointments to understand and feel with the bitterness and disappointments of others who have been rendered homeless. So much of art and culture, including religion, is devoted to this end. It aims to help us appreciate, remember, and relate. It aims to help us accept limits and yet go on striving. It aims to help us go back and forth in the space of our experiences without getting stuck. It aims to help us make new experiences out of our old ones and familiar experience out of our new ones.

When we want to talk in any way comprehensibly and comprehensively about homelessness and our responses to it, we must move back and forth between inner and outer, physical and symbolic, concrete and abstract. We must be able to talk at once about how we house ourselves within ourselves and the habitations we inhabit as we go about living with ourselves within ourselves and with others. Finding a home is a matter of inner action and interaction. It calls for a sociable solitude, a way to find a privacy that is not privation but rather makes possible the welling up within ourselves of the currents of love and need that help us get our bearings both with regard both to ourselves and to others.

We must weave all this together in order to sharpen and deepen our perception and appreciation of the problems and prospects involved in our quest for shelter. Given our culture's tendency to want to discuss all issues in materialistic terms, to turn to the realm of matter for answers to all our ills, such a discussion may seem unfamiliar and even disorienting. Given that we live in our minds and hearts, in our habits of understanding and responding (or not responding) feelingfully, it may produce a temporary sense of cultural homelessness in the reader. Hopefully, if this is the case, this brief encounter with cultural homelessness, this test dose of the homelessness experience, will serve to engage readers and their curiosity both more deeply and more immediately. Hopefully, it will stimulate a new kind of intuition and, therefore, inquiry about homing and housing. It will call attention to some urgent maintenance needs in our shared cultural habitation.

Homelessness as a Cultural Life Situation

Homelessness has to do with values as well as with other building materials. The homeless carry so much of our collective terror, doubt, and worry with them. Who can we count on? What are our responsibilities to each other? Why are our resources of collective good will seemingly so meager? Their homelessness represents our homelessness, our collective failure to get grounded within ourselves. Their homelessness is continuous with our own.

Nor can we make a better life for ourselves by fleeing it. If we fail the homeless, we are failing ourselves. Our material resources are sufficient so that the argument that the material sacrifice of taking care of the homeless is too great is scarcely persuasive. The material sacrifice of taking care of the homeless does not even begin to approach the moral cost of not taking care of them, a moral cost that will inevitably show itself as social disorganization with material consequences.

To widen the perspective on homelessness beyond issues relating to bricks and mortars or investment in dollars is not to try to declare either matter or money immaterial but to look more closely at the process of building and maintaining those very special places we call home. Compassion means being able at once to think feelingfully and feel thoughtfully. It does not exclude or slight issues related to efficiency and the instrumental use of resources. However, it keeps discussions of means always oriented within a broad perspective of human ends. It never forgets that the test of our actions and inactions, our collective will, is the subjective effects on real human beings. Compassion is not incompatible with sober intelligence. In fact, compassion requires the clearest form of vision, one in which identification with others and differentiation from them remain in balance. What compassion does is to forbid the use of intelligence in the service of cruelty. It never forgets that, when we are dealing with human beings, there is no way to get to the heart of the matter without getting to the matter of the heart.

A culture that does not know how to house itself meaningfully will have tremendous difficulty understanding the material and emotional plight of those who have no shelter, who sleep in the streets or in subway tunnels or at the edges of municipal dumps. The problem of homelessness is not new. A trip to a major art museum will provide a chance to see representations of figures from past centuries and many cultures who bear a haunting similarity to those we can see— or cannot avoid seeing—now not only in our large cities but on the peaceful wooded squares of our affluent suburbs. We have participated recently in social processes that have made so many homeless. It is staggering that, thirty years ago, in a much less wealthy America, there were so many fewer homeless. This is a fact known by inspection to every one of us of a certain age and clearly documented on the historic record. Is there not a prophetic voice in each one of us that speaks to us of the shame of this fact?

A first step in confronting the problem of homelessness compassionately is to look at ourselves and how we go about trying to make a home for ourselves, to look at our alienation and difficulty in putting down roots. The homeless are our kin, potentially ourselves, for, if we listen to the stories of the homeless, we will hear clearly enough that they were not always homeless, that they were not born meaning to be homeless. When we listen to their hurt and bafflement, we will feel it resonate with our own. Can it be that we have more things but less of ourselves? Can it be that the things we have, our appetites for having things, are crowding us out of house and home?

Compassion requires a realistic capacity to perceive and assess situations both inside and outside ourselves. We are, in fact, all at home less than we used to be. First of all, we spend less time physically in our homes. We are out and about, working, driving, and being driven. So much of what we do involves being driven, often relentlessly and ruthlessly, without any clear grasp of the ends we have in view. A young woman described the long drives that she took for solace in the evenings. She said it was so nice to be close enough to other people to be able to see them but safe inside her own separate metallic container. Is it that we have to go so far, to be on the go so much, because we, like this woman, cannot bear human proximity without an enormous threat? Why can we not organize ourselves inside to bear connection and intimacy more easily? Why is it that so many of us experience intimacy as a threat to the self rather than a promise, as a stimulus to disorganization rather than to integration?

We move farther and faster than ever before. Could it be that there is a competition between physical motion and the capacity to move and be moved inside in terms of feelings, not that, as dance (that so moving of human expressive activities) teaches us, this need be so? Could it be that we have set up a false competition between emotion and motion because we have forgotten that the mind is that form of transport that creates the landscapes through which it passes? Being able to be at home has to do with attachment, not just to others but also to ourselves. Attachment is an enormously

complex process involving both communion and communication, a way to get close and a way to get sufficient distance
so as not to be fused or swallowed up in the closeness and so
lose ourselves.

It involves a series of intricate adjustments of distance,
now closer, now farther, but never quite out of earshot of
the other. Successful and satisfying attachment, of which
there are many varieties, is an undertaking that requires the
full resources of an active and interactive culture. It has
to do with how we invest others and ourselves with meaning. It has to do with being able to feel and with being able
to express and understand feeling. It has to do with being
able to appreciate diversity of experience both within ourselves and outside ourselves.

The situations outside ourselves and the situations inside
ourselves are linked. There are so many different ways in
which we are all, concretely, home less and less. So many
more women work. They do not work so much simply from
choice, although that may be part of it, but from a necessity
that is related to the social arrangements we share, including our material priorities. These women are home less and
less. When they are home in body, they often have a difficult time being home in spirit as well, for they are distracted
by work responsibilities as well. Children, including so many
now of the children of the affluent and highly educated, start
out their careers away from home as early as just a few weeks
old. It is terribly sad to think of their work lives beginning in
infancy with before dawn dashes to caretakers, many of whom
are barely known as persons to the parents of these children.
How difficult it is for children to learn to keep their parents
in mind with any richness of texture! Of course, we must
remember that children's capacity especially to keep their
mothers in mind can be crucial to the development of the
richness of texture of their own minds. If this initial richness

of texture is not nourished, no amount of later material investment is likely to redress the ensuing internal poverty.

How many young school-age children come home to shelters that have no one in them at the time of their arrival? How long and strange must the wait seem to them before a parent arrives. What is so difficult and dangerous about being such a latchkey child is how easy it is to lose the key to yourself as you wait. Nor is it simply the concrete feature of being left alone that is telling. What is most dangerous is when this physical being left alone stands, as it all too often does, for being forgotten about, not continuously invested, not having a place of importance in the actual arrangements of everyday life. How many children seek solace in the alienated and alienating, that is, unconnected and disconnecting, presence of television? How many have to pretend, as one patient described to me he used to do, that the television is speaking personally to them in order to assuage their loneliness and keep from fragmenting? How many must shut down the channels of feeling altogether, preparing themselves for lives with only the most limited access to their own vital capacities? How many find attachment frightening later on because they have been so isolated and frightened early on? How many find denial of themselves their only tool for dealing with overwhelming experiences of helplessness and vulnerability? How many learn to treat others as nothings because their only recourse has been to numb themselves and treat themselves as if they did not matter?

It is striking how rich so-called primitive cultures are in social interaction with their children during the very first stages of life. Children are touched and passed around and never outside of a web of social interaction that provides support and definition not just for the children but for their mothers. In our social arrangements, we have made a striking break with the past, probably without being able to appreciate its costs and consequences in the depth they deserve. We may have made a break that expresses a misunderstanding of our fundamental disposition.

Is work really worth it? What is being produced? What are these "goods" that we are seeking so assiduously? Do we any more hear the problematic, if not prophetic, voice of Socrates asking us whether the unexamined life is worth living? Do we have any idea what it is to examine our lives? Have we perhaps so lost touch with the roots of our culture that when we think of examining our lives, we visualize some technologically advanced machine, beyond even a CAT scanner or an MRI device, that will buzz a bit, click a few times, and then print out a picture of our lives, while we are utterly passive? The question of what we do with our lives, what we think we are making and why, is not only for women who work. Home neglect is not a viable alternative in child care, either. This question is clearly for everyone and not an easy question. The force of social habit, of institutionalized power and predilection, no less than the force of individual habit, is extremely daunting to challenge. Houses are part of ways of life. We cannot think of homelessness apart from how we live our lives.

A teacher was trying to make a point in class to a group of teenagers from middle-class homes. He was trying to suggest that learning was something that went on all day long, that it was a matter of looking at the world in an inquisitive way, of touching and being touched by what was around you, of remarking on what you saw and heard, of being puzzled and finding ways to express and share your puzzlement. It was a matter of an attitude that was as natural and fundamental as breathing. He found himself trying to make his ideas clear by drawing on his own experience of growing up and being interested, challenged, exasperated, confused, shocked, and amused by what went on around the family dinner table. As he talked about this, he noticed that his students had that peculiar blank expression on their faces that indicated that they were not connecting with what he said, that, for whatever reason, it was quite meaningless for them.

The teacher's first idea was that they had no grasp of informal learning, that they associated learning strictly with school, textbooks, and tests. However, he knew from experience that when he saw those blank expressions, it was time to stop whatever he was doing or thought he was teaching and investigate what was going on in his students' minds. Closed ears, after all, hear nothing. He asked his students what was wrong with what he was saying. He said he really wanted to understand why he was not making sense or, if they disagreed with him, what their thoughts were. There was one of those long, uncomfortable silences, in which the teacher felt his basic good faith was being weighed by the kids. As he imagined it, they were wondering whether this was just another example of an adult asking a question without really wanting an answer, so that the asking was more an exercise of coercive force than anything else.

Finally, a student in the back raised his hand very uncomfortably. He said that he could not really relate to what the teacher was saying because his family had dinner all together about four or five times a year, and, when they did, they really did not talk about anything. The teacher asked how they did eat. The student said that both his parents worked, so that, usually, his mom left something on the top of the stove or in the refrigerator and everybody ate on his own, because their schedules were so different. He said his mom cleaned up the kitchen when she got home in the evening and that she was always mad about how messy it was.

Once this fellow had broken the ice, the others chimed in, too. The picture that emerged very much surprised the teacher. Of the thirty students in the room, only three reported having family meals with any regularity. Many, whether from one- or two-parent homes, said that they thought it would be disastrous if their families tried to eat together on a regular basis, providing only an occasion for more angry hurtfulness, if not outright violence. The experience that the teacher had been describing that had been so important to him as part of his growing up and education was one that his students in this next generation were not having. Far from making his ideas clearer, his discussion had had the effect of making his students feel that there was something peculiar about their families. The looks on their faces had expressed a feeling of hurt. The teacher felt badly about this and reminded himself once more of the importance of getting to know about the real lives of his students rather than making assumptions about them based on his own growing up.

For a long time afterward, the teacher found himself thinking about how different home was for these young people. He also noticed that, while about half seemed very eager to join in lunchtime sociability and conversation that included teachers at school, about half seemed to avoid this, possibly not only because of their adolescent developmental issues but also because it was simply unfamiliar to them. The teacher realized that for his students, nutrition was a different matter than it had been for him, because calories came without conversation. This look into his students' lives produced a real sense of dislocation in the teacher, giving a new detail to the picture of what it meant for people to be homeless. It made him grateful for his long summer vacations, helping him with the hurt of feeling underpaid in monetary terms as a teacher.

An elegant woman and her three children, the two oldest of whom were young teenagers, happened to be flying across the country. They were on their way to the fifth new city in eight years. All this moving had to do with her husband's swift rise in the ranks of one of America's largest food and beverage corporations. The family was building a new home in a fashionable suburb of this new city. At 37,000 feet just east of the Mississippi, the woman explained that it was really very exciting to build a new home because this was a chance to have a home that was just exactly the way that you wanted it. The contrast between this statement and the history of forced uprootings was stark. The two teenage children explained in tones every bit as sanguine as their mother's that going to a new school was not much of a problem, because they knew how to do it. Of course, you missed your friends a bit, but then you learned how to make new ones, so that it was better. You got to see so much more than most kids did. They presented themselves as experts in replacing people, using them as interchangeable bits. It was as if they had internalized a version of the most up-to-date corporate personnel policies, in which one unit of human resources, that is, a person, is represented as being easily replaceable by another unit. If you cannot count on constancy from people, then you have to form a new intimacy with things. Perhaps processes like this are what lead to a culture's excessive focus on material possessions.

To look at this family and listen to them was to form a picture quite at variance with the one being presented with such apparent poise, such insistence, such fluency. The woman and her children were both doing their best to present matters in the best possible light. This was automatic, a habit of character, deeply ingrained. Yet, the effect was chilling. If everything was so much for the best in this best of all possible worlds, why did the woman look so sad, so edgy beneath the mask of good cheer? Why did she cling so tightly to her youngest daughter, almost as if the youngest daughter were a teddy bear for her? Why did the two teenagers seem so dispirited, so lost in their enthusiasm for this new move?

Sometimes a snapshot, a brief encounter, can speak worlds. This family prompted questions about its future—among them, when would the idyllic veneer start to crack, showing a much more difficult reality underneath it? If this was good fortune, the best that could be hoped for—"success"—then all sorts of questions about how we live proposed themselves.

Shortly after separating from his wife and during the period that the divorce arrangements were being worked out, a doctor in his forties took to spending a night a month in a shelter for homeless men as a volunteer. Some of his colleagues thought that what he was doing, while also interesting and even admirable, was a bit peculiar. As much out of curiosity as anything else, one of them asked him why he was doing what he was doing. He replied, with a very slight quaver in his voice that betrayed both his heartbreak and his longing, that he, himself, was a homeless man. He did not happen to live on the streets but instead in a rather bleak and disorganized apartment, without the companionship of children and pets, not to mention his wife. He said that he could relate to what those guys felt like. He went on that it was sometimes hard to imagine just how far down on your luck you could get. You could, he remarked, get so far down that there really was not any way back up. Often after his night in the shelter for homeless men, he would find himself feeling sick and rundown for two or three days. But he was able to look squarely at his kinship with those men, to face the difficult emotional task of granting how fragile and in need of constant maintenance all our moorings are. He was also remarkably effective in his work with some very disturbed patients on whom many others had given up.

A teenager was talking about his life as a child whose parents had divorced while he was in elementary school. He moved back and forth between his mother's and his father's house. Each was now remarried. There were elements of baffling, even shocking unfamiliarity in each place. In each place, there was not only a new stepparent but also step-siblings to deal with. He was only too aware of the impor-tance of the new stepparent for his parent and of the dis-crepancy between his view of the stepparent and his parent's view of the new spouse. His metaphor for the trips back and forth was interplanetary space travel. Whatever was true in one place was not true in the other. Since his parents main-tained their involvement with each other by intense disagree-ments and mutual disparagement, he also did not feel safe to explore the differences in either place.

He pointed out that the particular article that he hap-pened to want or need seemed always to be maliciously out of reach, located on whichever planet he himself was not located on. He recognized that sometimes he played a part in this but also made the point strongly that it was an enor-mous organizational task to go back and forth between two separate houses each week when you were a teenager. He said he did not know where he was himself half the time or maybe all the time, so it was very difficult to keep track of his things. Perhaps the most agonizing difficulty was in his separation from his friends on the weekends. He felt it impor-tant enough to be with the weekend parent to choose that over activities with his friends, but he also felt keenly the loss of time with his friends and the damage to those relation-ships. He summed up the trouble by saying that whatever was important to him never came first, so much so that he had trouble remembering that there were things that were really important to him and that he himself could try to put them first. Needless to say, school was a terrible difficulty for him, being so thoroughly occupied and stressed with family matters as he was.

This young fellow's predicament, too, represents a kind of homelessness that is common among us, a situation in which two is much less than one. In his case, each candidate home was reduced to the status of a competitive fragment. Because there were two so much at odds with each other, neither one was quite habitable. It is perhaps not too enormous a leap to move from considering this predicament to noticing how odd it is that a nation with so much homelessness, so many people who do not have a place to call their own, should maintain a tax law that explicitly subsidizes the buying of second homes, most often vacation homes situated in the portions of the environment that are most fragile.

When we encourage people to own two homes as a matter of policy, are we not, perhaps, helping them along the way to an increased degree of homelessness? Might we not be helping them along the way to states of being in which they are neither here nor there? We are helping them divorce themselves not only from the needs of others but also from an awareness of their own rootlessness, of which this being out of touch with the needs of others is only one feature, if a central one. When we have no deep acquaintance with our own needs and their practical management in subjective depth, we have very few pathways open to us for understanding the needs of others. Do people need two homes (or three or four or more) because they do not know how to make themselves at home anywhere?

Homelessness, Dignity, and Autonomy

Homelessness is not unitary. It is a name for a vast kingdom of human experiences, manifold in its variety and with place always for new variations. Just as no two homes are alike, if we appreciate them in proper depth, so no two states of homelessness are the same. If we are to grasp the range and extent of the experience of homelessness, one feature that cannot be left out is the connection that often exists between states of homelessness and the individual's drive for dignity and autonomy. People can be homeless out of a refusal to settle for what seems to be offered them as a place in society. They can be homeless because they feel, often as inarticulately as ardently, a criticism of the surrounding modes of living. More ordinary, settled, and comfortable existence does not seem to them compatible with what they experience as being essential about themselves. Homelessness can be seen, in this sense, as the result of a failed negotiation, in which, as in the vast majority of all cases, all sides must shoulder part of the burden of the failure if any way is to be found beyond it. In this sense, homelessness may be seen as a criticism of a culture's failure to make places for its members.

A man in his late twenties had formed the habit over a very long time of getting along with himself by always castigating himself for having failed to live up to the standards of achievement and visible success in the world that seemed to him to have come relatively easily and naturally to his older siblings. While paying lip service to the idea that he had a neurological illness and that this might represent a serious handicap, at a deeper emotional level he gave this notion no credence at all. In fact, he resented it with a ferocious bitterness to which he rarely gave vent. He was absolutely not allowed to feel for himself within himself. It was as if, inside himself, whenever he encountered a difficulty, he repeated over and over a mantra like, "When the going gets tough, the tough get going."

He refused to compromise, at some level insisting that, unless he could resolve his troubles by brute force of will, he was not going to make any effort at accommodation. As he viewed himself, far from having a handicap, he was a rep-

robate who simply refused to do what he knew he should do
to claim a place as a member of the family. His conduct could
be exasperating enough to put the force of considerable cred-
ibility behind his claim. In fact, also, he was correct in feeling
that his family put an extreme emphasis on visible material
success. Certainly, this attitude had to do with the backgrounds of struggle and material deprivation from which his
parents and their parents had emerged. But it was also true
that their propensity to feel unduly guilty and responsible
for their children's difficulties made it very hard for them to
make a place for this child who had such real and tangible
troubles. They did what they could do, suffering along with
their son.

After a flare-up in his illness associated with the trial of
a highly touted new medication that, far from making things
better, made them worse, he ran away from home, destroying everything that would give a clue to his identity. In so
doing, he was putting into effect a long-cherished project to
be someone else, almost anyone else besides who he was. He
wanted to escape from a mold that he experienced as excruciatingly confining. He wanted to do something active and
to be in control of his destiny.

To the dismay and consternation of his family and therapist, he spent a number of days on the streets as a homeless
person. During this time, whether realistically or not, he had
no particular subjective sense of danger. He said that what
people did not realize was that, when you are homeless,
nobody wants to talk with you or hassle you. They just leave
you alone, as if they do not want to catch whatever you have.
This was, he said, really all right with him, because it was a
relief not to be under so much pressure.

He spent a night in Lafayette Park opposite the White
House and was surprised and touched that a man in a van
came by passing out free food to the people. He remarked

that it was nice to know that there were still people who were capable of being so kind and generous in a dog-eat-dog world. He spent another night sleeping near a steam pipe in another public space in Washington. This enabled him to stay warm. He was quite pleased with himself because of the ingenuity with which he had rigged up an improvised shelter. As he awakened the following morning, a very little girl, perhaps 4 or 5, offered him a pillow, which he gratefully accepted. He was impressed that she and her mother were out distributing pillows, performing another act of kindness that ran counter to the prevailing currents of his imagination and his way of treating himself as someone with no claim on himself for kindness.

Arrestingly, this young man summed up his experiences of being out on the street in a way that highlighted his trouble in making and finding a place for himself. "What people don't realize," he said, "is that when you're homeless, you get a whole new life." For him, going back to a more conventional living situation involved visibly mixed feelings, relief mingled with regret. In a way, he seemed to have gotten a lift from the experience, an experiment in autonomy that had also the benefit of allowing some fresh perceptions of good aspects of people, of human generosity and kindness, and, perhaps most importantly, of his own capacity for tenderness and genuine gratefulness. This young man's experience represented at once a confession of his difficulty in negotiating with his surround and a critique of the values and practices of the surround. Of course, this young man was very much at risk for much longer periods of homelessness, if not more dire trouble.

In order to conceive compassionate responses to homelessness, we must recognize not only that homelessness concerns us vitally but that it concerns us vitally in myriad different ways. Just as homelessness does not have a single cause but a whole range of contributing causes, and just as home-lessness is not one experience but as many different experiences as there are people to be homeless, so it does not permit of any unitary response.

Certainly, there are a host of social policy issues that arise in connection with homelessness. These range from the distribution of wealth to the treatment of minorities and others with differences. It is not merely coincidental that homelesssness became such a pronounced problem again during an era when there was an enormous net transfer of wealth to the richest among us. As I will discuss later, it is also not coincidental that homelessness grew during a time when a combination of idealistic fervor and cynical legislative financial penny-pinching did in the notion of a set of asylums for the seriously mentally ill. The peril of the family, the feminization of poverty, the growing disparity between resources available to the old and those available to young children, all need to be addressed at the social policy level. How we spend our money matters. But how we spend our money is determined importantly by how we think and feel and express ourselves, by what we regard as vitally important.

Homelessness is such a complicated set of issues that what is required is not so different than Velcro. Velcro is an adhesive material with thousands and thousands of small hooks that catch on each other. Each hook contributes just a little to the force of the connection. When we are talking about making places for people who are homeless, about decreasing the role of homelessness in all of our lives, we are talking about a myriad of small, local changes. We are talking about changes in values, attitudes, and intentions as well as changes in patterns of behavior.

We need to have small hooks to make possible the grounding of individuals in social life. We need to ask basic questions about work, family, and the organization of community life. We need to ask what constitutes progress. The care of the homeless depends on ongoing relationships and attachments. The making of a place for the homeless means making relationships with specific homeless people, becoming specifically attached to them and with them in specific circumstances, not lumping them into a category that renders them invisible, even as we have increasing trouble averting our eyes in the street from them. We must prevent people from needing to be homeless, and we must go about this prevention in myriad ways, personally. If we allow homelessness to go unaddressed, the literally and concretely homeless may even come to include ourselves. The "It can't happen to me" attitude is part of a denial of what is going on around us that only furthers it.

A very disturbed young borderline woman had graduated from a halfway house that had been a considerable help to her to a supervised apartment. Both she and I had good feelings about the halfway house, which, however, was having a hard time making ends meet financially. She complained with an unrelenting fury about the carpet in her new apartment. She said that she just could not get it clean, no matter what she did. First, the carpet was so worn that it was continually fraying and producing small strands of fiber that coalesced like dust devils. Second, the vacuum cleaner that the halfway house gave her did not work. She was enraged because she felt she was being ripped off. She was paying what seemed to her a lot of money for this apartment.

I suggested that she talk the matter over with the staff at the halfway house. I knew how much trouble she had communicating with people and how much she relied on being enraged to keep herself company. So I thought that it was important to help her at every turn to try to solve problems with others by talking. I had worked with her a great deal on this problem while she was in the hospital for a lengthy stay, and I had come to appreciate just how big and pervasive a problem it was for her. She did not trust talking in part because she was so afraid of being ignored or hit.

It came as no surprise to me that she was not able to work the matter out with the halfway house staff. I could not even be sure that she had done what she said she had done, namely, try to talk with them about the trouble she was having. I knew from experience that, when I suggested something that was hard for her, she could experience this as a tyrannical demand. She could get caught between her abject terror of trying and her conscience's uncompromising insistence that she do what she was supposed to do, no matter what.

The resultant impasses could easily produce a set of distortions in which she claimed that she had done what she thought she ought to have done. Sometimes she would cling with a defensive righteous fury to claims that were, viewed from the outside, clearly untrue. She did this because she had such a ferociously punitive primitive conscience that it prevented her from making sense rather than helping her to take care of herself sensibly. She was often thought by others who dealt with her to be manipulative. However, it was usually much more accurate to say that she was so out of control that her internal sense of reality was compromised.

Her complaints about the rug and the vacuum cleaner and the apartment continued, like a wind that rises and rises until it howls and shrieks in a frightening way. These matters seemed to me to have taken on the force of a defensive obsession. I knew that she had been terrified at home growing up in the midst of a violent and dangerous household. I felt that she was re-creating this all alone in her apartment in an expression of loyalty and loneliness that had its perverse aspects. I was also very invested in helping her make the transition from the halfway house. I knew how easily she could become suicidal and how lethal she could be when she was suicidal.

As the complaints about the rug and the vacuum cleaner and the apartment continued unabated, I became more and more bothered. Finally, unable to imagine that she was giving a clear picture of the matter, but also unable to understand why it was so hard to make any progress in helping her settle into the apartment, I asked her whether it would help if I came to take a look myself. Maybe then I could be more help to her in working things out. She accepted this idea cheerfully. After the next therapy session, I drove her back to her apartment so that I could see it. To my horror and astonishment, matters were just as she had portrayed them. The rug shed continually, as if it were a shaggy dog preparing for hot weather. The vacuum cleaner simply did not work. Certainly, her upset had to do with how out of control she felt internally, but there was so much that really was out of control in the outside world, too. My visit and the improved grasp of reality I derived from it were a significant help to both of us in helping her adjust to life outside the halfway house. By taking her complaints seriously enough to investigate them personally, I had made a contribution to her making a new kind of home, not only materially but also interpersonally and intrapsychically.

This halfway house, most unfortunately, no longer exists, having gone out of business during a period in which, while everyone has paid lip service to the importance of transitional care, it has actually become a service in much scarcer supply. This is the kind of paradoxical situation that calls for a basic examination of values and also for questioning of social good faith. If we make hospital care less available on the grounds that transitional care can be just as effective and then fail to provide transitional care in interpersonally rich surroundings, are we not simply involved in a cruel hoax that will produce more and more lost and homeless persons?

Asylum

A man arrived by train at Pennsylvania Station in New York City one winter's day in the late 1980s. He needed to use the rest room. He was shocked and dismayed at the sight that met his eyes. The rest room was packed full of homeless men in varying states of disarray. There was no free space in the entire room, which was warm. The men were in various stages of undress. Some had claimed small territories by spreading out pieces of cardboard or newspaper on the floor. Even the toilet stalls were occupied. Some of the men were talking to themselves. Some were gesturing. A few were fast asleep in the midst of the surrounding bedlam. It could have been, the man thought, a scene from a painting by Hieronymous Bosch. What disturbed the man most of all was that, living in comfortable circumstances, he could easily have gone on being absolutely ignorant of the situation. It was only because he had happened to need to use the rest room that he had stumbled into the midst of something that he found over-whelming. Needless to say, he waited until he reached his hotel to find a rest room.

According to some estimates, up to half the homeless persons in America have serious mental illnesses. Many of these persons are on the streets because of the woeful situation in regard to long-term care for the mentally ill. State hospitals for the mentally ill continue to close and to deteriorate, even long after it is quite clear that the ideology of the community mental health movement has produced a massive social failure. Patients have been discharged to communities that do not want them in their midst and that do not have or intend to create the means to receive them. Many seriously mentally ill persons have been not only allowed to exercise what amounts to nothing more than a right to complete destitution and victimization on the streets but compelled to exercise this extremely dubious "right." The resource in shortest supply has been practical compassion.

Admittedly, the history of state mental institutions has been often far less than admirable, but this does not excuse us from considering seriously the need of certain among us for asylum and protection from burdens in living that are for them unmanageable. Asylum, the making of a place of shelter and refuge for the disabled and incapacitated, does not work only for the benefit of those who take shelter and refuge in the asylums provided. The provision of asylum for such persons has enormous symbolic force for all the members of society. Such asylums embody a promise on the part of the group not to turn its back on the misfortunes of its members. Such asylums not only proclaim that a society is well knit but help to knit it together. Such asylums have enormous political meaning, as Sophocles makes so clear when, near the end of his life, he has Oedipus promise Theseus that the Furies will treat Athens kindly in return for his just act of providing Oedipus refuge in the grove at Colonus after his enormous sufferings (Oates and O'Neill 1938).

The cost of not providing asylum shows up in increased insecurity and mistrust among all members of society, which in turn powerfully reinforce selfish attitudes and even predatory behavior, which in turn intensify the feelings of insecurity and mistrust. This is how the failure to provide asylum helps turn the furies loose in a society. Providing asylum for those who need it is not a peripheral matter but rather central to a social group's definition of its own identity, purpose, and ethos. The cost of asylum is probably not much more than the cost of one electronic gadget, one toaster oven, one video game, one compact disc player, one automatic garage door opener per middle-class family per year. We should wonder whether foregoing one such device would actually be a cost at all but perhaps rather a liberation.

Probably very nearly each and every one of us, if we will only stop to consider the matter honestly and openly, has one or more reasonably close relative with a serious mental illness. The need for asylum is not someone else's problem. Rather it is our own. We need to know that we know people who are mentally ill, that is, to house them in our minds and hearts, before we can provide the cultural sustenance necessary to support a system of asylums. Mental illness, like so much other human suffering, is here to stay. It will always be present in our neighborhoods. The question is whether we can afford to know about it and do the complex and taxing work required to make a place for it that is safe, or whether we choose to live in terror of it and so make it a much larger problem than it need be. The most taxing part of the work is not the raising of public levies for asylums but the careful nurturing and growth of compassionate attitudes that will enable a system of asylums to take root and thrive.

Interdependence

Every human dwelling is oriented to other human wellings. No house exists alone without reference to other houses. Every home is part of a network that sustains it and in whose sustenance it plays a part. A compassionate response to homelessness depends on the practical human work of relating to each homeless person as an individual. The crucial housing task is getting into a position to ask individual homeless persons about themselves, recognizing that the process of making sense of each of them and of their diverse possibilities will require a great deal of back and forth. This crucial task involves listening and tinkering. The homeless are vulnerable. They need support and holding of the kind and quality that can come only from concerned others. When this concern is available on a broad scale, it will motivate the development of a social policy framework. We need to enlist the homeless as our collaborators in finding a way to find homes. In the process, we need to attend to the criticisms of our social arrangements that are implicit in their disappointments and fears and hopes.

When we treat the homeless as nonpersons, we are on the way to becoming nonpersons ourselves. When we try to avoid seeing them and taking account of them as individuals with real histories and aspirations, we are refusing to look squarely at our own histories and aspirations. We are refusing to see our own vulnerability. We are degrading the social nexus whose vertices our homes are. This is a major failure in home maintenance. How far back does any one of us have to go in the histories of our own families to find episodes of homelessness and dislocation?

The board of a philanthropic institution was considering the topic of a donation to an association of organizations that ran soup kitchens providing meals for the homeless and hungry. This board was composed mostly of quite wealthy individuals, many of whom were central to the support of a variety of community projects. One man who had been very successful in business raised a concern that he understood it was possible for a homeless or hungry person to get a meal, say, at dinner time, at one of the soup kitchens and then make his way to another one and eat a second dinner. He felt that, in the absence of stricter controls on this kind of behavior, there was no way to know whether the donated money was being used in the most cost-effective way. He suggested that perhaps the donation was not a good idea. This led to a general discussion of ways to monitor and control homeless and hungry persons' use of soup kitchens.

At one point, as an effort to meet this concern and remove it as an obstacle to making the proposed grant, another board member proposed earmarking some of the grant money for the purchase of indelible ink pads and stamps. People eating at a soup kitchen would receive a stamp that would identify them as having already gotten one meal, thereby rendering them ineligible for another. In this surrealistic discussion, there was no effort to imagine the plight of the hungry and homeless, certainly no sense that the enterprise required to get two meals was perhaps laudable and not so different than that on which many a successful business has been founded. Certainly, it was not an invidious form of greed.

A woman whose children were grown and off in college became interested in providing group homes in the community for retarded adults as a way of preventing them from becoming homeless. When she became aware of the many difficulties posed by the zoning regulations in her community, she took the risky step of simply acquiring a number of houses dispersed through the community in her own name and settling in each one a small group of retarded individuals. She was careful to discuss what she was doing with close neighbors surrounding each one of the houses. She was also careful to make sure that city officials were aware of what she was doing without asking them for any explicit approval. By persuasive moral diplomacy, very practical, very down-to-earth, but also rather implacable in its determination, she was able to present the community with a fait accompli that it could accept. She managed to help the community see her projects as small efforts to help real people who were much less frightening simply by reason of being known. She was, in fact, able to enlist a good deal of support from neighbors who felt she was doing the right thing.

In order to develop compassionate responses to the homeless, we have to ask ourselves, in a very quiet and determined way, what is important? What really makes a difference? What is enough in the way of material possessions? We have to notice the homeless as real people with real histories and real possibilities, even if these may not infrequently be very limited. We have to be able to see the homeless as being not so very different than ourselves and to understand that their plight is important to us, so that we can seek practical ways to collaborate with them in making their situations better. Compassion has to be activist, based on moral imagination and conviction. Homelessness is not a matter that can be resolved without bricks and mortar, but it is also not one that can be resolved by bricks and mortar alone. The toleration of homelessness has become a very unfortunate part of our way of life and needs resolute confrontation. We need to be able to look at the ways in which we ourselves are home less and less at home and the continuity of our own predicaments with those of the individuals who are literally and concretely homeless. We should not forget, either, that so many of these are small children with hunger both in their bellies and in their eyes.

8

Drugs

Orientation to Our Biology

Compassion is such hard work, in part, because it involves noticing and appreciating. It does not stop at superficial understanding. It requires understanding and engagement that are feelingful and thoughtful. This means that they are full of thought and full of feeling both. Thought and feeling both require commitments on the part of the self that require inner mobility, flexibility, and integrative force and discipline.

Whenever we take on the work of noticing and appreciating, we challenge ourselves. We put ourselves at risk. We ask ourselves to be both critical and intuitive, active inside and active in perceiving and relating to what surrounds us. We embark on a trip whose destination is a region of our own selves that is as yet incompletely known. Every creative activity involves risk, and compassion is, cardinally, a creative activity, one that depends on our continuous application, appreciation, and discovery of our inner resources. Compassion is engagement in real living.

No one has yet suggested a pharmacological approach to the nurturance of compassion, although there have been numerous pharmacological explorations in the not unrelated areas of attachment, affiliation, nurturance, and sexual attraction. So far, when we speak of compassion, we all recognize that we are speaking of qualities that lie within the purview of our own agency, therefore of our own freedom and responsibility for and to that freedom. We should not forget, though, that compassion is a biological process that is rooted in our physiological processes. It is a life process in human beings. It is one of the defining features of the domain of the personal. Of course, our genetic makeup plays a part in it.

We need to understand clearly that it is dangerous to turn the term *biological* over to those who wish to use it in a narrow and mechanistic way to refer to the doings of molecules. At or near the root of so many drug-related problems is practical and practiced despair about human agency. When we relegate agency to the doings of molecules, we prepare the way to be entirely ignorant of our own possibilities as people. Exaggerated and mechanistic materialism is morally and ethically dangerous. It leads to forms of human sloth based on entrancement with technology.

We do not explore and discover biology even principally in laboratories and field studies but across the whole free range of our labors and loves in life. We do not only explore and discover it. Rather, in association with our fellow creatures, human and otherwise, in association with the materials and potentials of this whole living earth, we create it, not only repetitively but also, inextricably intertwined with the reliability of the repetition, each day afresh.

Biology, not in the debased sense in which agency is turned over to unfeeling and unwilling molecules, has to do with everything that contributes to the sustenance and integration of life. It has to do, to go back to its Greek roots, with the "logos" of a "bios." *Bios* means "life." In Greek thought, *logos* referred to that which gave the world order, sense, and intelligibility. Deriving from an Indo-European root meaning "to collect" with derivatives meaning "to speak," it evoked all that made it possible for the world to speak to and through us as well as all that made it possible for us to speak in, to, and through the world around us.

With our conception of logic, even of psychologic, we

have radically narrowed this vast world spanning sense. If we wish to understand in a serious and compassionate way something about the problems of those who use drugs to destroy their chances in living, we must keep in mind that biology spans, includes, and integrates matter and meaning. It spans, includes, and integrates matter and what matters to us and in us. If we see our molecules as active and ourselves somehow as passive, absolved by material incapacity from the searching interrogations of responsibility, we have set forth on a most dangerous kind of drug trip ourselves. Certainly, drug abuse is licensed and supported by cultural attitudes that emphasize the power of substances over people, of the outside over the inside.

Who is active? Who is responsible? Who hears me? Where can I turn for response? Who will help me with problems of feeling overwhelmed, empty, dead, stuck inside? Who will help me with my loneliness? Who will help me with those quintessentially human maneuvers of attachment, intimacy, and self-esteem? Who will help me learn to miss myself and seek myself? How can I learn to help myself be active, responsible, feelingful, vital, and so forth? Who will help me learn to be my own teacher? What are the criteria for worth and satisfaction? Questions like these are at the core of the drug dilemma.

Drugs can take on the magical aura of a way that is sufficient in itself. Drugs can charm and beguile and stand instead of the promise of life. It is possible for people to get to the stage where they have given up any hope of knowing themselves or anyone else and become only intimate with drugs, inanimate substances they perceive as being the be-all and end-all. Drug abuse can be part of a fundamental error in the understanding of human being and doing.

Waste

In time the perception becomes the reality. Since our lives
are limited, all that we have, all that we are, all that we can
come to be is at stake in the passage of ordinary everyday
time. Drug experience, solipsistic, encapsulated, empty, and
increasingly desperate, can become all there is to the drug-
abusing person's life and not infrequently can end it. It can
be as dull and as matter-of-fact as the way individual grains
of sand flow through the waist of an hourglass. It requires
an act of inner animation to appreciate the horror of this
kind of waste.

A traveling salesman was on the road most days of the
week. He did rather well in making sales. He minimized the
stress of the job, the insecurity, the worry of always trying to
please and convince customers on whom he was very dependent. He did not express out loud sentiments like those of
the other salesman who said that being a traveling salesman
was like guerilla warfare, enormously wearing because you
had always to be on the alert. Nor could you necessarily count
on the people who were supposed to be on your side. They
might sacrifice you whenever that suited their convenience.
This man kept whatever he felt inside, made a good living,
and by his early thirties was a confirmed drinker. He was an
alcoholic in the sense that he relied on alcohol to get through
each and every day.

By his mid-fifties life had passed him by. Alcohol had
remained a constant. He had no relationships that were vital.
While his wife had stayed with him, there was little left between them. His children had all adopted the strategy of trying to minimize contact with him. All of them were in one
way or another involved with drugs and alcohol. In fact, for
more than a decade, he had been driving around blacked

out. Each time he got home and parked in the driveway, he performed the same strange ritual, walking all the way around his car to look for blood because he feared that he might have hit someone on the road and have now no memory of it.

No one bothered to ask him why he did this inspection job on his car, although not only his wife but the neighbors had seen him doing it. Needless to say, his work performance had steadily deteriorated, so that, as the years went on, he was moved to more marginal territories where sales were more difficult to make. His response was to drink more. He lived a haunted, terrified life in which the only active presence belonged to the spirits, increasingly malign, inside the bottle. His own spirit had long since been driven into exile.

As remarkable as his continued drinking, his progressive destruction of his own life, was the consistent failure of those around him to notice. If he was sometimes quiet and withdrawn, so they told themselves, that was normal, because at other times he could be so outgoing and vivacious, the life of the party. He made a good living, drove a nice car, lived in a nice house, wore nice clothes. If everyone who had lunch with him remarked that he had three stiff drinks, they did not discuss it with each other and tried hard not to be unduly alarmed by it. After all, who did not know other people who had that many drinks for lunch? Who, in fact, had not also on one occasion or another had three or even four drinks for lunch?

If his wife appeared unhappy, what was so very unusual about that? Did not everyone have their own troubles? Friends might even feel a bit sorry for her, noticing that the spark had long since gone out of her relationship with her husband, noticing that she looked more and more martyred and resigned. If he had been pulled over for a few motor vehicle violations, including one for driving under the influence of alcohol, he had taken care of these. If a few friends knew that he had paid some money to keep an accident quiet, if these few friends even knew that his wife did not know about the accident, was it not necessary sometimes to work your very hardest to preserve your reputation? After all, it was not easy to make a living. It was a hard world, and sometimes you had to bend a few rules to keep yourself safe.

If a few friends were aware that his sons had started drinking and drugging as young teenagers, did not all kids go through a wild stage? If some were a bit bothered by knowing that both his daughters had been in with the druggy crowd in high school, had not they still been able to graduate and go on to college? Who could be so righteous as to point the finger at another family? After all, being a parent was a hard job, and this man was a good provider. Just look at all the family had, the lovely home and so forth. Would not most people be quite content with that?

The ongoing failure to notice, the myriad rationalizations used to overcome the clear perception of danger signals, the widespread failure to react, point to the drug problem as having a basis not only in the individual but in the social surround, not only in organismic physiological vulnerability, but in social climate. If the measure of a person is what things he or she has, then it is all too easy to avoid noticing that the person has lost him- or herself totally. If we are out of touch with our own feelings, frightened to know ourselves, then it is very hard to notice someone else's ordinary living hell as it continues on a daily basis. When we do not notice our neighbors' and friends' and near intimates' perdition, our own failure speaks to an incapacity in ourselves.

A teenage girl passed out one day after lunch directly in front of the office of her school. She had clearly been drinking and drugging. The school principal brought her into his office and took her car keys. When she came to, she raged bitterly at him, claiming that he had absolutely no right to take her keys and that this was a violation of her constitutionally guaranteed civil rights. She proceeded to yell at him that he had no right to contact her mother about this because that was a violation of her right to privacy. He interpreted this as virtually an injunction to get in contact with her mother and spell out the drinking and drug problem. While she was clearly under the influence of a number of substances, she yet gave the impression of a small child who was very frightened and desperate for just the help that she was protesting so hard against receiving.

She had previously failed out of another, much larger high school. Her academic record had been progressively worsening. She came to school each day with a sullen and unhappy look on her face. She had given up all participation in extracurricular activities, including music and singing, which she had once loved and in which she had excelled. The history at the previous school was that her interactions with teachers and guidance staff had gotten angrier and angrier over time. Apparently, no one had been puzzled about the process that was taking place right in front of their eyes. The school, busy with so many students, had confined itself to making more and more demands on her that she could not meet. The question of what was interfering with her schoolwork, what was making it so difficult for her to use her evident abilities, was never posed. That she was so clearly unhappy and so much not enjoying herself did not get directly addressed, as if the implicit assumption was that it was normal for a teenager to be miserable and to stay that way month after month.

When she came in for a conference, this girl's mother, who worked full-time and was trying to raise three children on her own without even the benefit of regular and reliable child support payments, professed shock and dismay at her daughter's drug and alcohol use. She said she had not noticed a thing. She said her daughter was the last person she would have expected to use drugs and alcohol, because she had always been such a bright and sunny girl. For her part, the girl was extremely skeptical of her mother's claim not to have noticed a thing. She pointed out that she had been drinking whatever wine and liquor there was in the house for the past four years, since even before her parents had separated.

Her mother said that she had sometimes thought that things were disappearing quickly from the liquor cabinet but that she had not really zeroed in on this. She did not think she was the best housekeeper to start with and certainly she had not been a good housekeeper over the past few years when she was struggling for survival. At this point, the daughter looked up at the ceiling and rolled her eyes, as if to say, "What do I have to do, maybe burn the house down, to get you to notice me?" This gesture brought a hurt and anxious look to her mother's face.

The mother volunteered that it had made her sad to see her daughter give up her music, which had been such a source of pleasure to her. When her daughter asked her why she had never talked about that with her, the mother said that she had been afraid to do so because she got so mad at her just like her father had used to do. The mother said, with a kind of sad, suppressed fury, that she just could not stand anyone else being mad at her. This led to discussion not only of the father's drinking, which he had always claimed was not a problem, but of the mother's father's drinking. Of her father, the mother said that she thought he had been a nice man who just was not able to be there so much of the time. He had been in the war and never seemed, she said, to have gotten over it. She said she thought that he was just too sensitive for his own good.

The daughter protested that she did not know what was so wrong with getting high. People did things that were a lot worse. She said that sometimes she just did it because it was fun and that she was not sure that she could or would stop. Why should she mope around all the time? Surely that was not what her mother wanted for her. This provided a basis for a discussion of what the costs of drug use were in terms of the loss of so much that was so important in life. The anguish on the mother's face was more eloquent than anything that she said during this part of the discussion.

With her face mostly hidden behind the curtain of her long black hair, combed and shiny on this particular day for the first time in a long time, the daughter looked down at her hands folded in her lap. She was the very picture of shame. When this girl looked up to see the expressions on her mother's face and so showed her own, there was a fugitive tenderness in her features. The daughter did concede that she, too, thought that school was very important and that she was frightened of what her life would be like if she went on like this. Very soberly, she said that she was not sure she could stop using even if she might know that was the best thing for her.

It is hard to describe just what a difficult, painful, poignant, powerful conversation between mother and daughter this one was. It was at once reunion and surrender. It was charged with both hostility and love. It provided occasion for both disillusionment and for hope. These two had so much to say to each other that had been left unsaid and unresponded to for so long. In a very real sense, the daughter's drug use was a symptom of a far-reaching communicative impairment in the family, one that was transgenerational. This conversation did have the beneficial effect of starting a process by which the more realistic part of the mother and the more realistic part of the daughter could get back in contact. A very serious problem at hand, once recognized, made a bridge across which much could pass in both directions.

The daughter's drug and alcohol use stood for so much that had been neglected and avoided in the relationship between the two of them, in the life of the family, full as it was of difficult and devastating losses that represented such serious injuries to the self-esteeem of each member of the family. The two had been living in what amounted to a limbo of disconnection that had a nightmare quality because it left out so much that was so real and without which nothing else in their lives could make real sense. The crucial intervention of the school was simply to notice, to hear the thud in the hall as this girl passed out and to be bothered about it. This, however, was not so simple, because it involved not only alertness but a capacity to bear the girl's anger without retaliating.

With her mother's help and not without difficulty, the daughter was able to stop her drug and alcohol abuse. As she did so, her schoolwork perked back up. Her interest in the real possibilities of her young life returned. The change in her appearance, in her bearing, in her demeanor, in the sound and cadence of her voice, in the look on her face, as well as the change in her relationships to other students and teachers, testified to the fact that she was undergoing a real biological reorganization, both physiological and psychological. This biological reorganization was not without its spiritual dimension, if what we mean by spiritual dimension is the highest level of personality integration oriented toward meaning and human purpose in life. It was possible to observe other students looking at her differently now, including some others who were still using drugs and alcohol to excess.

The mother commented later on when her daughter was doing much better that she had not realized how much of a part drugs and alcohol had played in her own life since she was a little girl. Somehow, she said, she had just always taken it for granted that these things were there and tried her best to look away and to go on as best she could with her own life. She said she had learned to go numb so that she would be able to go on. She said she could see so much of herself in her daughter.

Trying to face her daughter's problems and to see her part in them had been a real help to her in coming to grips with some of the things that she most disliked about herself. She said she was afraid that she was really a coward. If it was hard, she tended to try to avoid it, probably because she did not have much confidence in her abilities to cope. She hoped that her daughter would be better off for taking the risk of bringing so much to the surface. For this pair, daughter and mother, it was not too late.

Contact

Compassion is not timid. In the cases of persons who are mired in the confusion of drug experience as a substitute for more authentically self-generated experience, compassion demands of us the boldness to take a stand and the firmness to stay with that stand in the face of what taking a stand will unleash. In the case of the young girl just described, her wrath was in direct proportion to her shame. This may be so often what keeps people from noticing drug problems and paying real attention to them. The person involved in drugs is so hard to reach. There is an aura of menace in the devotion to the drug, as if the person were to say, "Whoever tries to interfere between me and my drug had better be prepared to bear the brunt of all my wrath, all my disappointments, all my need and my greed, all the scorn I feel for myself as I watch myself lingering here in the land of the lost. If you mean to part me from my drug, it is up to you to give me something better, which I will do my best to spurn just as I have so long felt spurned in so many ways."

Menace is forbidding. We often back away from those who have an aura of menace, even without consciously knowing why we back away. This will be especially so if we are so daunted by the difficult side of life that we try to look at the world through rose-colored glasses. It will be especially so if we lack the conviction about our own values, point of view, and purpose to take the brunt of someone else's feelings. It will be especially so if our own anger and disappointment, our own capacity to be cruel frightens or, what is much worse, is unknown to us and yet essential to how we are organized psychologically. It is not uncommon for people in trouble to push others away with a force directly proportionate to their need for them.

Compassion for those with drug problems is a contact sport. This is so precisely because drug use is so often both (1) a symptom of a lack of satisfying internal contact with oneself within oneself and of a lack of satisfying contact with others and (2) a powerfully reinforcing cause of this being out of touch. The beginning of any hope of a different way of living comes in contact with the real facts of the effects of drug use. This contact can not happen in the abstract. It almost always involves interaction with others who are willing to take the heat that inevitably is part of conveying to drug users that they are on a shortcut to nowhere. Drug use blinds people, so that they fall into the habit of blaming everything on the world outside them, as if it were by mere perversity that that world refused to come fully under the sway of their sovereign wishes.

To confront a drug user successfully requires an attitude that goes beyond blame and self-righteousness. If we wish to get through compassionately to a drug user in deep personal peril and lacking the self-awareness to be fully cognizant of the peril, we must believe in our point of view and represent it with the same steadfast consistency we would use if we were trying to convey to someone else a fact of nature, as, for example, that no matter what anyone might wish or pretend to believe, the sun will continue to rise in the east and set in the west. We must be able to be adamant without animus, acting like the messengers of truths that are of the deepest consequence and bigger than any small one of us. We must be prepared to be hated for taking the trouble to love. We must be able to understand that the drug user's fury expresses a struggle around paying attention to a message whose force feels devastating, especially in proportion as the one trying to attend to it knows somewhere deep inside him that the message is right for him or her. The icy cold fury can be the hardest to bear. All the while that we meet drug abuse, we must remember that only the drug abuser can stop using drugs. We can try to provide opportunities, never solutions.

Drug and alcohol abuse have the power to turn us away from life to a never-never land in which things never get better but only worse. They can steal our nerve and our verve both. This is as true as that, if we put our hands in the fire, we will have painful burns. We need, if we are to be able to take on persons who are endangered from substance abuse, to have looked inside ourselves and brought to mind the occasions on which we have turned away from what is real and important. We need to remember when we have sought to take succor in magical pretending because we despaired of being able to deal with the real challenge in a way that measured up to our standards. We need to remember what qualities in ourselves and in others, what home truths, we have shied away from recognizing over periods of years because they threatened cherished illusions in which we were so invested that they bordered on delusions.

We need to be in touch with our own tendency to revise our perceptions because we cannot bear the news they bring us on a moment-to-moment basis. We need to remember what it feels like to be shamed and enraged and helpless and trapped in a cycle in which these feelings reinforce each other and wall out any possible access to other feeling states. We need to remember how vast and variegated are the opportunities that life provides us to be disappointed. This remembering will not make us any less firm. What it will do, however, is to protect us from self-righteousness, that despairing sport in which our consciences, having given up hope of benefiting us, make a hostile game out of pinning blame on others. Repulsively, self-righteousness pins the tail on the wrong donkey.

Demand for Drugs

Drug abuse represents a default state for so many people. They use drugs to excess because there is so much else that they do not know how to use. They use drugs because there is so much of themselves they do not know how to use and because, as a consequence, they feel so useless. We live in a culture that values highly an ideal of sobriety at the same time that drug use is rampant. It is certainly not unusual. Statistically, especially if we include alcohol and nicotine, it may be normal. One of the greatest illustrations of the power of market forces in the last thirty years is the inordinate increase in the supply and availability of cocaine as the price has dropped. This drop may actually have been more precipitate than the fall in the prices of computers.

The vastly increased supply at dramatically lower cost has represented a response to explosive demand for the drug. If we wish to respond in a clear and compassionate way to the problems of drug abuse, it is the demand for drug experiences that we need to understand. What services do states of intoxication perform in our psychological and spiritual economies? What is it that makes the undrugged life worth living?

A locksmith in his late thirties who was in the process of trying to kick his habit said, "I've felt lower than whale shit all my life. You know how low that is? That's so low you can't get no lower. There's nothing lower than whale shit. I just use because I feel so low, and then I feel so low because I use, and I don't know any way to get out from it." This man was successful in changing his way of approaching life, although probably neither he nor anyone else would have predicted success for him. In fact, it seemed to be the case that success, while ardently desired, was also something he ardently feared. As he found himself on better terms with the wife who had threatened to leave him if he did not make changes, he found himself struggling with his feelings of being so low. The struggle was more open and more agonizing after he stopped his drug abuse. It was not so much that he felt better but that he had gotten much better at feeling across a much broader range. He also got much better at communicating, but, as he put it, only because he felt he had no alternative.

Karl Marx proclaimed that religion was the opiate of the people. He felt that religion, with its focus on transcendent rewards in worlds to come, not in the world that was com-

ing to be right now all around us, deprived believers of crucial capacities to see clearly, rouse themselves, realize what
was happening to them, and rally themselves to contend
responsibly with it. Might we not now wonder whether drugs,
not only the opiates, but also the energizer cocaine and the
disinhibiting depressant alcohol, had become the people's
substitute for religion? Do not many people turn to drugs
for relief from their misery, in quest of meaning and for some
way to come to terms with the essential mysteries of life?
Perhaps they seek a chimerical chemical destiny because they
despair of anything more personal. Do not these efforts even-
tuate in ever more misery with less and less sense of meaning? Do not they take people farther and farther away from
contact with the genuine mysteries of life?

How much of the current use of prescription mood
modulators is actually quite continuous with other forms of
substance abuse in that it seeks solutions in drugs for problems created by defaults in living that are at once personal
and cultural? Is not our material craving for more and more
so-called goods, things of all descriptions and kinds, also a
form of substance abuse? If our goal is to create a culture in
which we can buy whatever we want and we can only want
what we can buy, why should not agents that alter mental
states be among the most marketable of all commodities?

Some years ago a consulting expert in psychopharma-
cology was interviewing a teenager as part of a teaching conference for resident doctors in a psychiatric hospital. This
boy was said to be depressed and had been abusing drugs.
His father was a prominent religious leader. The boy stopped
the proceedings in their tracks with the following argument,
made very boldly, with striking clarity and confidence.

"Look," he said to the psychopharmacologist, "we agree
that I feel terrible. We agree that I should take drugs because
I can't do a thing about it myself. You think I should take

the antidepressants they prescribe for me. You believe in them. I don't think they do a thing for me. You won't let me take what I want to take, and I don't want to take what you want me to take. So it's a stalemate."

As he concluded his sally, the boy's face was a bit flushed, and a small smile of satisfaction, if not triumph, played about his lips. For a seriously depressed person, the zest with which he spoke was notable. Certainly, it was tempting to believe that the clarity and zest with which he made his argument augured well for his future. However, the fear and loneliness in what he said were also notable. Even as he argued so clearly, he seemed terribly vulnerable, a lost little boy.

Compassion requires breadth of vision. It requires engagement with people in their full human contexts. This boy presented a treatment issue as a clash of opposing doctrines. He spoke about a clash of faiths and world-views in a way that immediately evoked his conflicts with his father. Unfortunately, perhaps cooperating all too unwittingly with the driving dynamics that moved the boy, the psychopharmacologist became nonplussed and began to argue with the boy about how he, a mere youngster, could presume to know better how to go about treating himself and his difficulties. Here again was the issue of agency, the psychopharmacologist taking the position that the boy was not qualified as an authority.

This sounded to the boy's ears as if he were being told that he was not qualified to take a genuine role in the authorship of his own life, a proposition he could not help but fight. The boy had put his finger on the stalemate, as if he were hungry for some way of looking at and speaking about his problems that went beyond considering the actions of molecules to a more integrated view of his human situation as an extremely frustrated and conflicted agent. Unfortunately, the opportunity to look at matters in a wider context was lost.

To make the point that so much is neglected in an inter-action like this one is not to claim that medicines for mood disorders are superfluous or without use but rather to insist that a compassionate approach to the problems of drug use requires considering them in broad human perspective in each individual case. More is spent on illegal drugs than on the whole gamut of prescription medicines in this country. Illegal drugs do not even include what remains our culture's drug of choice, alcohol. The economics make clear what an integral part of our culture drug use is. Compassion means looking for the feelings, the promptings, the possibilities that are buried in the drug use.

A successful African American in his forties sat on an open porch one spring night in the late seventies in a large midwestern city reflecting that of all the guys he had gone to junior high school with in that same city, he knew of only one other who was not either on drugs, in jail, or dead. His voice sounded tired as he talked about this. This man wondered why so few had escaped. He said that going into the Army had been a help to him. He recounted how, during a leave in Germany, he had happened to go into an art museum where he saw a picture of a black knight in armor on a horse from centuries and centuries ago. The picture had stunned him. It had made him feel that he did not know who he was and that he had best be finding out, so that he had used the rest of his leaves in Europe to travel around to art museums, looking for more traces of black history.

He said he had been lucky, because when he was growing up it just did not seem like there was much out there. It just had not seemed that there was any place at all for the black man. Nor was this a despairing man who was talking. He was simply describing how the world had seemed to him growing up. He said he could not exactly understand why he himself had not gotten hooked on drugs. It was not that he had not tried them. He said that some of his friends who had gotten hooked had been pretty decent guys before they got hooked, but not really afterward.

A New Way of Life

Getting off drugs is a classic chicken-and-egg problem: in order to get off drugs, a person has to find another way to participate in life; and in order to find another way to participate in life, a person has to get off drugs. It is hard to grasp just what a persistent and harrowing struggle this can be. Drug use has to do not just with dreams deferred but also with development deferred. Getting off drugs calls not just for a sense of possibilities but also, just because so much development has been deferred, for a sense of practicalities. It calls for a sense of how to use small actions, feelings, and thoughts with no great immediate impact to stitch the minutes, sometimes even the seconds, of the day together so that yawning abysses of despair and panic do not open up in them. This is why group experience and the holding environments provided by organizations like Alcoholics Anonymous can be so important.

Drugs usually have represented a nonsolution to so much for the person who abused them that they retain their seductive potential to offer nonsolutions to real problems long after the person has given them up, probably even for the rest of his or her life. If reality is to compete with them, then the former drug user must accept a much higher degree of frustration in the quest for a different and more enduring form of satisfaction. For many people, this is the fight of a lifetime, one in which their very lives are at stake quietly day after day after day. The person struggling to get off drugs and stay off drugs needs a constant sense of danger that does not go beyond that to panic and hopelessness. Nothing in the long run can reassure the person save his or her own consistent actions.

The seductive potential of drugs, the way they offer glib nonsolutions to problems, is a cultural issue, not simply a personal one. Despite the claims of the television commercials, we know, if we pause to think for a moment, that there is no such thing as "Miller time." We all live in the same kind of time subject to similar frustrations. Beer is not going to take us to the refreshing freedom of pure and pristine mountains. It is not going to give us the gusto of doing what we will without risk, any more than heroin will transport us to the land of milk and honey and build us a mansion of perpetual entranced tranquility there.

Responding compassionately to drug use calls for creating practical forms of fellowship that are at once fellowships of the difficult and fellowships of hope. A fellowship of hope must be a fellowship of the difficult, and a fellowship of the difficult will not endure unless it is also a fellowship of hope. We should not forget how alone the drug abuser has been with and within him- or herself. This aloneness is a dangerous perdition because it represents such a fundamental deprivation. We need, in order to stay attuned, to remember the pain of our feelings of loneliness. Our biology is not a biology of isolation but a biology of sustained attachment and interaction.

A fellowship of the difficult is one that faces what is enduringly and irreducibly problematic in human life squarely. It is one that is able to help us work at the task of looking our smallness in the eye and seeing that wherever we go and whatever we do, we will meet limits not of our choosing, so that what is fateful for us is what we do with that experience.

If we do not have the capacity to face the facts, we will never be able to make out our own features clearly. If we cannot make out our own features, our own presences, with any clarity, we will have a terrible time finding a future. A fellowship of hope never forgets our capacity for action and invention even in the most difficult and straitened circumstances.

A fellowship of hope never forgets that, while there is no way to mitigate our own fundamental responsibility for our own life as an individual without doing crucial damage to our inner sense of agency, possibility, dignity, and worth, we need to have others available to us in order to help us avail ourselves of ourselves. We need to have them as available as possible. Here, again we meet limits not just outside ourselves but within ourselves. In order to have others available to us, we must participate actively in providing them access to us.

Compassion calls for an unending quest for understanding. There are neurochemical, physiological, and genetic factors that have an important impact on the vulnerability to drug abuse. Research on these is very important. We have to understand not so much drug abuse in general but drug abuse in particular cases to impact the problem. There are other factors that mediate vulnerability. Many forms of abuse and distorted relationships are continuous with drug abuse. Just as depression is more common under conditions of high danger and stress, so drug abuse is more common in environments of high danger and stress, for example, in poor and hopeless inner-city areas. Drug abuse is part of a complex puzzle, all of whose pieces interlock to imprison so many.

Many people turn to drugs to try to manage inner states that they find unbearable. They turn to drugs when they are subject to inner storms that interfere with them giving themselves a form they can accept. A teenager who had started to use had memories of being sent to buy his father beer when he was as young as 7 years old. Once, when he got home carrying the six-pack in his hand and found himself locked out, he totally lost control of himself to the point that he used his head as a battering ram to try to break down the offending door. The noise finally roused his father, who opened the door and was enraged at him. His mother came along just in time to keep the father, on this one occasion at least, from beating him. This memory was not an isolated one. We can infer with considerable confidence that there is so much more from much earlier that this boy does not remember, at least in any consciously accessible declarative form. Nor will we help him by trying to assist him in remembering what was unbearable, Instead, we must help him to a more ordered way of living in the present to provide a template for inner reorganization.

When this teenager starts to use, he is doing what is familiar to him. He is exercising what seems to him an adult prerogative. The task of stopping substance abuse for a boy like this one means nothing less than finding a different way of life. He has a task of inner emigration to perform before he can find his way to a more liveable inner land. Like all immigrants, he will experience terrible loneliness, a missing that reaches deep into him and that states itself in terms of sights and sounds, smells and touch. The compassion he needs does not involve efforts at compensating him because he is such a poor fellow. This will only undermine his efforts.

What he needs is a new form of community that *really* works differently in the *present* and *really* helps him work differently in the *present*. He needs a community with decent standards that lives its standards decently and, when it fails, not only acknowledges its failings but tries to correct them. He needs a new form of community that helps him to grieve what has happened to him and his father and remember what the risks are that are associated with the drug-abusing way of life. This boy knows them too well even to bear to know them without solidarity from others who are fundamentally interested in knowing him as he really is, that is, both as he really has been and as he can come to be on the basis of his own efforts.

He needs a community that helps him work and helps him do the work of finding valid ideals. Work is so important because we do not make our way to self-respect except through our efforts in meeting and mastering not so much what comes easily to us but what is difficult for us. Work is so important because it lets us give to others. Work is an essential part of relating to reality. This is where joblessness becomes such a crucial part of the culture of drug using.

This community must be implacably resourceful in meeting despair and providing practical livable alternatives step by step. It must have an implacable resolve in its defense of real living with real people and real responsibility. It must understand that so much has already gone wrong that it is simply impossible that the way out of the drug-abusing life should be without strife, struggle, reverse, bafflement, and moments of despair. It must be tolerant and also have real limits to its tolerance, so that there is always real choice and a shared awareness of the reality of choices about how to live.

There is no such thing as compassion from a great distance. There is no such thing as passion from the remoteness of unconcern. Compassion means providing *space* and *presence*. It means developing the capacity to stay with people step by step, practically, inventively, intuitively. The task of caring about people who have serious difficulties with drugs is a notoriously difficult one. It is not a task of an hour, a day, a month, or even a year. It is an ongoing task, because there is no way to say no to drug abuse, without finding ways that are practical and persistent to say yes to more related and more responsible ways of living.

A young woman had come very close to destroying herself completely with alcohol. She had started drinking in high school. She only stopped after she had had more than twenty hospitalizations, some focused on her drinking, some focused on other symptoms. She had been a very talented student who did very well in college, which she had completed. She had been down and out in a variety of different ways. She had betrayed the trust of virtually every single person who had ever tried to help her. For her, sobriety was a fight all the way. She hated the limits. She hated anyone who stopped her in her flight from feelings.

Throughout the time that she was struggling for her sobriety and for her sanity, she swam compulsively. She described swimming so that she would not think, so that she would not feel. She also ran in the same spirit, a search for oblivion. She could not bear to feel her need for other people. At one point, she hurt her hand, which, realistically, needed to be bandaged to protect it from infection. She described wanting to slug the nurse who was about to bandage her hand or to just pull the bandaging materials from out of the nurse's hands and do the bandaging job herself. She said the impulse had been so strong that she was surprised that she had not done it. She had in fact slugged family members when they tried to intervene in her drinking. The impulse had to do with abject terror of dependency. The feeling of being in the least dependent—that is, on a person, not on alcohol—brought on a sense of helplessness that took her swiftly over the edge of panic. She raged to stay organized. To be around her was no easy job.

After more than a year of a sobriety that felt to her like a passage through somewhere that might just as well be hell as purgatory, she began to notice some changes. The character of her swimming was different, as was the character of her running. She found herself, with some surprise, being able to think while she swam, being able to think while she ran. She was present in her swimming and in her running in a way that she had not been before. This puzzled her and even disturbed her, but she also enjoyed it. Sometimes afterward she remarked that AA meetings were different for her than they had ever been before. What other people said meant something to her. She could listen and she could connect. She could connect because she had become present to herself within herself.

It was not that her terror of dependency had ceased to be. Rather, she had started to understand that it was hers and that, given her life experience in an extremely chaotic family with a terribly disturbed mother and a completely overwhelmed father, it made sense. She shied away from intimacy, because it felt to her like a loss of autonomy. She began to get the idea that, inside, she was not only terribly needy but also terribly greedy. This frightened her and made her look down her nose at herself, but she also saw that, like it or not, these qualities were hers and here to stay. She tried over and over to invest in the fiction that there were people who were free of need, but these fictions always developed difficulties, forcing her at least to entertain the notion that there was simply no escaping neediness and a measure of greed if one were to be human.

She was able to work and to begin efforts at rapprochement with many of the people she had pushed away so cruelly and furiously. A major part of these efforts had to do with being able to look at these people more realistically and to accept how disappointing many of them were to her, despite the qualities that she loved and cherished in them. As she grasped what a mixed world it was, she looked more and more sad. She looked years older, but in a way that engaged one rather than repelling one. Her sense of humor returned, and she was able to turn it back on herself. She could open the mail that she received and make a good-faith effort to manage her own affairs. She could take care of her teeth and eat.

The truth that compassion knows is that the alternative to drug dependence is human interdependence, that realistic and imaginative interchange among limited people that gives spirit and zest to life. The plight of drug-abusing people is that they have lost touch with their own sense of agency in the real world, with their own spirit. They have become alienated from themselves in an inner world that they cannot even call their own because they cannot reliably call it into being on their own. In the distortions of drug experience, users cannot find either the truth of their own pain and loss and rage or the truth of their own possibilities.

Such individuals need help not only in finding the real world but in calling into being within themselves a world that is more authentically theirs. They need to fight and curse and moan and struggle with everything that besets them on the road back out of the never-never land of drugs. They need to fight mighty battles to get out of bed in the morning. They need to fight mighty battles to stay on the bus that is taking them to job interviews. They need to fight mighty battles to be able to admit when they have erred. They need to fight mighty battles to bear the pain of connection with other people, whether the connection is a small conversation or an ongoing relationship. They need people to be with them, people from whom they can set out and to whom they can return, as they fight, moan, curse, struggle with everything that comes along. They need people who care for what is at risk in them but do not take it upon themselves to control them. They need people who are not afraid of their helplessness or of their own helplessness. They need people who can understand what a mighty struggle it is for them to enjoy themselves and think well of themselves without thinking too well of themselves.

Perhaps we may close by wondering why blame and righteousness so often creep into discussions about drug abuse, why people who abuse drugs are so often seen as not quite human or worthy of our deep concern and engagement. Could it have anything to do with our own temptations? Could it have anything to do with our awareness of how much the rewarding struggle of realistic involvement in the world with other people tries us? Could it have anything to do with the depth of our own wishfulness, our own strivings to be sovereign and have what we want when and as we want it? Are we afraid that, if we recognize the humanity of our fellows who abuse drugs, then we will have to look into a mirror that shows us images of ourselves that frighten us? Are we, perhaps, more ashamed of our limitations, more ashamed of our urges to float off into a magical dimension than we like to admit? How much of our own rage, our own hatred of ourselves for being real and limited, do we cover with our righteousness? How many of us have fantasies of vengeance and escape we hardly dare share even with ourselves? When an apparently very successful physician with three small children is found dead as a consequence of his heroin habit, what does this mean to us?

One cold December day, a drug-abusing mother threw her tiny baby out the window of her apartment. She had been turning tricks to pay for her fixes and found herself at a point where she had no more resources to cope. The baby happened to have on a jacket with a hood. As the baby fell, the jacket just happened to catch on a fire escape, where it dangled, the white snow falling down on it in the cold. A passerby happened to see it. This person climbed up the fire escape, carried the baby down, and alerted protective services. This baby concerns us all. To understand how the baby got where the baby got, we have to understand how the mother got where she got. We need to understand that there are many such babies and many such mothers, that every one of these babies has a father, too. We need to understand our own ongoing parts in giving birth to a world in which babies meet such predicaments.

9

Compassion and Institutional Life

Institutions Produce Life

We all live our lives in contact with institutions that give shape to our cooperative efforts. The ability to cooperate in complex endeavors that require coordination in space and time is one of the distinguishing human characteristics. It draws on our capacity to share information and images, feelings, plans, and purposes. It draws on our talent for making and sharing simulations. It draws on our fabulous capacity to make virtual reality actual.

Schools, businesses, hospitals, and our other human cooperative institutions all share the characteristic that they produce two distinct kinds of product. They produce the product it is their purpose to produce, say, education in the case of schools, steel in the case of a steel mill, medical care in the case of a hospital. However, they also have a major role in producing the lives of the people who work in them. Working conditions condition people and shape their lives. Work and cooperation are central life experiences for virtually all of us. Meaning and meeting both depend crucially on context, and institutions provide so much of the context of our lives. We need to remember that we produce ourselves in the course of producing the products we produce.

We need to remember that we radically modify the environment that is a part of us and of which we are a part in the course of producing the products we produce. Our work does not only keep us in touch with reality and the struggles that reality imposes. It also produces very important parts of the reality that touches us and with which we must contend. With work we make not only things that are outside ourselves but so much that lies within ourselves. We might expect that a culture of appreciation might view work quite differently from a culture of acquisition. One of the large pieces of work that goes neglected in our culture is precisely the understanding of work and its role in our lives. Work is a form of human relationship.

The first step toward compassionate engagement with the myriad and complex realities of institutional life is awareness. When we consider what we mean by compassion, we note that we are not describing anything mechanical. We are not discussing a quality that can be delegated. We are not discussing an attitude that can be compartmentalized and assigned to a committee. We are discussing a quality that pertains crucially to individuals *as* individuals, no matter what group settings they are in. Groups can only display compassion if compassion as an attitude and orientation to the practical tasks of living is deeply rooted in the individuals who make up the group and if the individuals accept their full responsibility for active and initiating engagement in the group, not simple passive acquiescence.

Compassion pertains crucially to individuals *as* individuals because it depends on such complex tasks of integration and valuing. Compassion depends on knowing and feeling what experiences of various types mean to persons who are seen as valuable in themselves as themselves and for themselves. We cannot feel with others, suffer with others, rejoice with others, seek and doubt and occasionally find with others, unless we ourselves are able to feel, suffer, rejoice, seek, doubt, and find for ourselves in ourselves. We cannot be compassionate either in the abstract or in the absence of experience deeply rooted in ourselves and in our senses both of autonomy and of responsibility. A cog in a machine is not capable of compassion. We cannot deed our responsibility for compassion to a surrogate, much as we might wish to do so to lower our level of inner conflict and concern. We must live, breathe, and speak as individuals in the groups of which we are a part, which is no small task.

Compassion depends on the existence of a vital and striving communicative culture within the individual. The word *striving* is important here, because the kind of communicative inner culture we mean is not one that is free of conflict and doubt but one that is able to contend with conflict and doubt, and use them as stimuli to growth. An inner communicative culture is one that takes in real news of the outside world and responds both feelingfully and thoughtfully inside. Compassion strives both inside and out. It is active in the real world that it meets and makes. Consideration depends on the capacity to consider and on the regular, even habitual use of this capacity.

Compassion is crucially different from compliance. Compassion has to do with the authority, authenticity, and autonomy of the individual not as an ending point but as a beginning point and as a point of reference throughout. An autonomous individual, we might make clear, is not isolated. This is why compassion is a problem of critical importance not only for individuals in institutions but for the life and influence and destiny of social institutions. Compassion, too, involves cooperation, but it always subjects collective actions to the criteria of individual thoughtful and feelingful judgments. Compassion will not submit to the tyranny of a "go along to get along" attitude but rather always attends not only to the destination but also to the mode of transportation. That is, it asks, "Where are we going?" and "What must we pass through to get there?" and "How are we going to make this trip?" It asks these questions not so much negativistically and oppositionally but critically, that is, with an awareness that the answers make real differences.

The lives of individuals in institutions and the lives of these institutions will be crucially impacted by the capacity of individuals for compassion *even if* this capacity puts them in opposition within the institution and sometimes to the institution. Such opposition is crucial to the health and dynamism of any institution. Compassion has a prophetic dimension that is bound to be at odds with motivation based on the quest for profit and power and prestige. Compassion has the capacity not only to blow whistles when they need to be blown but also to blow trumpets, if that is necessary. Compassion also has the capacity to lead us into the wilderness where, sometimes after a great deal of confusion and anguish, we can see new possibilities and new prospects.

Compassion can abide, but it also knows how to tell in simple and direct human terms what is not to be abided under any circumstances. Institutions, after all, have enormous creative and constructive power but also enormous capacities for stifling people and for frank destruction. Enormous power for good and enormous power for evil are combined in our human institutions. We need to stay in touch with our awareness of both these ranges of potential. We cannot be passive in our participation in institutions. This passivity, which is not only so prevalent but also so comprehensible, is a declaration of irresponsibility, which cannot help but have the most serious consequences. If we are passive too long, when we finally perceive the peril we have allowed ourselves to get into, it may well be too late. Certainly, passivity in communication, in judgment, in thinking and feeling works to produce lowered self-esteem.

Complexity and Autonomy

Our institutions are complex groups that undertake complex tasks. It is extremely hard to overstate the complexities involved in current institutional organization, in the tasks assigned to and undertaken by our institutions, in the relationships of each institution to other institutions charged with other tasks, in the continual strivings of institutions to reassert and defend their claims to social legitimacy, prestige, and support. The richness and complexity, even the luxuriance, of the organization of our current institutions is one of the distinguishing features of our culture. Never in history have the efforts of so many been so intermeshed. Never have problems of coordination created such thorny dilemmas or called forth such creative and sometimes highly convoluted efforts at solution. Never have individuals within institutions found themselves confronted as individuals with such large, anonymous, and powerful institutions, making it only too easy for such individuals to feel dwarfed and passive and without responsibility or voice. The complexity of our institutional arrangements, as well as the confusion and quandaries they generate, are both here to stay. Arriving at some human mastery of these complexities is one of the major challenges facing our civilization.

Every task group, every institution must have ways to define its task. It must have ways to break larger tasks down into smaller and smaller tasks. It must have ways to define and assign roles within the institution. It must have fairly efficient mechanisms for making decisions. Every institution must confront the difficult trade-off between gathering information and allowing exploration of options and consequences on the one hand and coming to closure and implementable decisions on the other hand. However an institution resolves this dilemma, there are important and real opportunity costs.

If closure is premature, actions taken may be terribly ill advised, involving enormous waste of resources and threatening not only the surround but the life of the institution itself. If closure cannot be reached in a reasonable way in a reasonable time, possibilities for useful and vital action may vanish. Neither swift reaction nor deliberative consideration is always indicated. Each has its place. Nor is it a simple matter to decide which is indicated when or even how to go about deciding which is indicated in which situations. The whole temperament of a culture is involved in struggling with these questions, which can never be definitively resolved in a once-and-for-all fashion. These questions of enormous practical import have ethical and philosophical dimensions, even religious dimensions.

Institutions rely heavily on hierarchical forms of organization and on delegation of authority and responsibility. Institutions have elaborate ways not only of assigning accountability but seeking to evade accountability. Institutions all have ways of asking allegiance and varying degrees of obedience of their members. Institutions have ideologies and cultures. Institutions have elaborate ways of channeling the flow of information. It can be fascinating to watch those who work in an institution develop allegiance to a similar view of the world, hold certain propositions with deep conviction together, restrict consideration of certain kinds of information, and restrict contact with certain kinds of people and exposure to certain kinds of life experiences.

Institutions have a way of restricting the amplitude of dissent. Institutions have a way of regarding of paramount importance not only their survival as institutions but their survival in their current form. Institutions make claims on individuals. They restrict individuals' freedom of action and

thought, both for the best of reasons and for the worst of
reasons. In fact, the common situation is that the best of
reasons and reasoning and the worst of reasons and reasoning are all mixed up together. The boundaries of allegiance
can present enormous quandaries and conflicts for individuals. A culture's identity depends not only on its members'
capacity to identify with its basic purposes but, decisively, on
its members' capacities to be conflicted in their identifica-
tions and strive to inflect the culture's basic purposes and
program in new directions. There is no compassion without
creativity, and there is no creativity without inner conflict.
Life that seems to flow along too smoothly within the banks
of an institutional setting probably is life from which the
creative principle of compassion has been excluded.

Finding and holding a place in an organization is no
simple matter. It presents different difficulties in different
institutions at different levels and at different times. An issue
for so many is that the institution can make such far-reaching
demands on them. Individuals want and need to be part of
an institutional setting, but they must retain the capacity to
scrutinize not only the ends of the institution but the processes by which the institution goes about reaching those
ends. In the name not only of compassion for others but also
of compassion for themselves, individuals must keep an identity that is not wholly subsumed in the institution or even in
a set of institutions. They must always retain the possibility
of seeing separately and differently from the ways proposed
by the institutional cultures. They must not just give allegiance but keep the question of whether their allegiance is
merited continuously under review. Institutions present individuals with fusing dangers, subtle, everyday avenues to the
compromise and loss of self and self-identity. Of course,
without a fairly comprehensive sense of self, without a relatively intact set of those complex integrative capacities we

call identity, an individual's capacity for compassion is compromised.

A gifted therapist found herself in an ongoing conflict in the midst of an institution that was struggling for its financial survival and continually putting pressure on her to increase her productivity. Increasingly, she felt that her productivity was being defined in terms of the financial return to the institution rather than in terms either of service to the patient or of her own personal and professional growth. She had difficulties with self-esteem and also difficulties regulating how much work she did, so that she often found herself tired and overcommitted, resentful of this and not knowing quite what to do about it.

She valued her attachment to the institution for a variety of legitimate reasons. First, she had learned a great deal and grown as a person and as a therapist within the institutional setting. Second, she enjoyed the contact with colleagues and the enrichment it brought. However, she worried that, with the fiscal pressures the atmosphere was being changed so that discussion was likely to become much scarcer. Third, she enjoyed the prestige of being associated with the institution. She worried that in a private practice setting she would feel isolated and bored.

She understood the institution's need to survive but felt that she was not being heard or respected in the discussions of what was necessary for survival. She worried that, if she went along with the policies of the institution, she might find herself crossing ethical lines in her practice. In her dissent, she felt very exposed and very doubtful. She wondered whether she could make a living in private practice. She wondered whether she could manage to be part of forming a group that would provide a collegial atmosphere for her and also an environment for learning. The thought of changing her work situation grieved her because she had so much invested in the work she did in the institution. On the other hand, she felt a deep need to be active in doing work of which she could be proud and retaining enough autonomy to be able to ensure that she was true to her standards.

As a private supervisor retained by her to help her with a difficult borderline treatment, I tried to help her have this conflict, while not acting impulsively to solve it prematurely. I was aware that the conflict simultaneously reflected the real situation in the institution *and* important conflicts over autonomy, acceptance, standards, and safety in the patient whose treatment we were discussing *and* similar important conflicts with complex histories in the therapist herself. At none of these three levels were the issues involved either simple or comfortable. I tried to help the therapist stay in touch with the discomforts, often noting that I had similar conflicts and that any resolution involved important choices and sacrifices.

In the course of struggling with this conflict, the therapist was led to consider much more deeply her own motivations in doing the work of therapy. She wondered how many hours she wanted to work, how much money she felt she needed to make, how much she valued prestige and professional standing, how she went about developing her own ideas and theories about psychotherapy, how much she did this work to help herself with her own conflicts and how much enjoyment she got out of the struggle to be useful to other people. She began to wonder how much she needed to feel comfortable and how much she could bear to be in conflict in fundamental ways about her work and her orientation to it. She found herself questioning many of her professional loyalties. In linkage with many of her old personal conflicts, she was reworking her professional identity, her integration into the institution, and her relationship with her patient all at the same time. Eventually she started to wonder about the question of her capacity to be present in a real way to her-

self and to others, a conflict that was her patient's most prominent one as well.

The most chilling example of excessive integration into
institutional processes is the cooperation of so many Ger-
mans in the execution of the plan utterly to destroy the Jew-
ish people and others regarded as defective using the full
technical resources of the state. So many people took such
grizzly orders without examining their own consciences to
see what the orders meant in human terms. They acted as if,
having been fused into some superordinate whole, they did
not have individual consciences. They seem to have experienced very little anxiety. So many people allowed themselves
to enjoy what they were doing, feeling a sense of pride and
purpose as they went along a road of horrors. They had
defined themselves as takers of orders rather than as people
of conscience and compassion. This example of human cruelty is notable because of the way the entire integrative force
of modern instititional processes was pressed into the service of virtually psychotic thinking and feeling. Boundaries
of professional ethics failed notoriously.

What was demonstrated were the practically demonic
possibilities of such systematization. While so far this extreme
state of institutional systemization and translation into action
of the impulse to do evil remains arguably historically unique,
the revelation of the dark side of the potentials of modern
institutional integration retains an enormous relevance. We
ignore it in everyday life at our extreme peril. Our institutions are vulnerable to the same sort of perversion and can
be made resistant to it only through ongoing vigilance and
the active concern of individuals and groups of individuals
at all levels both inside and outside these institutions.

This concern cannot afford to remain private but must
be expressed in ongoing discussions of the purpose and integ-
rity of our various institutions. Within every institution there

is a drive to create a closed world-view, to streamline and systematize in the name of more efficient claims to power and prestige. We need, for just one example, to be able to ask ourselves seriously whether we feel we may be participating on an everyday basis in the devastation of the environment that will appall and stagger future generations. We need to be able to ask ourselves whether our allegiance to our institutions and our passive acceptance of the role of fellow travelers do not express an excessive degree of integration into these large institutions. What comes after these institutions and our own pattern of living that lays such emphasis on material resources and neglects the resources of human relationship so drastically?

Limits and Wider Responsibilities

We need institutions that are integrated and systematized but that are not too integrated and not too systematized. We need institutions that leave people room to breathe and that can recognize limitations, including their own. We need institutions that can chart a course and change their course. We need institutions that provide not only freedom to speak but freedom to ask questions, to think, and to feel. We need institutions that have the capacity to make room for doubt, not only about the outside world but about the world inside the institution and the world view of the institution. We need institutions that are able to keep themselves under scrutiny and with open horizons to a human future. Can we imagine a large company that decided simply to stop producing cigarettes and devote its efforts and resources to conversion to more socially useful ends? Can we imagine a company doing this in response to pressures not just outside its borders but within its ranks?

We need institutions that respect human attachment, growth potentials, and needs for security as well as for challenge. We need institutions that are able to take a coherent look not only at the products they produce for consumption but also at the impact these institutions have on the lives of those who work in them. Ideally, this integrative view of the life of the institution would be developed through participatory processes within the institution. What, for example, are the responsibilities of an institution toward the families of those it employs? How should these responsibilities be explored and defined? These are issues that have crucially to do with compassion. We cannot see ourselves as compassionate persons if we do not assign compassion a role in charting the course of our institutions. If we confine our view of the exercise of compassion to a circle of very small radius including only close relatives, friends, and neighbors, we have virtually abandoned the field to the ever-vigorous forces of cruelty and human indifference. Compassion must have the courage to oppose to the ruinous overweening voice of the untrammeled profit motive the still-small voice of the prophet.

The question of an institution's responsibilities toward those who make it up is no simple question. One view, basically, is that the institution provides a paycheck to its employees in return for the work they do. It buys a commodity called labor. It pays taxes and, through this mechanism, discharges its full responsibility toward the community and toward its employees and their families as members of the community. According to this view, any other method of proceeding is likely to saddle the institution with costs that will erode its competitive position. The institution is specialized to produce just the products it produces and should keep out of the business of meeting "extraneous" social needs. These are separate and should be met by institutions specialized in meeting them. While many business institutions have gotten deeply involved in some areas, as, for example, the provision of health care and retirement benefits, these involvements are problematic because of their impacts on the bottom line. Those who worry about the costs of health insurance for small businesses now express this concern about the impact on profitability.

There are some serious problems with this view. For example, suppose the institution is in a position to provide some solutions that are better than could be provided in any way outside its purview. We have in this country what amounts to a child care disaster. Over the last thirty years, there has been an explosion in the number of women participating in the work force, as well as an explosion of women trying to raise children on their own. Currently, most institutions do not provide day care on site. They certainly do not even consider whether it would be in their best interests to make special efforts so that mothers (and fathers) and their very young children could have contact during the day. The line of thinking that this might be essential both to the quality of the child's development and to the mother's health and productivity, that it might positively impact factors like the child's future performance in school, is not even discussed. In fact, most child care now is provided in a system that is not only free market but absolutely helter-skelter.

Our institutions, businesses, schools, hospitals do not consider this particular class of problems to fall within their purview. In the exceptional cases in which the issue does come up, the institutional response is likely to be something along the lines of doing a survey to see whether there is a demand for on-site child care from its workers. The survey is likely to be done by an instrument like a questionnaire that asks whether those associated with the enterprise would use child care if it was provided by the institution at a certain cost. This questionnaire approach has a certain impersonality. It proposes an unknown arrangement in a bland way that is the very opposite of what most parents want for themselves and their children. They want a high measure of autonomy, a high sense of concern and a sense of the availability of channels for regular communication. They want a high-touch approach to child care.

So it is no surprise when the questionnaire yields the result that there is not sufficient "demand" to justify the creation of the proposed facility. In almost no cases are employees actually given a chance to participate in a process that would allow them to say what they would like the institution to provide in the way of child care and access to their children. Very rarely does a grassroots design process like this get going. In part, this expresses the prevailing patterns of communicative limitation in our institutions, where the focus is so often on the manipulation of things, the exploration and exploitation of the outside world to the exclusion of the interpersonal world and the worlds within people. When we talk about alienation in the workplace, we are talking about the lack of linkages between work and other important human concerns. We are talking about systems that are not only hierarchical but also relatively limited in their capacity to consider their impact on how people really live. This is a cultural lack, not simply something to be laid at the door of management. Suppose, for example, that an institution made the decision to start a day care center after discussions by and with employees and then devoted ongoing attention to trying to get it to work well, to trying to help mothers (and fathers) integrate contact with their small children into the work day. Is it naive to believe that mothers and fathers might be capable of making creative contributions to the design and sustenance of such a project?

In so many institutions workers will be given off a day for the funeral of a close relative, somehow expected to return to work immediately after the death of a parent, a spouse, or even a child. This expresses a tremendously limited understanding of the scope and importance of grieving. It represents a very short-sighted policy based on a very narrow view, again, of the relationship between worker and institution. It almost certainly has real costs in terms of productivity and health and of the workers' own individual capacity to make sense of their loss and preserve their own capacity to relate to other people and to themselves within themselves. We could go on producing examples of this kind in terms of arrangements around pregnancy, the need for flexible scheduling, support for increased training, and a host of other issues.

It could be objected that to raise these issues is utopian in that our institutions cannot be expected to take on such a variety of concerns. It can also be objected that the expense involved would be prohibitive. It could also be objected that what we seem to be asking of our institutions is that they adopt a paternalistic stance (or should we say, "a maternalistic stance"). While each of these positions can be argued, the fundamental questions of how we expect our institutions to work and how we wish to construe in practical terms the relationships between individuals and these large institutions will not go away. We need to keep asking what our institutions are for. A compasssionate approach to the question of the life of institutions and of life in the context of institutions will insist on looking at the links between life in the institution and a broad array of human concerns, both individual and social. We must ask ourselves what kinds of people our institutions produce. A measure of Gross National Product that avoids this question is gross indeed.

Currently, social solidarity and social support are both

being substantially eroded by decreased stability in relationships between workers and workplaces. More and more
positions are part-time, with no guarantees or even realistic
prospects for full-time employment with possibilities for
advancement. They also carry either no benefits or reduced
benefits. This is justified in the name of cost cutting and of
the imperative to compete. However, justification along these
lines begs the equally real question of the short- and long-
term social costs of these kinds of employment policies. Social
cost is an abstract term that refers to a staggering array of
excruciatingly *personal* injuries.

Social support has crucial practical implications not just
for the quality of life but for matters as tangible as health
and productivity. We lose an enormous amount of human
potential as the result of this kind of policy. Where social
support and social solidarity are low, violence breaks through.
A cycle of demoralization with consequences of the greatest
magnitude can become entrenched. Certainly, this seems to
be what has happened not only in inner cities but in much
of Appalachia. We would be quite naive not to believe that
this can spread, too. Compassion demands that we try to look
these problems squarely, practically, and actively in the eye.
Compassion always looks askance at compartmentalization.

A veteran of the Second World War mused very mov-
ingly in a cemetery in France on the fiftieth anniversary of
D-Day on what had been lost with the deaths of all those
young people so long ago. What inventions, what creations,
what relationships, what contributions, tangible and intangible, to the great stream of life had been lost. He reflected
that he had been thinking about this ever since the war. He
concluded by saying in a sad and resolute tone whose mel-
ancholy melody bore the stamp of wisdom won from all too
difficult living and losing that, if you thought about it, there
really was no such thing as winning a war. Similarly, if we

think about it, cruelty, whether imposed actively or passively through neglect, always brings enormous losses in its wake. It always issues in losses of self-esteem that can become culture-wide and dim the gaze and sap the vigor of the whole culture.

Institutions are cultural media for growing people every bit as much as they are devices to make possible the production of certain products. They are cultural media in the sense that they mediate between individuals and their culture. They are cultural media in the sense that they provide crucial social and psychological nutrients for individuals. How people grow or are stunted in their growth in institutions is crucial not only for the individual people but also for the institutions, because the growth and development of the institutions depends in the long run on the growth and development of individual persons. Institutions are also media for growing a culture. A culture must grow through its expression by real individual persons in institutional settings.

Compassion is awareness from the point of view of kindness. It is a secret or not so secret assumption in many institutions that kindness, a real regard for the individuals involved in doing the work, is incompatible with the efficient production of the product the institution produces. This is an exceedingly dangerous assumption. In so many institutions, as the institution aims to take unfair advantage of those who work in it, the management regards those who work in the institution as having attitudes of greedy entitlement. A pernicious atmosphere develops in which no one trusts anyone else to make a good-faith effort to look out for any interest but his or her own—and that construed as meanly and narrowly as possible. This has terribly destructive effects on communication in the institution, on investment in the institution, on quality and creativity within the institution, not to mention the destructive spillover effects outside the institution as this model of human relations is propagated.

The late eminent Swiss zoologist Adolph Portmann remarked to a student that never in his long career had he hurt an animal in order to find out something about it. He said this had never prevented him from finding out what he wanted to know but rather had simply required that he take more time and think more deeply and more clearly. He felt that he had profited from this way of going about things. It made him both more thoughtful and more perceptive (Carter 1986). This attitude was based on an appreciation of the link between him and the animals, on the sense of both as "living," having a particular inwardness and exploring and creating within the vast bounds of a particular prepared relationship with the world. This point of view also expressed a worked-out appreciation of the relationship between claims to knowledge and claims to power that deserves the name compassionate (Carter 1990). While Portmann's claim is perhaps an extreme, yet it certainly proposes a standard, a challenge to notions of expediency that only too easily become habitual.

We need desperately to look at life in our institutions from the point of view of the validity of seeking kindness, that is, from the point of view of compassion. We need to appreciate what it is that we are making. The goal of an ever-expanding Gross National Product is, unfortunately, perfectly compatible with an expanding product of human misery, part of the misery being a despair over what it is to be a person. If we produce the wrong things, things that are hurtful to ourselves and to others, to the human and natural environment of which we are a part and apart from which we make no sense, then more and more is worse and worse. More and more, in human terms, is less and less.

If we produce in the process of producing attitudes and patterns of human relationship that emphasize the disposability of people while deemphasizing human attachment, growth, and capacity for kindness and mutual regard, then we are making ourselves less and less. Put this way, these issues have a ring that is quite unfamiliar in our culture. This does not deny their reality but simply emphasizes the work that is to be done to help ourselves and others appreciate what the critical light of compassion shows. This is not work that can be delegated but work that must be undertaken on a moment-to-moment basis, in small ways as well as large, because this is where the human frontier lies.

A skilled and effective high school guidance counselor was reflecting in therapy on the fact that the school he worked in had no vision of what to offer the substantial minority of students who had no particular flair for the manipulation of symbols and for book learning. Vocational programs were not as available as they had been in the past. In addition, it was no longer clear what pathways could lead reliably to stable employment. This segment of the school population was one the school was quite aware that it did not serve adequately. Interestingly enough, in the discussion of the school's point of view about this difficult question, the possibility of educating teenagers for jobs that involved taking care of people did not come up. Vast human needs are simply hidden from view.

When we speak of compassion, it is vitally important to appreciate what work is, that, fundamentally, it is a collaborative interchange among valuable individuals of goods. Work is for the benefit of people, not people for the benefit of work. A recent editorial in a medical journal found the author of the editorial expressing his satisfaction that medicine was still one of the altruistic professions. This satisfaction reflected a much deeper blindness concerning the fact that all work, properly construed, has an altruistic dimension. Work does not involve only taking care of ourselves but also taking care of others. Work, life in institutions, properly constructed and properly understood, is about the links among ourselves as essentially responsible and valuable agents and others as essentially responsible and valuable agents.

The plumber, the farmer, the professor, the assembly line worker, the programmer, as well as the physician, all have equal claims to the altruistic motive. Institutional life, work, is not only about what we get. Fundamentally, it is every bit as much, and inseparably so, about what we get to give, about the fulfillment we get by giving. In our culture, the acquisitive temperament is based on the appallingly mistaken and, therefore, destined to be disastrous psychological construction that giving empties us out, when, in fact, it is the satisfaction we get in human giving that is coordinated with human getting that fills us up. This is what fulfills us, links us, overcomes our tendencies to isolation and alienation, gives us access to a deeper and more far-reaching appreciation of what it is to be human.

The purpose of our institutions is to actualize and realize this form of exchange. Compassion demands of us that we work our hardest not only to hold them to this standard but to elevate them to this standard. This approach offers the promise of giving more substantial and more intimate meaning to notions of raising our standard of living. It gives a more human meaning and less simply "thingish" meaning to the increasingly debased phrase "standard of living." We need the help of compassion in hoisting a new flag over our institutions, not one that is incompatible with efficiency and productivity but one that asks questions along the lines of "Efficiency at what human cost under what system of human relations and for what human ends?"

An Imaginary Exercise

The vignette that follows is imaginary, with its roots in actual encounters. It aims to suggest important classes of conflicts that are rarely fully voiced. It aims to evoke some of the complexities of participation in institutional life and of the relationship between institutional participation and personal identity.

A middle-aged man in a very responsible position discovered himself in unanticipated and very complex conflict about his work. He looked back on how he had come to be a manager and policymaker. He traced this to having become very taken as an adolescent with the powers of abstraction. He recalled that even in high school and college he had always been impatient with forms of solutions that applied only to single cases. He wanted to look more deeply into things and to find forms of solutions that could be applied more broadly and was, in fact, very good at this. He said he had been interested in the generation of algorithms long before he knew the word. He liked to think, he said, that you could set up mechanisms that would hum along and take care of things so that you did not have to be bothered.

He reflected that he had always been rewarded for these tendencies and wondered whether he had perhaps not been seduced into regarding them a bit more highly than he should have done. He had, he said, become very good at defining options and choices and formulating rationales for taking one course of action or another, especially in situations in which he was a bit detached. He laughed and said that he thought he was some kind of unscientific scientist, trying to maneuver in situations in which there simply was no such thing as certainty. He said he thought he got a certain thrill from the uncertainty. He also thought he got a thrill from trying to persuade others of his point of view, always under the guise of trying to let the so-called facts speak for themselves. He had loved mathematics in college but felt liberated when he noticed the problems at its core that seemed to rule out certainty even there.

It was precisely his detachment that now troubled him. He felt that he had become very good at seeing things, as it were, from above, from perspectives where technical efficiency and organization were emphasized. He said that he was afraid that he had developed the soul of a manager or a policymaker, that he was capable of thinking about most any kind of a problem in this particular mode of detachment, as if he were not at risk himself. He wondered whether there were perhaps not other ways in which he had become incapable of thinking. He also wondered why it was that he should have become bothered about all this, even preoccupied with it, just now. He wondered whether it was perhaps his age, or the deaths of his parents, or some of the troubles that his children had had and the ways in which he felt he had failed them.

Or, he wondered, was this kind of doubt and difficulty something that had always been present in him but whose expression he had deferred for so long? If he had deferred it, why had he done so? He wondered whether there were not a kind of secret sharer who had been living along with him inside himself silently for many years. He said that it was troubling to take all this up, now, but that he felt that, possibly, he had been a coward long enough. He reflected that it was not that he rejected the position of a policymaker or manager. He recognized the need to formulate policy in broad terms and to manage efficiently. But he said he often felt like a horse that had worn blinders for so long that it had almost forgotten that it was wearing them. He worried that he had been taken captive by his role, by his responsibilities, by the form of organization within which he worked. He wondered whether, by being responsible within this particular framework, he was not being actually irresponsible in a wider framework.

He said he did not talk about this at work. He felt this line of thinking was not one that many of his peers shared, or at least not one that they seemed to share. They tended, he said ruefully, to think much better of themselves than he did. He wondered whether, perhaps, there was something that they got that he did not get. He wondered whether, perhaps, they were simply more realistic than he was. He wondered whether he were not so ambitious that, in a world defined by the art of the possible, he was prone always to ask the impossible. He said he thought it was possible that he was a dreamer who had been very successful at presenting himself, even to himself, as the very opposite of a dreamer. But he wondered also how a person or a company or a society was to know just where the edge of the envelope of the possible was located. Was not dreaming part of the discipline of locating this edge? But why did it scare him so much?

He remembered that the woman who was his freshman composition teacher had told him that his essays were interesting because he seemed both to enjoy his imagination and to be in terror of it. He wondered at what point it really became necessary to dissent from the projects of your own institution. He said he could not imagine working for a tobacco company but that he wondered whether there were not perspectives from which what he was doing looked very much like what the tobacco companies were doing. He said he knew that he had a case of bad conscience, but he could not quite convince himself any more that having a case of bad conscience was simply a matter of self-indulgence.

He said that he really thought that, at heart, he was a very frightened person. He did not know why that was so, but he felt he had been this way since he was very young. He had learned, though, to be very private about his fears. He said he had learned long ago that, when he met someone who seemed extraordinarily calm and self-possessed, he was probably in the presence of someone who was very frightened but had learned to dissemble just as he, himself, had. It had often struck him, he said, how frightened his children had been when they were young. He felt that he could see that both his son and his daughter had made a number of decisions that came out very badly because they had made them in the grip of their fears. When they were little, he had responded to their fears analytically, trying to help them see options and consequences. He had responded, he reflected, just the way he was used to doing at work. Looking back, he worried that what he had really been doing was to lie to them, acting as if he, himself, did not know what fear was. Perhaps he had lied to them because he had gotten into the habit of lying to himself.

He felt that, if he were honest with himself, he had turned to abstraction as a way to deal with his own fears. He had been sick a good bit as a child. He had always worried that he would not be able to live up to his parents' expectations, not that he could have said with any precision what his parents' expectations were. He felt he had breathed them in, taking them as much for granted as the air itself. Abstraction had provided him with a kind of thought armor. But now he felt like a knight whose armor was growing heavy because he had worn it too long. It felt more confining than protecting and seemed at least as much to wall himself off from himself as from any outside dangers. He was struck by his own success and by how much these qualities that he now began to question were valued by those around him.

It seemed to him that it was possible that they valued these qualities for just the same reason that he had—namely, because they could not cope with their own vulnerabilities and chose mostly to remain unaware of them. He said that he had tried to talk to his wife about how he was feeling about his work, but all she did was reassure him, when he was not at all sure that reassurance was what he wanted or needed. She pointed out that he had gone through periods before where he had seemed down for a few months but that he always perked up. He thought that, perhaps, what he needed was just the opposite of reassurance, help in moving in the direction of his fears. Talking to her had made him feel especially lonely, as if he had successfully deceived her to the point where she did not want to know him in any way that was uncomfortable for her. He said that he thought that the world looked very different from the point of view of vulnerability than from the point of view of efficiency or organization.

He wondered whether it were possible to get an institution to look simultaneously from the points of view of efficiency and organization on the one hand and vulnerability on the other. Institutions, he said, were like people, in that they could only bear to see so much at any given time and, if they were asked to see more, they might become confused and disoriented and sometimes not only distressed but dangerous. He said that it was curious that he was so aware of his own limitations and the limits of institutional life all at the same time.

With a certain amount of awkwardness, he noted that he felt there was a religious dimension to what he was experiencing. He said he was not even sure what he meant by religion in this context. Wryly, he wondered whether he did not mean something like the ultimate dimension of personal policymaking in which some intuition much deeper than logic ruled. He wondered whether vulnerability was not really a name for a set of cues too complex to sort out. He said that he recalled reading Kierkegaard's *Fear and Trembling* when he was in college and having a strange feeling in his stomach. He wondered whether sometimes it was with your digestive system that you recognized core truths. He did not feel that he was undergoing anything like a conversion experience but more a confusion experience, one in which nothing seemed quite what it had been before.

In the midst of what had been to him a very familiar and comfortable setting, he now felt very much alone. He said that what bothered him as much as anything else was a radical sense of lack of community. He felt that he was at least in part responsible for this radical sense of lack of community, because he was so tongue-tied. How could you expect others to understand you, if you didn't know how to speak?

He wondered whether, perhaps, this predicament was not a new one. He wondered whether there had not been much that he had wanted to say all his life that he had not found any way to give a form that was intelligible to others. He said there was part of him that just wanted to drop out and search for another way to live but that he thought that was romantic, the expression of just the wish that he had not allowed any expression when he was younger. He feared, however, that dropping out was just a way to make absolutely sure that he was never heard. He found himself, within the organization, being more and more the voice of doubt, the voice of caution, usually not so much on grounds that were clear to him but more because of a diffuse unease within himself.

He was particularly surprised that people respected him for his doubts and would sometimes take the time to rethink matters about which he expressed doubt. He thought this had to do only partly with his status in the organization and his reputation for being able to think clearly. He said that he found their receptivity strange because he had such an inner sense of the dangers of doubting and of how a person might get completely lost in it. He said he had never allowed himself really to think this before but that he thought he was so frightened of doubting precisely because doubt fascinated him.

Once you started doubting, how were you supposed to stop? If you let yourself doubt, how were you to know when you found something of value in your doubting? He felt that, if he wanted to devalue it, he could declare that his questioning had a sophomoric quality to it. He supposed that, in a private inner dialogue of which he had been never more than subliminally aware, he had made a habit of putting himself down. He had chosen a kind of conformity, he felt, because he was afraid to appear clumsy and tentative. What bothered him now was the power of this urge to conform that postponed real consideration of just what it was that you were conforming to. He said ruefully that he felt he had been a lump of cookie dough longing for a cookie cutter because he was so unsure inside himself. He had never had the courage of his lack of convictions.

He said that he had gotten more and more interested not just in the careers of some of his younger colleagues but also in their lives. It stunned him how sure and committed and confident they could look. He said he found himself dazzled by their technical abilities and their capacities to size up complex situations, at least in the way that was asked of them in the course of their normal work. He imagined that that was what he himself had looked like some years earlier. When he looked at them carefully, he wondered whether they did not have to look so sure and committed and confident just because they were so frightened of being unsure and uncommitted and diffident. He wondered whether the underpinnings of their technical clarity were not elements of real blindness particularly about themselves and their personal connections. He said that he found himself struck by how much pain there was in their personal lives and how much of it he felt was of their own making, not that they had set out deliberately to cause it but that they had so much trouble making themselves available on an intimate basis.

He said he wondered whether he was seeing straight or whether he was simply making them up in his own image. The possibility that he was seeing straight, he remarked, was the one that struck him as truly frightening. He reflected that, if you looked at the world from the point of view of vulnerability, there was so much that you might abstain from doing.

He remarked that he was particularly puzzled by time. He said he felt that he had lived the past thirty-five years in a kind of trance. It was for him now as if all that time had vanished in a twinkling. He felt as if he had just woken up, as if he were some sort of Rip Van Winkle. It was a shock to him to recognize that the trance in which he had been living was not, as he put it, the only trance in town. He found himself going back over and over to the question of what his trance had helped him avoid. He thought perhaps that he had found the trance so seductive and so alluring because of its monotony, which, he felt, would also explain why it seemed to him that the thirty-five years had vanished almost without leaving a trace. Had he collaborated, he wondered, in reducing himself to the state of some servo-mechanism for so long? Was it because the servomechanism made a comforting hum? His colleagues, he remarked with some wonder, tended to think of him as a person capable of strikingly original thinking. In an odd way, this made him feel both complimented and mocked and exiled. Respecting someone, he pointed out, could be part of a subtle effort to avoid the necessity for listening not only to the one being respected but to oneself.

10

Compassion and Evil

The Denial of Evil

The topic of evil is not only a painful one but a terrifying one. We often wish to close our eyes and close our minds and close our hearts so that we do not have to meet the challenge of evil. We all too readily can be led down the dangerous path of trying to make the world a better place to live by pretending.

While the appeal of this pathway is easy to understand and itself undeniable, this strategy of neglect has nothing benign about it. It provides precisely the conditions in which evil can flourish, not only outside us but in our hearts as well. We cannot solve or combat problems we are not willing to have. There is nothing at all innocent about the pose of innocent bystander. In fact, it licenses evil and may provide many opportunities for those who adopt this pose to indulge in covert sadistic pleasures.

The innocent bystander seen more realistically is a guilty collaborator who cannot achieve even sufficient animation to know about his or her guilt. Many, of course, adopt an "innocent bystander" pose with regard even to their own cruel and destructive acts, as if these pertained somehow to someone else. We do better to do the hard work of trying to bear a fuller knowledge of our own capacities and inclinations.

The premise of regarding ourselves as innocent bystanders is that we can disconnect from what goes on around us, when nothing could be farther from the truth. We are implicated in what surrounds us, because our borders can never be truly closed. Semipermeability is a fundamental fact of life from the membranes of cells, which regulate what goes into the cell and what comes out of the cell, all the way up through how our minds and hearts and souls are made to work. Compassion belongs specifically to the realm of our efforts to understand and take care of our connections. It belongs to the realm of our responsibility for maintaining the common nexus in which our differentiation and our articulation of our personalities and acts and hopes and loves and losses can take place.

If we notice evil, then we take on a responsibility to combat it. If we notice evil, we cannot help but be aware not only of its enormity but of our own capacities to participate in it. If we are not aware of the allure of participating in evil, then we have already begun to fall victim to the pernicious inner disease of self-righteousness, a distancing maneuver that starves the self of its real potential and actually makes it available to do and support the doing of what it claims most to abhor. We see, for example, so often the child of the rigidly righteous parent acting out at adolescence just those impulses the righteous parent claims most to detest. In fact, his disgust disguises a secret taste.

Self-righteousness has to do with inner alienation, an inward lack of links that produces inner stalemate. When we hear the note of self-righteousness in our own voices, then it is incumbent upon us to stop ourselves and ask ourselves what of ourselves we have left out of account and why we have done so. Self-righteousness is the corrupting and often sadistic sport our consciences engage in when we have despaired of our own capacity to guide ourselves and to correct what is troubling us inside ourselves. Whenever we are self-righteous, there is a way in which we know we are in the wrong and that the wrong is in us, but we refuse to admit it.

If we notice evil, we become aware in a new and chilling way of how enticing the idea of remaining blind to it is.

When we notice evil, we will notice again, with renewed force, how small we are as individuals. We will notice how much that is how dreadful lies outside the scope of our control. Not only that, we will be led to question again our formulation of our own identities and our commitments in life. We will be led to question how we spend our resources, how we spend our time, our concern, our money, and our life energies.

When we notice evil, we are led to fundamental questions concerning our scale and significance. If we can bring our moral and ethical imaginations to bear on the problem of evil, we will feel how it rankles and be moved to try to make a creative response. Evil is here to stay, and its abode is often nearer even than our neighbor's house.

Some Perspectives on Evil

What do we mean by "evil"? This is an ancient question to which there is no short or simple answer. Evil is a presence in our lives that is always changing, always seizing on new opportunities to make new initiatives. Evil intent is always with us, and so are evil actions, not that evil intent need always issue in evil action. If compassion is intelligence in the service of kindness, then intelligence in the service of cruelty is evil. If we stop to consider for a moment, we will realize just how common the employment of intelligence in the service of cruelty is. Nor is it common simply in places like Rwanda, Bosnia-Herzegovina, and Lebanon. It is common right here, right under our own noses. Evil is the practical negation in everyday life of one's hopes for oneself as a loving creature.

Rwanda, Bosnia-Herzegovina, and Lebanon were all pleasant enough places to live at one time or another, places where all manners of civilities and courtesies were practiced, places where attachment and culture flourished. What went wrong? What led to their terrifying decay, their explosion into a violence and brutality that is unspeakable, because no speech act can convey the degree to which these are overwhelming and traumatizing? After violence, after brutality, after evil, there comes an awed silence, in which men and women struggle to bear witness to their own losses and hurts, their own hopes and despairs. This silence can hold them in its tight grip for decades, keeping them mesmerized by what was too painful for any symbolic account. There are at all times many more people in the grips of this kind of silence among us than we find it convenient to know. This terrible silence, too, can be passed on from generation to generation.

It is daunting to realize that no one among us is wise enough to give a complete and convincing answer to the question of what goes wrong in places like Rwanda, Bosnia-Herzegovina, and Lebanon. The fields of Maryland are green and inviting beneath the warm summer sunshine where once the gory battle of Antietam was fought. Why could not this civil strife have been averted, the conflict resolved in a manner that was peaceful, if painful, rather than issuing in the incredibly bloody and foolish and shameful American Civil War? Do we not have the right, even the obligation, to ask more of ourselves in the way of the practice and pursuit of peace? But how? That is the question that should stir us on a daily basis, stir us minute to minute, even breath to breath.

A patient said of his long-divorced parents and their civil war, "I really don't know what went wrong between my mother and my father. I know they were both lost, that they had no idea about themselves. When I think about how they grew up, I can start to understand it. But it's still so sad, because, if they had just stopped for a moment and seen what was there right in front of their eyes, they would not have had to hurt each other so much. Not to mention me. But they couldn't. They couldn't. They couldn't stop and they couldn't look. They're still mad at each other, too."

Compassion begins in awareness and returns over and over again to the well of awareness for refreshment and challenge. We can give broader definitions even than that evil is intelligence in the service of cruelty. What takes apart pleasant places to live, civil accord, the peaceful pursuit of life, liberty, and happiness? Each time we reduce a person to the status of a thing, ignoring the crucial dimension of the other's inner experience, hopes, strivings, and need for love and respect, we put ourselves in proximity to evil. Each time we think of another as only an instrument rather than an end in him- or herself, we put ourselves in the proximity of evil. When we use people as if they were things that existed solely for our appropriation and use, we are on the road to abusing them, because we have misconceived both them and ourselves. Clearly, we can even take up this stance internally in regard to ourselves.

This is a very difficult line of thinking, because, even as we embark on it and notice its validity, we cannot help but be aware that we regularly use people, that we regularly consider them from an instrumental point of view, that we regularly exclude from the field of our awareness any deep appreciation of their inner experience, their hopes and fears, their needs for love and respect. Indeed, so much in human cooperation, much of it carried on under the sign of competition, would be impossible if we were not able to consider others from an instrumental point of view, from the point of view of what they can do for us and our projects rather than what they are in themselves and for themselves. Much of the common good depends on the capacity to see each other in an instrumental way.

But, ultimately, the common good depends crucially on our capacity to keep the instrumental point of view, with its tendency to regard people as interchangeable parts, from being our ultimate point of view. We must always be able to see persons as ends in themselves, as local centers of value and mystery. We must continually exercise this vision, which is so inconvenient from the point of view of large organizations and their projects, which so easily push rationality to a point that is, seen from the point of view of the individual as a center of meaning, utterly irrational. When we insist on seeing individuals as centers of value and mystery, we find that we are led to listen to them, to hear what they have to say, so to enrich our points of view by allowing the points of view of others to goad us to new syntheses and new forms of appreciation.

We must, individually and relatively intransigently at times, take the responsibility for resisting the tendency of the pooled power of the many to become a tyranny over each one. This can happen subtly and insidiously, until everyone feels isolated and confronted with a power against which they are powerless. When we abdicate individual responsibility, we collude with the evil of reducing the individual to the status of a thing, an "it" rather than a person. The difference between things and people is precisely that things do not respond. Things do not have the capacity to appreciate, evaluate, and respond.

When, as persons, we fail to use these gifts that pertain to us so crucially as persons, when we become unresponsive, then we collaborate in reducing ourselves to the status of things. While there is a certain anesthetic luxury in this position of unconcerned passivity, it regularly and reliably has dreadful consequences. When we respond, we often notice that our responses have effects other than those we intended. They can be ineffectual. They can lead us to believe that we acted in error. But, if we exercise our responsibility as persons, if we remain alive and vital and responsive, our capacities for response can develop and become both defined in new ways and more refined.

Compassion requires of us that we take things personally and examine not only how they connect with ourselves and others like us but with others who seem *unlike* ourselves yet are like ourselves at the deeper level of being persons with personal interests in matters that affect them and their possibilities and prospects in living. Not all musicians write and perform the same sorts of music, yet all are able to recognize one another as musicians. Similarly, not all persons live the same kind of lives or cherish the same kinds of aspirations. Yet, as we all hang by the same slender but powerful threads of breath, we need to be able to recognize and respect the kindred shaping spirits that animate all of us, however diverse the surface forms of our living may appear under relatively casual scrutiny.

The problem of understanding, addressing, respecting, integrating, and even enjoying differences is a vital one for human destiny. It is a vital one for anyone who is sincerely interested in peace. As history has shown over and over again and as we all have had opportunity to witness over and over again in our daily lives, differences and insecurities can all too easily be condensed together to produce fault lines where people are divided one from another in ways that are, while arbitrary, extremely powerful and often grimly fateful. Over time, these divisions can come to seem indispensable, even though they are not. They provide a focus for aggressive interactions with untold destructive potential.

Negativism

We define ourselves not only positively but also negatively. There is a wise saying to the effect that we should be extremely scrupulous in the choice of our enemies, because as time goes on and we invest in the enmity, we will come to resemble them. We find out what we are, at least in part, by finding out what we are not. We seek security often behind negativistic ramparts. We seek security in a failure to identify with certain qualities that we define as being outside ourselves. The horror of difference that is so common is really a horror that we might lose our sense of shape and be transformed against our wills into something we are not, something radically unfamiliar.

We need our horror of difference because our inner anchorage is so shaky. Our insistence on not identifying with what is different is founded in a sense that we are as malleable as wax and so dare not even try on a new shape because we might solidify in it and have no way open to going back to being ourselves. The horror of differences that we see as located outside ourselves bespeaks a horror of our inner diversity, our sense of the plenitude of our own potentials as a nightmare. We would not have such horror of difference if difference did not speak to us of something in ourselves, of a potential, a possibility, a way to be that has a measure, if not more than that, of subversive appeal for us. We change in life and yet often resist the awareness that we are persons in the making, beings in question until the very moments of our deaths.

A man in his thirties had as his defining passion in life a hatred for his father. His psychological project, as he understood it, was not to be like his father in any way at all. He described the world as he knew it in terms of two formally simple propositions. The first was that, if it was like his father, then it was bad. The second, the converse of the first, was that, if it was bad, then it was like his father. He accused his father of having treated him harshly, of having always been unable to hear him properly, of never accepting blame for anything, of being utterly selfish, of being utterly inflexible and unbending. He accused his father of being pompous and righteous and unable to relax and enjoy himself. He accused his father of having absolutely no sense of humor.

In short, his world was utterly patricentric. Gradually, he did start to notice that his view of his father was rigid, unyielding, humorless, and tense. He also started to be able to notice, if only fleetingly, that his view of his father was in fact as uncomplimentary to himself as it was to his father, because it spared him not only any blame but also any capacity for responsibility and initiative. As he nursed this monumental grudge against his father, it nursed him, too, reducing him to the status of a suckling without any greater ranger of initiative than an infant.

His relationship with his mother and his felt need to please her, to be the way she wanted him to be, to conform always to her view of him even when he knew better, came gradually under scrutiny. His grudge against his father covered over a deeply enmeshed style of relationship that kept him in an internal exile from himself. What was often a feeling of intense hatred against his father represented the conflict over how and whether to break free not only of his father but also of an identification with his mother that was so global, so extensive, so infiltrative as to amount to a virtual merger. The intensity of the hatred was in proportion to the internal feeling of helplessness and hopelessness over achieving a new status of increased autonomy and personal scope not only in the external world but also in the internal world.

The major problem was that instead of the anger and rage helping to power realistic, that is, limited initiatives in the direction of achieving practical autonomy, the anger and rage had coalesced into a habitual and habituating form of hatred that had an autonomy of its own and ruled the inner roost. The patient had trouble letting go of it, even momentarily, because then his experience of himself became too confusing and chaotic. His negativistic rage and anger had control of him because he could not make his way to any other hold on himself besides this exciting and inciting internal stranglehold. It is always an issue whether negativistic relating creates warmth through friction, making possible a closeness that still is abrasive enough to guarantee separateness, or whether the situation goes on farther to a rage that is more purely destructive and much less related.

Compassion understands prejudice, because it understands the agony of coming to a judgment slowly, deliberately, with due process and with the internal changing and rearranging that goes along with coming to a provisional judgment. Prejudice, judging too early, coming to premature closure, is a default position. It expresses states of inner insufficiency, inner bafflement, inner lack of confidence that are, alas, only too common. As such it forecloses on so many possibilities for enrichment, so many possibilities for a more integrated and deeper understanding of human potentials, not only those of others but also our own. Prejudice prepares for evil, licenses it, gives it inspiration. The tragedy of prejudice is that, by dehumanizing the other, it dehumanizes the self. Prejudiced people express the poverty of their own opinions of themselves, the poverty of their own inner inclinations to articulate their own human shapes in their full richness and depth.

Evil as a Process

When we speak of evil, compassion knows that we speak of a *process* by which people misunderstand themselves, make themselves morally misshapen, and wreak havoc not only on the world around them but on the world within them. Compassion knows that evil is a set of existential mistakes with dire consequences.

A 10-year-old boy was asked to define greed. After just a moment's hesitation and with just a slight tilt of his head to indicate the intensity with which he was applying his attention to the problem at hand, he replied, "Greed is when you want more than you want." Implicitly, this young boy obsessed with baseball made a distinction between authentic desire and desire gone awry, between a want that is attached to an authentic image of the person's becoming and a want that aims to fill out a horribly flawed and misguided design.

Compassion knows that we cannot approach the problem of evil without a deep scrutiny of what humans are and what humans can become, of their hopes and their despairs, of what is necessary and what is contingent. Compassion knows that we cannot approach the problem of evil without trying to understand how we make mistakes about what we are and about how deeply our mistakes can affect ourselves and others. Evil not only causes suffering, but evil is suffering in the sense of a failure to live up to what a person can come to be. Evil is also suffering for the one who does it in the sense that it closes off inner pathways to a different and fuller and freer realization of what it is to be a person. Evil is always linked to a failure to understand and to appreciate.

Evil is not simply a matter of monstrous deeds, acts of a violence and perversity so extreme that they chill the spirit.

Awful as these are, they are the points at which series that seem much more ordinary, more everyday, more habitual pass to their savage limits. In rural Africa in a tiny store in a tiny town, the following scene transpired. A man from one ethnic group brought in a basket full of eggs that he wanted to sell. He said there were twenty-five eggs in the basket. The shopkeeper, a member of another ethnic group, engaged him in a bit of banter with a tense edge. Finally, he asked the man whether he could wait for just a moment because he had some business to attend to in the yard behind the little store.

The man who wanted to sell the eggs turned his back to the shopkeeper, wandering toward the door. As he did this, the shopkeeper reached his hands into the basket, not once but twice, removing some eggs and slipping them under the counter. The shopkeeper then disappeared out the back of the shop into the yard. He was gone for ten or fifteen minutes, apparently quite indifferent to the man waiting for him. When he returned he made a show of carefully counting the eggs in the basket. When he reached twenty-one, the shopkeeper had a few unkind things to say about the other man's intelligence in trying to cheat him in this crude way, as if he did not even know how to count. He multiplied the number of eggs by the price he was prepared to pay and went to his cashbox to take the money out.

The other man was furious. He muttered something to the effect that he knew perfectly well that there had been twenty-five eggs in that basket when he brought it into the shop. The implication that it was the shopkeeper who was stealing was clear. Then the man fell silent, a look of utter bitterness on his face, despair and rage mingled together as he reflected that this shopkeeper was the only buyer for miles around. If he wanted to sell his eggs at all, he had no alternative. He had to accept what was offered. He stood still as the shopkeeper counted out the coins he owed him, making a show of being very precise. The man took the coins, walked slowly to the door, then, just at the door, turned and said very quietly, but with unmistakable menace, "Some day I am going to kill you." The force of this pledge was such as to make it only too believable.

This encounter was so chilling, so memorable, so terrifying because it was so personal, so direct, so intimate, a tragedy in the making over a matter of four eggs, not that four eggs are necessarily insignificant but that here they served as the mediators of a mutually destructive interaction between two individuals neither of whom seemed to have a way out. Neither murder nor theft happen all at once but rather arise in a seemingly sudden way out of a lifetime of urges, griefs, grievances, slights, self-indulgences, misconceptions, and errant desires. Our impulses, however they may seem to take us by surprise, are prepared. They are accidents and incidents waiting to happen. This is as true of our impulses for good as of our impulses for bad.

If we pause and consider the terms of trade between the richer nations and the poorer nations, the way in which the richer nations are able to dictate them, keeping the prices of the products of the poorer nations artificially depressed, thereby keeping the rewards of labor in the poorer nations artificially low, we may wonder whether this encounter over the eggs, so grim and intimate, so desperate and terrifying, cannot stand as a parable. The terms of trade between the rich nations and the poor ones have to do with the hunger in the belly of the 2½-year-old son of the widowed Dona Olga dos Anjos Santos who lives with her eight children in the *favella* of Alto do Cruzeiro on the red laterite hills in northeast Brazil. The terms of trade in our own society have to do with the hunger in the bellies of children who live within blocks of the most luxurious sections of many of our own cities.

Are not these unequal terms of trade really a form of theft? Is not theft that has such devastating effects on real human lives just like ours a form of evil? Are we not complicit in such evils if we allow them to go on without becoming a focus of our concern? It does not matter whether they are shrouded in habit, disguised as movements of markets, mostly referred to under the guise of numbers with their fabulous ability to remove the qualitative from view.

A prominent professional man insisted on being disappointed in his teenage son, remaining quite oblivious to the destructive effects on his son's self-esteem despite his wife's increasingly desperate efforts to intercede with him on the boy's behalf. Her intercessions were met with accusations against her for having failed in her job of producing an appropriate son for him. This man demanded that his son be like him and be able to make him feel proud and pleased with himself. His view of the son's role in life was that the son should be a prized possession of his own that reflected well on him.

What the father did not see was that the pressures he placed on his son had to do with his own enormous self-doubts as a man and as a parent and his resulting enormous need for self-justification. The father, a very hard-working fellow with a very narrow emotional focus, had a character structure that was entirely and effectively devoted to warding off his own sense of his inadequacy. When he started to feel badly about himself, he would turn to a mixture of alcohol and combativity, latching on to a new goal outside himself and pursuing it with a ferocious energy. His son was a more thoughtful, softer kind of person, with a greater tendency not only to open self-doubt but also to depression and self-destructive behavior.

In many ways, he understood his father's deep emotional problems much better than his father did, but his resentment of his father ran deep. It was as if his father had confided in him just the particular character problems around self-esteem and self-justification that the father dealt with so automatically and ruthlessly by denial and deprecation of others. The father's disappointment with the son had, in fact, very little to do with the son but much more to do with the father's own conflicts.

One way of looking at the conflict was that the father required of the son that he sacrifice his own individuality and personal inclinations and prospects to provide the father with the kind of supplements the father needed. In fact, this was an old theme, one of the dominant issues in the marriage, where this man saw his wife as mainly a support device for him and his ambitions without being able to recognize the cost to her because he needed her so desperately that he could not recognize her as an independent center of need and experience. Part of the son's peril was that he was very tempted to try to be exclusively for his father instead of for himself in the vain hope that this would lead to the recognition he desperately craved.

Intimately conflictual situations like this one can be thought of also as having to do with terms of trade, with balances of power, with allocation of resources, with balances of awareness and blindness. Of course, in these situations there is an enormous potential for violence, for destruction that is both psychological and more literal. What we want to call evil, we must remind ourselves, grows out of an ecology of human understanding and misunderstanding, grows in a context of human relationship and alienation, grows out of a set of judgments and illusions that can pass over to be delusions. One perspective on evil is that it is collaboratively and transactionally created in ways that can have a complexity that make them difficult to map as well as a stark simplicity that makes it hard for us to see and register and respond to them. These ways have to do with the terms of exchange between people and within people.

Awareness

Compassion asks always that we be aware, that we understand our gift for awareness, for doubt and difficulty, for risk and innovation, for taking ourselves and others seriously. In our daily lives, if we dare to be aware, if we can accept this awesome challenge without losing a sense of our own scale, we notice that we are caught in a web of evils large and small, just as we are also caught in a web of goods, large and small. Evil is both intricate and ordinary. If we notice that our comforts are purchased at the cost of someone else's chance at a decent life, then we must be able to take the risk of asking ourselves how comfortable these same comforts ought to make us.

This is not to say that we need believe that others need the things we have, that they should have some entitlement to the identical things we have. Poverty and plenitude of existence are not simply a matter of things and of material possessions. They are as much, if not more so, about self-possession. Our wealth is a form of poverty itself if we cannot imagine how we might live with less, how we might be active in the creation of our own internal goods through appreciation and the imaginative extension of our participation in living.

From the point of view of compassion, the sloth involved in unawareness, in a studied passivity that refuses to extend the self on behalf of others, is a major evil because it abdicates responsibility and so also abdicates the fulfillment of more fruitful human possibilities. When we are aware of evil, whether in the intimate realm or in the public realm, we may become frightened. We may become daunted. We may wish to withdraw. We may be overambitious in our hopes of others and of ourselves in the near term. We may be naive in our assessment of the hold of evil and unfairness, cruelty and terror on people, but we have embarked on a path that will change us and challenge us, that will give us occasion for reflection and meeting with others who reflect and who are available for being troubled. We will play a part in keeping alive in the world a vital set of hopes for justice and peace and mercy and reconciliation. Also, not unimportantly, we will enter into a communion over time with others who have cherished similiar hopes and been alive and awake to the difficult, indeed soul-searing and soul-searching, challenges of evil.

The understanding of evil presupposes the creation of an image of something else, a notion of the good to throw down a challenge to it, to engage it in hand-to-hand and heart-to-heart combat. This notion of the good serves to deprive evil of its place as something normal, something to be expected, something ordinary and acceptable, a matter of habit. The development of the awareness of evil is like the rising of a new sun to illuminate the human landscape. As we are more aware of the possibilities of good, of kindness and compassion, and as we are more aware of the pleasures of the good, of kindness and of compassion, then we will also be correspondingly and painfully more aware of that falling short that is evil, that is the predilection for cruelty and disrespect of the other, that is the failure to care and take care of what touches us, whether it be animal, vegetable, or mineral.

Certain kinds of discomfort are very good for us. In the face of evil, it is simply shameful to be comfortable. This does not mean that we should automatically fly into a rage or that

we should ambitiously and exhibitionistically devote ourselves to the pursuit of immediate solutions that are more
fantasy than reality. Compassion demands of us that we live
in the world as it is, while at the same never falling into the
idolatrous mistake of believing that the world as it is is the
only way that the world can be. This is not the best of all
possible worlds. There is no hope without discomfort, no
hope without the capacity to sustain tension and conflict as
just as much part of our lives as the winds and currents and
tides with their shifting fluxes are part of the life of the ocean.

If we are going to be active and engaged and open to
the difficulties of the world around us, its possibilities for evil
as well as for good, then we must be active and engaged and
open to the difficulties of the world within us. In particular,
we must be willing to know about the flaws and fault lines
that exist within us and how they influence our orientation
in the world. We must be willing to undertake the difficult
work of trying to make a response to our own insecurities
and our own urges to disavow large territories of our own at
least potential selves. We must be willing to try to make some
such response that does not infringe on the rights and needs
of others.

Compassion asks of us that we know our own potential
to do evil and that we be able to look upon the fact that we
actually have done evil and are complicit in doing evil with
an honest desire not so much to punish and castigate ourselves but rather to change so that we do not need to do it
more and so that we can make amends where we can. Making amends can be an enormously satisfying job, because it
not only confirms that we have changed but helps us grieve
for the serious flaws of our previous self. Compassion asks
of us that we do everything in our power to make the here
and now habitable, not only for ourselves but for others, not
only outside ourselves but within ourselves.

Compassion is opposed to evil, is opposed to cruelty, is opposed to the misuse of thinking, creativity, and enthusiasm in the service of destructive aims, as, for example, the reduction of people to the status of things, the failure to grant full scope to persons' legitimate claims on resources and opportunities, the prejudicial construction of others as somehow inferior, defective, deviant, or not able to be worked with as real human partners.

Compassion asks of us first of all that we give up the defenses of unawareness and indifference, the quiet collusion with evil, in favor of a more committed stance of engagement with evil as a reality that spans a vast continuum from matters outside ourselves to matters inside ourselves, from matters that appear in global-historic perspective to matters that matter on the most intimate and near scales. What compassion asks of us in combating evil is not that we as individuals control in some historic and heroic manner what lies beyond our scale but that as individuals we take seriously the job of putting our small weight in the balance on the side of kindness and mercy and peace, with the hope and conviction that our doing so will influence others both near and far. Compassion knows that the leadership of the heart is a leadership of example.

How we construct ourselves, how we choose and pursue our values, how we arrange for what measure of security is possible in human life, how we construe what is at the core of us, what we resemble, and what seems to us to be different and challenging all matter. Evil is a matter that pertains to our hearts and minds, to our hearths, and to our involvements in all the diverse institutions of our communities and the maze of dealings in which we are vicariously involved. Compassion asks of us that we take seriously both our effects and our defects as they show themselves near and far.

Doing What We Can

A middle-aged man was admitted for inpatient psychiatric care because of depression and suicidality. His case proved to be a complex one, with a troubling mixture of psychological and ethical problems. He had an indolently progressive neuromuscular disease. In order to secure employment, he had concealed not only the fact of his illness but also certain material facts about the limitations of his educational background. As he was quite talented in what he did, he had become a valued employee. As time went on, he had revealed his illness but not the truth about his educational background.

His employers had been very understanding about his illness and had, in fact, helped him compensate by providing special exemptions from certain physically taxing tasks and, generally, tailoring his job to suit him. A recent stress, along with some progression in his disease, had been a demand on the part of his employers for more productivity from him. This had to do with financial reverses the company had suffered and its efforts to cut costs to improve profitability. He was both very resentful of these new standards for his performance and very fearful that he would not be able to comply.

His insistence on living independently and taking care of himself verged on the fanatical. He had a great deal of trouble admitting to himself either the truth about his illness or the truth about his own capacities. He seemed to have two diametrically opposed attitudes. The first was that he should and could be able to do everything for himself, because the illness was not quite real. Certainly, he could not grant realistically its power over him. The second was that he was entitled to have done for him not only whatever he needed but whatever he wanted. If others, especially women, did not meet his demands, he would have fits of rage and pique that were often complicated by drinking. He felt easily betrayed, currently focusing this on work.

This man's view of his illness was also complicated. He had many guilty secrets, one of which was that more than twenty years ago he had run over and killed a little child. He had been going too fast at twilight and had hardly seen the little child at all. The child had darted in front of his car. He had been aware that he had hit something, but he had kept right on going. Not only that, but he had had a bit to drink and was a bit agitated, so that, as he looked back on it, he felt very guilty. The police had later found him. He had not told the police that he was going too fast, that he had been drinking, or that he was agitated and perhaps not paying adequate attention to his driving. He had, as he described it, kept all that to himself.

A number of people had seen the child dart in front of his car. The consensus was that there was nothing that he could have done. No charges were brought, but he had always felt guilty and ashamed of himself for not being able to be forthcoming about what he knew about himself. In one sense, he felt that his illness was a punishment that confirmed the verdict of murder he had brought in against himself. What was most peculiar about his discussion of the accident was that it did not seem to be in the service of resolving anything, whether internally or in the world, but rather in the service of declaring himself hopeless and helpless and therefore exempt from trying.

As a matter of fact, at the same time that he demanded a good deal of special attention and help on the unit, he had given up doing the regimen of exercises prescribed by the rehabilitation doctors who had followed his case. These were designed to help him maintain as much function as he could for as long as he could. His implicit attitude was that he was

deteriorating quickly and that this was someone else's problem, one that did not concern him in any way that might call
for activity on his part.

This man's depression and suicidality existed within the
context of a very difficult set of character traits, one feature
of which was a lifelong difficulty in bearing painful feelings
and in making realistic assessments based on the capacity to
bear painful feelings. I told him very directly that, if he could
not be bothered to do the exercises that he knew were helpful to him, then it was very hard to see what anyone else could
do for him. I said that I thought the issue of all the ways he
had not been honest with others and with himself along the
way was also important but not really as much as the immediate practical importance of the exercises, which were something he could do.

This focus on the exercises, on the small concrete and
practical beneficial thing he could do for himself and by himself wherever he was, proved useful in opening a much wider
dialogue about his current situation and what the reality of
his disease and his capabilities were. It raised the issue of
whether he was unfairly taking advantage of other people and
unfairly neglecting himself right now. It brought him up
against the reality that there were separate classes of things
he could do and things he could not do. It gave him an immediate and concrete exercise in trying to bear something that
was difficult. So it gave him an opportunity for improving
his self-esteem in the present.

I was surprised to receive a number of calls from him
at odd intervals over the year and a half after he had moved
back to the state from which he had come. In each one of
these, he referred to the exercises and assured me that he
was keeping up with them. He also told me about his work
status and the status of both his rehabilitation and his psychiatric treatment. I saw him as a very damaged man who

had also done a good bit of damage to others in his life. The story of his running over the small child stayed with me.

Compassion is not about guilt but rather about self-examination and self-animation. In the deep resources of our hearts there is an inventiveness for the good as well as an inventiveness in the pursuit of evil. The pursuit of kindness, of the good that matters in the dealings of individuals with individuals and their surroundings, requires an appreciation of these dimensions of creativity and firmness of resolve in their application on a practical and day-to-day basis.

We are not required to do more than we can do, but there is something central and essential in ourselves that is deflated and defeated if we allow ourselves to do less than we can, to consider less than we can, to live on a less intimate footing with ourselves and our fellows and our common problems than we are capable of doing. Evil is our common practical problem, but we need not allow it to define the shape and breadth of our communities or of our communion with ourselves and each other. Compassion, the knowing pursuit of kindness, takes on the problem of evil in all its diversity from the most intimate and inward scale to the historical scale. It takes the problem of evil on by helping us to do what we can, which is so often more than we like to think.

— 11 —

Compassion and the Self

Kindness to the Self

When we talk about compassion and the self, we focus our awareness on the complexity and consistency of the relationship between ourselves and ourselves. In other words, we focus on the fact that we are split within ourselves into two parts at the very least, a subject and an object. We take ourselves in a staggering variety of ways as the objects of our own actions, intentions, feelings, and inventions.

In fact, how we treat ourselves, how we cherish ourselves or mistreat ourselves, how we are able to muster kind responses to our own troubles or brutal and denigrating ones, has the most decisive impact for our living and for the kind of people that we will become. How we treat ourselves has a decisive impact on how we treat others, just as how we treat others and how others treat us have important impacts on how we will treat ourselves.

In a certain sense, we are never more defenseless than we are at our own hands. A corollary is that we have at our disposal thousands and thousands of ways, subtle and not so subtle, of being offensive to ourselves. If we have a disposition to be cruel and turn it inward, we can cause enormous suffering, enough suffering in fact to seriously blight a life. When we bite our nails, when we deprive ourselves, when we put ourselves needlessly at risk, when we punish ourselves by choosing what will hurt us, when we hold grudges against ourselves in the name of fantasied omnipotence, this has real effects and leaves real traces. When we speak of compassion as the knowing pursuit of kindness, this knowing pursuit of kindness must extend to the knowing pursuit internally of kindness toward ourselves.

The topic of kindness toward ourselves is a vast and complicated one, not one that we can deal with exhaustively. But it makes a difference if we are sensitized to this issue and understand that the cruelties we do to ourselves matter every bit as much as the cruelties we do to others. We are our own most intimate neighbors, so that our dealings with ourselves internally come under the inspiring and demanding provisions of the golden rule. We need to do unto ourselves as we would have others do unto us, as much as we need to do unto others as we would have them do unto us. We need to do within ourselves as we would have others and ourselves do outside ourselves. If we reserve our kindnesses for others and treat ourselves with a harsh spirit, then we show a hypocrisy that probably has at root a difficulty in accepting our own vulnerability. Why else would we want to figure ourselves as being either above the need for kindness or below it, two forms of dreadful and unappealing human exile?

A woman in her twenties described how, much to her chagrin, she had discovered the problems that had confronted her growing up continuing on within herself. She said that, as she had perceived them, her father had been a monster and her mother a martyr. Both her parents had been, she said with a complex mixture of pride and shame, very good at what they did, and neither of them had had any mercy for the other. Each had counted on the other to do the worst possible thing, and neither had been disappointed. She had, as a very frightened and lonely little child who always had to wait too long for everything, admired and envied both of them, because they had seemed both so powerful and so adamant, so free from doubt and terror.

As a result, she had grown very good at being both a monster and a martyr. When she lost her temper she could be a monster who had absolutely no regard for the impact of her actions on others. At other times, she could get involved in relationships where she was badly mistreated and make no effort to get out of them, protect herself, or even protest. She had repeated this pattern over and over again. Knowing about it did not seem to make any difference. The need to repeat felt to her more powerful than she was, herself.

The war that had gone on in her household as she was growing up continued on in her head on a daily basis, even on a moment-to-moment basis. Neither the monster nor the martyr within was capable of yielding at all, so that she was alternately too cruel and violent not only to herself but to those around and much too complicit in allowing, even taunting, herself and others around her to make her suffer much more than made any sense. Between the monster and the martyr, her psyche was turned into a battleground in which no more peaceful and promising approach to life could emerge. As she put it, there was no room at all for herself. She said it was a new idea for her even to imagine that she had a self separate from this system.

She said that she found that as a rule it simply did not occur to her to treat herself in a more kindly or forbearing way. If it did, it came as a tangential thought that always seemed somehow unreasonable and suspect to her, not the kind of thought at all that she could recognize as having any validity as her own. If she had such a thought, she was most likely to have a twinge of contempt for herself as a wimp. If she were just stronger, she thought, she would not have to give in. She had been raised to believe that it was unseemly to feel self-pity. So, whenever she had a thought that involved a prompting toward some genuine compassion toward herself, she invoked the commandment not to pity herself, not to feel sorry for herself, in fact, not to feel for herself or as herself at all.

After much labor, she got to the point where she could report these thoughts, these very slender and marginal shoots of the impulse to be tender toward herself, and how she had dismissed them. Her reports came with a mixture of puzzlement and despair. She said that she was shocked to notice that she experienced any inner promptings to take care of herself as acts of betrayal, almost criminal acts. She said that the very idea of taking care of herself or being kind to herself made her so sad and upset and angry. It provided her a window through which to look upon just how needy and desparate she felt, not just sometimes but all the time. Monsters and martyrs, she remarked, did not really have needs or worries. They simply had automatic ways of going about things, as if they were robots. She envied robots, because they did not have to feel as lost as she did.

She could not imagine the joy of spontaneity because the only spontaneities she knew were the spontaneities of rage and terror, awful surprises that took her over and shook her up so that she found herself dazed and withdrawn for long periods of time, sitting in silence waiting for the world to come back to order, wondering what had happened and why it had happened, wondering always what she had done to bring it on herself. She pointed out that it was very new for her to be able to think about any of this, to be able to make a try at describing it. She had spent so many years with nothing so formed as thoughts.

This woman said that, when she did have the impulse to do something that involved being neither a monster nor a martyr within herself, she found herself feeling very lonely. The world of the monster and the martyr was the world she knew, and she did not know any way to proceed to knowledge of any other world. If she started to treat herself kindly inside herself, this would mean disconnecting from her mother and her father and from the world of her childhood. The monster–martyr paradigm kept her in touch with the images of other people about whom she had cared deeply, treasuring and loathing them in patterns as complicated as those made by a tangled ball of yarn. She did not know how to make different connections inside herself with these people who were so important.

She was in the internal dilemma, one from which she was never able to find an exit, of not knowing how to live with them and also not knowing how to live without them. What internal structure she had was caught up in the drama of the monster and the martyr. Her unkindness to herself and also to others in the process was a memorial, a linking device, a form of clinging with a very high cost. The tragedy of it was that the impulse that prompted it was not only one of rage and despair but also one of love and loyalty. It was an impulse to repair what had been beyond repair for much more than a single generation.

When we speak of kindness toward the self, we are not speaking of self-indulgence. We are not speaking of coddling ourselves. We are not speaking of seeking a life of undue comfort or ease. We are not speaking of seeking a life of obliviousness and unconcern. We are not speaking of building a fortress or the psychological equivalent of a castle defended by a moat. Rather, what we are speaking of is caring for the self, mind and body both inseparably united in the mysterious seeking that is life. We are speaking of understanding ourselves as persons with needs and vulnerabilities, frailties and failings.

We are speaking of suiting the stresses to the resources available to meet them, even as we seek to increase those resources. We are speaking of trying to meet the adventure of living with calm and vividity and clarity, with a sense of its uniqueness and a sense that the everyday provides an enormous realm of opportunity for the exercise of our creativity. This includes our faculties of creative appreciation that can make marvels be present to our own eyes in the apparently uneventful torpor of a peaceful afternoon.

We are speaking not of flight from the challenges of the self but rather of integration and responsiveness. It is unkind not to know ourselves across a wide range of our aspects, sad and glad, good and bad. To leave ourselves unknown by ourselves is to cultivate an inner numbness that is worse than any kind of loneliness, because loneliness is at least a seeking and searching, whereas numbness is a withdrawal that forecloses on the possibilities of living. It is unkind not to bring our different aspects into relationship with each other, letting them question and amplify and change and reorder each other.

Accommodating Change

It is unkind to oneself to cramp oneself in design, to seek to assimilate oneself to some external standard alone rather than to seek the touch and feel of authenticity, its challenge and freedom and promise and difficulty. When we find the paths that belong to us authentically, we can have the good fortune of experiencing that sense of the old that renders it breathtakingly new and also that sense of the new that renders it breathgivingly old and so familiar, as if it had always been there waiting for us.

When we speak of being kind to ourselves, an important part of this kindness is the capacity to find the thread of the self's becoming and to follow it through the labyrinth of experience, meeting and responding to what tests one along the way. Or perhaps the singular is not appropriate to such a complex task with such varied possibilities. Most likely it makes more sense to think of ourselves as having selves of many strands, potentially an infinite number of strands, some of which are highlighted in different ways at different phases of our lives. So the task becomes to find the many and diverse threads of one's own authentic becoming and follow them through diverse labyrinths of experience, all the while seeking ways to weave and reweave them into patterns that are appropriate not just to our meetings with the outside world but to our inner meetings with ourselves.

Another important part of compassion for ourselves is to be able to find a way to acknowledge and accept that we change as we go along our ways, so that what suited us yesterday may not suit us today and what suits us today is not required to suit us tomorrow. It is an odd truth that we take hold of ourselves as we let ourselves go. We can hold on so tight that we run the risk of strangling ourselves, of shutting off the access to anything new, of literally as well as figuratively making it impossible for ourselves to breathe. The free flow of breath, after all, depends on a degree of relaxation that allows the lung its natural elastic capacity to resonate, preparing for out with in and for in with out, so setting up the life-sustaining alternating rhythm of inspiration and expiration. It is unkind to ourselves not to let ourselves breath freely and fully. All this can be taken at once literally and metaphorically.

Along these same lines, the nearly universal gesture of the relaxed open palm has such resonance because it is poised midway between offering and accepting, receiving and letting go, supplicating and giving. It expresses gesturally, that is, in a natural, if also highly elaborated language of the body, the existential middle point in which we find ourselves when we appreciate what surrounds us within and without. Kindness toward the self has to do with finding a home even as we leave the home of what has been familiar to us, what has seemed natural and inevitable, what has seemed essential and unchangeable. Kindness toward the self involves a spirit of adventure, not only or perhaps even principally in the outside world but in the world within. Kindness toward the self involves appreciation of the self, of its sources and its resources, the way in which it can renew and reclaim even what has been long lost. Kindness toward the self evolves from an adventure of the spirit that is available in everyday ordinary life and only in everyday ordinary life.

Compassion for the self presupposes a certain mobility, a certain sense of scale, a certain sense of perspective. These are not easy to come by. In order to feel compassion for oneself, one cannot be too humiliated to be humble. One cannot be so overwhelmed by what has transpired that one has to be in a state of continuous revolt against it, as if one felt that, if one simply lacerated oneself with sufficient force, one could change what had happened, change what one had felt, change what one had done and what one had come to know. Compassion for the self involves the acceptance of limits. It involves moving beyond futile protest to inner reconciliation with what has happened and what one has felt in response to it. It involves in particular the acknowledgment and taming of one's rage.

Atonement, so often the prelude to self-forgiveness, almost always involves an inner gesture of submission that is part of a movement from the more concrete and literal to the more abstract and symbolic. This inner gesture of submission is also a psychological act of mastering the truth of our own scale. Only very rarely in life is it possible for us to make amends by setting to right just the situation that we got so very wrong in such a fateful way not only for ourselves but for others. Much more common is the situation in which we have to accept that the harm we have done is done, that any repair we could make in that particular situation is only very partial. We have to look to what we have learned about ourselves and the world to instruct us in ways to make amends by doing well in other situations that bear a variety of kinds of resemblances to the situation in which we have done ill. Amends are, in this sense, metaphorical more than literal. The comparison to the original situation is implied, not necessarily explicit.

When we can acknowldge our failures, then we acknowledge our own fallibility. We acknowledge and accept something central about the human condition and about ourselves. When we can acknowledge and accept our own fallibility, we cannot only know remorse and regret but use them to help us prepare a readiness for making reparation. If we are ready to make reparation, we will find an opportunity. In order to prepare for reparation, we have to become more separate from the particular circumstances of our original error. We have to recognize the kinship that exists between many different situations and many different people. Our errors and our hurts, as well as our loves and our joys, can serve to lead us onto the ground of the more universal, where we can find both new degrees of inner freedom and new forms of expression. In the process of moving from error to atonement, from damage to reparation, there is a profound creativity at work.

The currents of life and time never stop flowing. They carry us along with them, moving us always into circumstances that, while undeniably changed, also bear undeniable echoes and remembrances of what once was familiar. Compassion for oneself involves being able to make active and real in new circumstances what one has learned from the prior circumstances of one's living, however difficult those have been. Compassion involves being able to remain present enough to oneself to establish a sense of continuity in change through the enormous shifts that make up a lifetime. This is no small job, involving an inner awareness and a willingness to do the work to keep this awareness changing and rearranging and still organized.

Learning always involves an inner change, a new take on what has gone before. In this sense, a basic aspect of compassion for oneself is to allow oneself to learn, that is, to let go in one's mind and heart enough to take hold in a new way. Of course, whenever we let go there is always the fear of falling, so that real human learning, the learning that makes an inner difference, is never accomplished without fear and trembling. Real learning is not bland but personal and passionate. Real personal learning is what can keep life seeming new and fresh, not without sorrow but still full of an allure that is not simple but substantial. Real personal learning is what brings us into authentic relationship with life as infinite opportunity and challenge.

Fortunate enough to have escaped just in the nick of time from a land ravaged by war and hatred, a man had promised himself that he would get his older brother and his older brother's family out, too. This man was the youngest of ten siblings. This particular older brother had been specially important to him as he grew up in difficult and dangerous circumstances. This older brother had protected him, sponsored him, taught him, and believed in him. There is no way to overstate the earnestness with which this man had promised himself that he would help his brother out of mortal peril. As it happened, events moved too fast. There was simply nothing that this man could do. To his enormous sorrow, his brother and his family were lost. Only many years later did he even learn the gruesome details of how they came to perish.

In the privacy of his own heart, this man not only felt great sorrow over the loss of his brother and his brother's young family but also held a grudge against himself that he had not been able to make good on his promise to come to his brother's aid. After all, the brother had so often come to his aid. As he built a new life for himself under circumstances that were, while still difficult, very much changed and improved, the images of his brother and of his brother's family were always with him. He dreamed for years of his brother's children, and, when he looked at his own children, the sense of what might befall them was never far away. In knowing them and enjoying them, he yet suffered for his brother and his brother's children.

The resolution of his grief and the grudge he held against himself took decades. He always looked at life through a lens both clouded and clarified by sorrow and his awareness of what could really happen to people, an awareness that most of his prosperous and self-satisfied neighbors shunned with a diligence that was as instinctive as it was remarkable. His lot in life was a lonely one, especially because under the hold of the grudge he bore against himself he did not allow himself to speak about what he had been through. Certainly, part of the grudge's function was to express his own sense of humiliation that he had ever been so small, so frightened and so much in need of his brother's help. How much inner vindication he would have felt had he been able to come to his brother's aid! To say that he felt guilty about his own survival only substitutes a psychological formula for a vast, difficult, and daunting tapestry of intimate human experience.

One part of the resolution of his grief and his grudge against himself was a gradual change in what had been a feisty and combative stance toward other people into a more gentle, protective, and sponsoring attitude, especially toward those who were struggling against the odds in life. This change came when he was already older than his brother had ever been lucky enough to become. Yet, in this adoption of a protective and sponsoring attitude toward others who were younger and facing various kinds of peril, he had managed, by finding it in himself and allowing it much freer expression, to bring something of his brother out to freedom and to life.

This exodus was not literal but metaphorical. It did not serve to remove the sting of the loss and the self-disillusionment that went along with this man's powerlessness to prevent it even after he had pledged himself wholeheartedly to the task. Rather, it served to transform the hurt and express it in a reparative strategy in current everyday living. It made it possible for this man not only to speak about it but to speak to it within himself. It made it possible for this man to experience a better sense of fit with himself both within himself and in the world. It acknowledged a deeper and also differently sad and joyful continuity thrown like a bridge across the awful chasm of the discontinuities of his life.

Accepting the Real Self

When we think about compassion for the self, we are always led to notice that it involves an acceptance that the self is often different than we would have wished it to be. In life, we are not infrequently shown to ourselves in lights far different than we would have imagined. We come to know aspects of ourselves in hard ways that take us by surprise and send us searching for some means to reconstruct avenues that can lead us to experience again a sense of at least relative coherence and self-acceptance. Compassion for the self is always at odds with inner grandiosity, always engaged in difficult dialogue with that part of ourselves that refuses to accept just how little we control. Compassion always insists that we stay in the difficult area of doubt. Compassion requires of us a healing measure of felt uncertainty that allows us to keep on trying. Compassion for the self always maintains its respect for the small action and the intimate initiative.

Compassion for the self does not tire of the old questions, the old difficulties, the old impasses, but instead keeps reminding us that decisive changes come from the smallest new insights that give rise to a series of new actions and new feelings. Compassion for the self keeps reminding us that we are not restricted to being alone in our questioning and in our quest, however profound our solitude may be, however profound our sense of communicative isolation and inadequacy may be. In the depths of our discontent, compassion for the self keeps reminding us that in order to have what we want, we must be able to make initiatives in the direction of wanting what we have, of moving toward increased flexibility and amplitude of inner appreciation.

Compassion for the self does not leave us alone, even when we feel most terribly alone. In this sense, we may experience it as a terrible nuisance, a pest that will not allow ourselves the luxury of the perfection of our misery. Compassion for the self will not quite allow us to get rid of ourselves, in action or in inaction, in a fixated concentration or in fixated inattention. Compassion for the self keeps us company and insists on inner dialogue, a private examination of the practical possibilities of our living.

We might say that compassion for the self is like the voice of a small echo, heard from an ever so slight remove, that presents to us the music of ourselves in a slightly changed tonality or with a slightly different harmony or rhythm or orchestration. Or we might say that compassion for the self is like the pillar of cloud by day and the pillar of fire by night that lead us along through the desert when we have sought to abandon ourselves there.

Or we might say that compassion for the self is like a skilled weaver who insists on showing us that there is more to our past and its patterns, more to our future and its possibilities, more, therefore, to our presence than we, with our so much too constricted design intelligences, have been willing to see. Compassion for the self simultaneously reflects and inflects, accepts and challenges with the implications of its acceptance. It will not let us have the last word but helps us reverberate within ourselves. This potpourri of figures is only suggestive because actually the process of accommodating and making real in that *process* we call self is too complex to be contained in any single figure.

Compassion for the self can be strict and even demanding but not in the manner of an excitement that helps us keep a distance from ourselves. The pleasure of compassion for the self is not in the edge we can make through inner pain but in the exit from terrible inner pain that can come through sustained effort at integration of the kind that comes from reminding ourselves over and over again that our current perspectives are limited and partial, incomplete. This incompleteness is not a grounds for despairing, not a grounds for devaluation, but rather a grounds for effort, no matter how difficult, even baffling. This effort, this inner taking on and sustaining of what is difficult and confusing and what situates us even at the brink of despair, can issue in a deep kind of self-respect and self-appreciation that is available no other way.

Compassion for the self helps us learn to forgive ourselves for being small as we are, helpless as we are, prone to

error as we are. It helps us learn even to forgive ourselves
our hopeless ambitions, our projects of restitution and res-
cue that are doomed from the outset. When we can forgive
ourselves for being what we are and as we have been, then
we are released into a new future with new possibilities not
wholly unlinked to those of the past but still arranged in new
arrays. This new future is not a future on a grand scale, but
it is a future that can have its own internal and local and
personal satisfaction because it is intimately formed, intimately linked and available for intimate scrutiny and appreciation. As one patient said, "I'm trying to cast enough light
on myself so that I can be famous in my own mind."

A Privileged Moment

Here is the story of a memory. One sunny spring Sunday
afternoon when the lilacs were in full and glorious bloom,
a 5-year-old boy watched his older relatives arranged around
an island of flowers in the middle of what seemed to him
the green paradise of his parents' home's backyard. At the
center was a pale and worn woman who looked now much
older than her years, incomprehensibly and frighteningly
older, in fact, than her years. The little boy breathed in the
atmosphere of concern and solicitude that surrounded her,
producing a kind of hush in which she was the focus of
attention.

What most impressed him, though, was her own demeanor. She sat very still in a flimsy lawn chair of woven
plastic. As she looked at the lilacs, she adjusted her cheek so
that the sun fell on it. A small smile played about her lips. It
seemed to the little boy as he watched this scene that it was

as much true that she was caressing the sunlight ever so gently and appreciatively with her cheek in a gesture that was at once welcome and farewell, as that she was allowing the sunlight to caress her cheek. This scene of simple and yet quite extraordinary mutual embrace between a mortally ill woman and the life-giving sunlight stayed with him.

He returned to it over and over again as his understanding of himself and others deepened, seeing more and more in it as he looked with the eyes of more and more experience. At times of special difficulty in his life, when he was deeply stressed and distressed and found himself despairing of the meaning of life, this scene would come back to visit, carrying with it what seemed to him a fundamental message—namely, that light and life, warmth and presence were still available to be appreciated even under the most dire of circumstances, even when life was very much on the wane and pain was a near constant if not constant presence. He remembered the special silence that surrounded this woman in the garden, a silence that was at once worried and fearful and embracing.

His memory of this scene helped support his own efforts to be compassionate with himself, to remember that what was most fundamental and most important could also be very simple and direct and available, as near as a beam of light no different than any of those that fall to earth in a steady cascade each day. He understood also as time went on that small children can have a way of seeing and feeling all at once in a single panoramic instant that is so comprehensive as to be almost incomprehensible to adults whose seeing and thinking and feeling have become sometimes tragically compartmentalized in the service of maintaining the capacity to deal at least marginally with the exigencies of everyday life.

Integration

As we search for ways to suggest something of the realities and possibilities of compassion for the self, as we search for figures with which to describe it, one that comes to mind is that compassion for the self can be thought of as a sort of internal elixir of decompartmentalization. Compassion for the self makes room for what a person has known, what a person has felt, what a person has been, what a person has done within that person. It does not indulge in acts of internal bigotry or persecution, envy or ostracism.

To mention just a few, compassion for the self allows for the feminine in the masculine, the masculine in the feminine, the fearfulness in bravery and the bravery in fearfulness, the shame in pride and the pride in shame. It knows that the only purity in experience comes when everything has been allowed its place in the mixture and changing forms and patterns appear, show themselves, and then cede to what comes next. The purity of the inner experiencing self is set in a rhythm of acceptance and inclusion, not avoidance and exclusion. Compassion for the self makes an eloquent and robust diction of experience out of what without it can appear as contradiction and dismaying disarray.

Compassion for the self has to do with making limitation, loss, and love habitable. A professional man discovered very painfully that he lived in terror of those he needed. His efforts to deal with this predicament took many and diverse forms. He tried to maintain the illusion of self-sufficiency in a fantasy life that was ornate, rigorous, exuberant, and secretive. He was himself sometimes shocked to discover what a hold his fantasy life had on him. Occasionally, he would catch himself drifting away. When he wrenched himself back into touch with reality, it would seem strange to him, as if he had just landed in a foreign country and was not yet quite oriented.

He would have the sense that he had been passionately and deeply involved in a world that had nothing to do with the actual one surrounding him. There would be a shudder of pleasure and terror both, as he became aware of the threat that just the fantasy life that he counted on to protect himself against the loss of those he needed might take him so far away as to make it impossible for him ever to get back to them. He wondered at what point the territory of comforting and sustaining illusion crossed a vast and unmarked border into the realm of treacherous delusions. He wondered whether, perhaps, he himself had not made many trips back and forth across this border, whether he did not, possibly, wander back and forth across this border as a matter of habit. He found himself doubting his own sanity.

Another strategy he had for protecting himself against his terror of those he needed was to make the most thorough and detailed study of these most intimate associates and enemies. He wanted to know what they were likely to feel, think, know, do better than they did themselves. He wanted to turn prediction into a controlling fetish, endowed with all the magical power he knew himself so painfully to lack. The same resources that supported his fantasy life were engaged in this effort, which, in fact, did produce a remarkably nuanced and deep knowledge of other people, if one that bore also a slightly paranoid and obsessional flavor.

But, again, the same danger showed itself, indicating the futility of the strategy. To the extent that his simulations seemed too perfect to him, to the extent that he was tempted to fall in love with them, to this extent they threatened to supplant the real others, to cut off any possibility of genuine and spontaneous interaction with these real others and so remove him from any possibility of novel self-discovery. Far from making him free, they subjected him to a new form of tyranny. In fact, it seemed that whatever he did to try to protect himself from his vulnerability and terror of those he needed seemed only to compound his predicament.

What shocked him was the affective awareness—that is, the presence in terms of visceral emotion—of his rage at the point of separation from these others on whom he depended so terribly. As he felt it, he could not tell whether he wished more to hug them or to decimate them, so strong was the pull they exerted on him, so deeply did his knowledge of their separateness from him and his needs and wishes disturb and disorganize him. He went through a period of despondency in which his rage frightened him so much that he felt he was simply hopeless and pathetic, a person who could not bear either to be with other people or without them. He saw himself as always trying to replace people, if in subtle ways, before he had even lost them, because he just could not bear to feel all that he felt about them. He worried about his own capacity to destroy just the people he loved, even in so direct and primitive a way as through physical assault.

He was aware that what he had been doing for so long was a despairing dance of disavowed dependency. He hated himself both for needing what he needed and for trying to pretend in so many different ways that he did not. Whichever way he turned, he saw himself involved in some project for self-perfection that was tantamount to an effort to shut out the outside world. Every act of his seemed a lie, a deliberate and aggressive manifestation of his own double-dealing and bad faith. Even his self-hatred seemed to him a project for self-aggrandizement.

Gradually, through a painstaking examination of his own history, of how his dilemma had arisen from a combination of the disappointments and insults he had suffered and his own creative efforts under conditions in which he was regularly and steadily overwhelmed, he began to develop a more ambivalent view of his own characteristic ways of going about things. He realized that he was, himself, one of those people whom he needed and of whom he was so terri- fied, that he had so many different ways of trying to replace himself and determine himself and generally keep any flex- ibility, spontaneity, or surprise out of his relationship with himself. He began to wonder whether he knew himself at all as he realized that he actually enjoyed not only caring for himself but caring for others.

He found himself thinking about his own mortality and realizing that, in the long run, any project he might form of definitively assuring that his needs would be met or of de- finitively assuaging his terror of others and his rage at them for being separate, reluctant, retiring, intrusive, and unreli- able was doomed. This filled him not only with a sense of pity for himself but with a sense of pity for them as well. He was able to accept that there were real flashes of insight in his terrors and that he need not use these terrors in the ser- vice of taking himself apart but might rather, if he could grant the reality of his own fears, use them instead in the service of putting himself together. He felt that he had made some headway in not lying to himself quite so much.

He found that he was puzzled as to what had always made his own vulnerability so unacceptable to him. He found himself newly able to bear the awareness that sooner or later he would lose all those he loved and cared about, that sooner or later, even, he would lose himself. The fact that everything was temporary seemed to him grounds for savoring it, because nothing could hold him permanently in its thrall. He was struck by how much more separate he could bear to feel and how much more he could bear to allow himself to feel because he felt himself to be more separate. He also found it mysterious that he should ever have come to be able to grant himself what semed to him like a second chance at life.

Compassion for the self has to do with second chances and third chances and fourth chances and fifth chances. It has to do with the reformulation of goals and the reformulation of reformulated goals. It has to do with taking bearings and with bearing with what has been taken from one. It has to do with an internal awareness that the self is at once frail and enduring, fragile and resilient, terribly eccentric and linked in all sorts of commonalities and communities.

A very large teenage boy flunked out of high school. He was at home basically making his mother's life extremely difficult. This poor lady, whose resources were limited, already had enough trouble, given that her husband was in jail for a particularly clumsy swindle that had swiftly unraveled on him. The boy enrolled in an alternative school, where he had a very hard time working. His opinion of himself was very low. He treated his mother with almost no respect and felt less and less respect for himself as he did so. He did develop a relationship with one of the teachers in the school and, on the basis of this relationship, tried to make a contribution to the school, performing a number of repairs on the old house in which the school was located.

His struggles to learn did not go well. In the middle of elementary algebra he complained that it had always been true that the minus signs and the plus signs had it in for him. He said they seemed to like to play tricks on him in order to make him feel bad about himself. His other studies did not go well, either. It became clear that, while he was interested in machines and quite good with his hands, he had enormous difficulties in anything that involved manipulations of symbols. He struggled for three years, making relationships with other students and teachers, participating in many school activities and functions, but not doing what was required to earn a degree.

At one point when he was quite despondent about his troubles in school, he came to discuss his future with the teacher with whom he had made the firmest relationship. The teacher was very much aware of the boy's longings for his father, of his disappointment in his father, and of his worry that he himself was doomed to follow in his father's footsteps, becoming an ineffectual loser with few prospects and even less self-esteem. The teacher had also been very touched by the boy's efforts to help the school, to take care of it and to keep it in good repair.

When the boy said that it seemed to him that he and high school credits just did not seem to mix, the teacher just nodded sadly. When the boy said that it was not that he did not try but just that he had never figured out how to try in the right way and that he felt embarrassed to be going on 18 and still trying to figure out how to try in the right way, the teacher responded by saying that he did not think there was anything holy about high school credits. They were, he said, only a means to an end. The same, he went on, was true of a high school diploma.

The boy's face showed sudden eager attention. He wanted to know what the teacher meant. The teacher said that school was to help you in your efforts to learn what you needed to know in order to be a useful member of the community and to treat other people decently and enjoy relationships with them. He went on to say that, as far as he was concerned, if somebody had figured out how to get a useful job and do it well and how to be involved with other people in a way that was mutually satisfying, then that was more than the equivalent of graduating from high school. The boy looked thoughtful and said that he had some serious discussions he had to have with himself. He refused to say what these were but said that he appreciated the teacher's help very much.

After a few weeks, the boy came to the teacher and said that he had been thinking things over and did not feel that high school was for him. He felt that it had been helpful in getting his head straightened out and in helping him do some growing up but that if he stayed too much longer, all he would be doing was avoiding the growing up he still had to do. He said he had found their serious conversation a real help. He actually did leave school, sadly and amicably, a few months later.

Six years later, when the teacher was living in another city, he was surprised to answer his telephone one evening and hear this particular former student's voice on the other end of the line. He said he had called because he had gotten to thinking about how his life was going along and had decided that his teacher would be interested in hearing. He had relocated to the Southwest where, at six feet four inches tall and close to 280 pounds, he had apprenticed himself to a silversmith. It turned out that he had a talent for making delicate jewelry pieces. He was now making good money and living quite happily with his girlfriend of the past two years.

"So," he concluded with a warm grin in his voice, "I've done what you told me I needed to do, and now I've decided that I should award myself a high school diploma so I don't have to feel bad about being a dropout any more. But I didn't want to do it without telling you about it and making sure that you agreed with me that I've done the work required."

Needless to say, the teacher was only too happy to agree. He said that, if he recalled their conversation correctly from all those years ago, what he had said was that that much work and progress in life was more than the equivalent of a high school diploma.

"Maybe even college," said the former student on the other end of the line.

"Maybe," agreed the teacher, "but I'm not much of an expert on that."

"Well," said the student, "I guess I better stick to one kind of school at a time. I wouldn't want to get ahead of myself, here. I sure do feel better about myself than I did back then. Those were hard, hard days for me."

This story illustrates how a boy in serious trouble found a way to develop a more compassionate approach to himself, a way forward that suited him and allowed him to accept his troubles and limitations while making something very appealing and admirable out of his own authentic resources.

Compassion for the self comes into play in different ways in different life situations and at different phases in life. It is at once a requirement and a supply. Compassion for the self is a creative challenge. We need to understand our possibilities even when we are in disarray and our weaknesses even at moments when things seems to be going extraordinarily well for us. Among the kinds of kindnesses to which we may aspire, compassion for the self is a specially important one.

At a certain point in our lives, we pass beyond the tutelage of our parents, even as we have internalized and redesigned them in our minds and hearts. In assuming the parental function toward ourselves, in acting ourselves as the trustees of the possibilities of our own growth, realization, and refinement, we need the discipline, the comfort, the challenge, the inspiration, and the sustenance of the spirit of compassion toward ourselves with us within ourselves. There is no higher imaginative function than the conception of a kindness that can be made actual and active, no greater reward than to know that we have loved and sustained not only others but that most intimate and strange other we are ourselves for ourselves.

References

Aristotle. (1941). Rhetoric. In *The Basic Works of Aristotle*, ed. R. McKeon. New York: Random House.

Carter, R. (1986). Personal communication.

——, ed. (1990). *Essays in Philosophical Zoology by Adolf Portmann*. Lewiston, NY: Mellen.

Frost, R. (1949). The death of the hired man. In *Complete Poems of Robert Frost*. New York: Holt.

Goethe, J. (1782). *Schriften uber die Natur*. Liepzig: A. Kroner, 1932.

Gribbin, J., and White, M. (1992). *Stephen Hawking: A Life in Science*. London: Viking.

Job. (1946), ed. V. Reichert. London: Soncino.

Kay, C. (1988). *Political Constructions: Defoe, Richardson, and Sterne in Relation to Hobbes, Hume, and Burke*. Ithaca, NY: Cornell University Press.

La Rochefoucauld, F. (1977). *Maximes*. Paris: Garnier-Flammarion.

Lewin, R. A., and Schulz, C. G. (1992). *Losing and Fusing: Borderline Transitional Object and Self Relations*. Northvale, NJ: Jason Aronson.

Michels, R. (1983). The scientific and clinical functions of psychoanalytic theory. In *The Future of Psychoanalysis*, ed. A. Goldberg, pp. 125–136. New York: International Universities Press.

Oates, W., and O'Neill, E., eds. (1938). Sophocles's *Oedipus at Colonus*. In *The Complete Greek Drama*, vol. I, pp. 613–669. New York: Random House.

Rosaldo, R. (1993). *Culture and Truth: The Remaking of Social Analysis*. Boston: Beacon.

Shaw, G. B. (1925). *Man and Superman*. New York: Penguin, 1987.

Sullivan, H. S. (1953). Conceptions of modern psychiatry. In *Collected Works of Harry Stack Sullivan*, vol. I, ed. H. S. Perry and M. L. Gawel, pp. 3–298. New York: Norton.

Yovel, Y. (1989), *Spinoza and Other Heretics: The Adventures of Immanence*. Princeton, NJ: Princeton University Press.

Index